ROAD TRIPPING

South Africa

Endless back roads to discover...

MapStudio

CONTENTS

INTRODUCTION

'It is good to have an end to journey toward; but it is the journey that matters, in the end.'

Ernest Hemingway

Unlike Hemingway, I've never been one for road trips per se; the attractions of the destination have always been more important than the journey. But researching this book and hearing the many anecdotes of my fellow contributors changed my views. I headed to the Cederberg and started exploring.

Suddenly I saw landscapes that I knew so well with fresh eyes: the incredible rock formations; lofty peaks; orderly vineyards and orchards; little flowers that lined the roadways; the state of the farms and small-holdings. I started to notice the seasonal changes, the condition of the roads, the quirky signs, the picnic spots and viewpoints; little things that I'd previously sped past. Best of all, I stopped and chatted to the people that I met along the way – the watermelon sellers, owners of the farm stalls, the craftsmen and women and the wonderfully enthusiastic staff in the tourism offices. And I fell in love with road tripping.

This book is a selection of 20 great South African road trips. They traverse the country from north to south, east to west, but are by no means comprehensive. Rather, my fellow contributors and I have chosen some iconic routes that take you to places that you might otherwise never visit.

The two things that all the routes have in common are that they follow back roads wherever possible, and that they are all perfectly manageable in a normal sedan. Sure, you might have to drive carefully on occasion – but you certainly don't need a 4x4.

Like slow food, slow travelling is an immersion, resulting in a very different level of satisfaction. I hope that these suggested routes will be the inspiration you need to hop into the car and discover back roads that you've never journeyed before.

Using this book
We've tried to make planning as easy as possible by dividing each journey into manageable 'sections', providing detailed maps, distances, driving times, highlights, regional tourism contact details, useful websites/further reading, and suggestions on where to eat, drink and stay. We've indicated whether the routes are child- and pet-friendly, and how suitable they are for your low-slung BMW. But a few words of warning and explanation are necessary:

Journey times
The times given are DRIVING times and do not take stops into account. If you are bumbling along looking at the scenery, doing a spot of birding or shopping en route, stopping to admire the view, to take photographs or for padkos, the journey will clearly take significantly longer!

Some routes also include optional detours, which are not included in the overall driving time. Driving time is also hugely dependent on the state of the road. If travelling on gravel roads it's worth phoning tourism info centres and accommodation establishments to check the status quo. Generally, gravel roads are worse in the rainy season, and much more pleasant to drive if recently graded.

Try to plan your journey in advance and decide whether you'll take a detour or stick to the main routes. Factor in plenty of time to enjoy the scenery and a leisurely afternoon lunch – you don't want to arrive at your destination in the dark or miss the B&B check-in times!

Place names
South African road signs are not consistent and take some getting used to. Place names often alternate between English and Afrikaans – so you'll be happily following the N2 to Cape Town, only to find the next sign indicating Kaapstad!

Many of the old names – like Louis Trichardt (now Makhado) or Lydenburg (now Mashishing), etc. – have been changed. But in practice you'll probably still find occasional signs with the old place names along the way.

Logistics and toll roads
The nearest airports, major cities and possible links into other featured routes are given.

Several of the national roads have tollgates and these, too, are noted in each route description. Toll plazas accept cash and credit/garage cards.

At the time of going to print, the situation regarding toll roads in Gauteng was still uncertain.

Up-to-date information on toll fees can be obtained online at www.aa.co.za/on-the-road/calculator-tools/toll-fees.html

Rules of the road
South Africans drive on the left-hand side of the road.

Speed limits
Unless otherwise indicated, the general speed limits are:
- 60km/h on a public road within an urban area;
- 100km/h outside an urban area on a public road that is not a freeway; and
- 120km/h on freeways.

If you speed you are likely to be caught. There are sneaky fixed cameras at the sides of roads and on many robots (traffic lights), and you'll often see traffic police hiding in the bushes to trap the unwary.

Seat belts
The wearing of seat belts is compulsory. Even if the kids are sleeping in the back, make sure they are strapped in properly.

Cellphones

Using hand-held phones while driving is against the law, so invest in a phone attachment or hands-free kit if you plan to speak on your cellphone while you're driving.

Drinking and driving

Drinking and driving is prohibited. The maximum allowable blood alcohol content is 0.05% (roughly one glass of wine for an average woman, and one and a half or two for the average man).

Yellow-line driving

On single carriageways you'll often see slow vehicles pulling into the emergency lane (inside the yellow line). It's common practice on South African roads for faster vehicles to come up behind you, flash their lights and almost force you over.

The only time that the use of the emergency lane is permitted is if you are travelling **on a single carriageway road with one lane in each direction**, in which case you can pull into the emergency lane to allow faster-moving cars to pass you. It is considered courteous to do so. However, venturing into the emergency lane carries the risk of hitting pedestrians, cyclists or stationary vehicles, so should be undertaken with extreme caution; the onus is on you to make sure doing so is safe. And even then there are certain provisos. The Road Traffic Act clearly states that if you are moving aside to allow vehicles to pass, **you can only do so during daylight hours and you are required to make sure that you have at least 150m of visibility ahead before you move over**. So, if rain, fog or mist limit visibility, or if you are on a blind rise, you may not enter the emergency lane.

On any other roads the only time you are allowed to use the emergency lane is if you have a real emergency, such as if your car breaks down, if you are rushing to the hospital, or need to stop immediately in the event of a medical emergency. The emergency lane needs to be kept clear to allow access to emergency response, rescue, ambulance and fire-fighting vehicles.

Four-way stops

Cars should proceed in order of arrival at a four-way stop sign.

Safe driving

You'll often come across tractors, heavily overloaded or unroadworthy vehicles and vehicles without lights, particularly in the countryside, so keep your wits about you.

Drive sensibly, taking other road users into account. Taxi (i.e. minibus) drivers are notoriously aggressive and often flout the rules of the road.

On many of the routes described the roads are not fenced, so watch out for dogs, sheep, cows, horses and chickens on the road.

Wild animals can also be a danger, so if you see a road sign depicting a leaping antelope, take it slowly, especially at dawn or dusk. And if you see a sign depicting a tortoise, keep your speed down and your eyes open – they will not be very quick to get out of your way!

Do not stop and feed wild animals such as baboons. Not only is it dangerous, but you will incur a heavy fine if caught.

Avoid driving at night in rural areas; there is a high chance of encountering vehicles without lights as well as people and animals wandering on the road.

Opening hours

Most national parks and nature reserves observe daylight opening hours.

Most restaurants and B&Bs/guesthouses close by 20:30–21:00, so you are likely to fall short if you pitch up late.

While service stations on major highways and around big towns are usually open 24 hours, garages (petrol stations) in small towns will probably keep regular 'office' hours. In addition to cash, garages will take garage cards and, generally, credit cards. Many garages have ATM machines.

Note that distances between towns (and therefore between petrol stations) are considerable in some parts of the country, so keep an eye on the fuel gauge and fill up if it looks as if there's a long journey ahead.

General safety

When driving through towns and cities, and when stopping at traffic lights, it's a good idea to keep your doors locked and windows up.

Never leave anything visible in a parked car. It invites a break-in. Lock everything in the boot.

For further information on safe driving, see www.aa.co.za or www.arrivealive.co.za

National Emergency Numbers

Police: 10111
Ambulance/Fire: 10177
Crime Stop: 08600 10111
ER24: 084 124
Fire Brigade: 998/999
LifeLine: 086 132 2322
Other specific emergency numbers, such as NSRI, Mountain Rescue, Diver's Alert Network, etc., are given in the relevant chapters.

Your vehicle and paperwork

Ensure that you have 24-hour roadside assistance cover either through your insurance or by joining the AA.

Before you leave home, check that your vehicle is ready for the trip. Check oil, water, brakes, windscreen wipers, tool kit, emergency equipment, the condition and pressure of all the tyres including the spare, and if you are planning on venturing into neighbouring countries, bring the necessary vehicle registration, insurance documents, etc.

Snow-capped peaks between Clarens and Golden Gate Highlands National Park

Is there enough space in the car? Do you need a packing aid such as a roof rack, trailer or bike rack? Make sure that you have clear visibility out of the back window and that driver and passengers are comfortable and can access their seat belts easily.

What to take

- Always carry a fully charged cellphone (mobile phone). **The custom in South Africa is to have the contact number of the person who should be contacted in the event of emergency saved as ICE (In Case of Emergency).** Car chargers for most cellphones are widely available and are handy for those long drives when you don't want to be stuck with a dead battery.
- Driving licence and insurance details (an international driving licence is not required)
- Passport/ID document
- Credit cards **and cash** – some small towns won't have card machines or easily accessible ATMs
- Medical and auto insurance cards
- Small change to pay car guards
- Road atlas
- Water in a cooler box for those long, hot days in the car (it's important to stay hydrated)
- Tyre repair kit – make sure you are familiar with the kit and know how to change a tyre on the vehicle you are driving. Working out how to deal with a flat tyre as you are stuck out in the middle of nowhere or beside a busy road is not fun!
- Jumper cables
- Basic toiletries – wet wipes, tissues, hand sanitiser, etc. – and first-aid kit (with a stock of anti-nausea pills in case of travel- or carsickness)
- Head lamp or torch
- Spare camera batteries/memory cards, just in case you can't get to a power point every night
- Binoculars
- Flora and fauna field guides
- SATNAV – can be hired with rental cars
- iPod or CD collection with your favourite tunes for the road – the radio service isn't always reliable in more remote places!

- Padkos – a South African tradition. It's always important to be well stocked with biltong, chips, snacks, fruit and sandwiches! You can sometimes pick up fresh local stuff in small towns along the way, or buy fruit on the side of the road.
- Entertainment for the kids – if you are going to be spending lots of time in the car, remember to have some fun stuff for the kids to do so that they don't get bored. Colouring or activity books, novels or a Game Boy are good options. Or make a game up in which they can participate – spotting landmarks, counting cars or an old-fashioned game of I Spy!
- Swiss Army knife or Leatherman multitool
- Toilet paper, tissues and a garbage bag for the car so that you can easily throw everything away when you get to your destination
- Pillows and blankets
- An inverter is probably overkill for most of the routes described, but is useful if you won't have access to somewhere to charge your electronics
- Comfortable shoes that you can wear for driving long distances

Climate

South Africa is a big country, so general advice on climate and when to go is fairly meaningless. Rather take note of the advice in individual chapters and pack accordingly. Generally, however, the Western Cape has winter rainfall while the remainder of the country has summer rainfall.

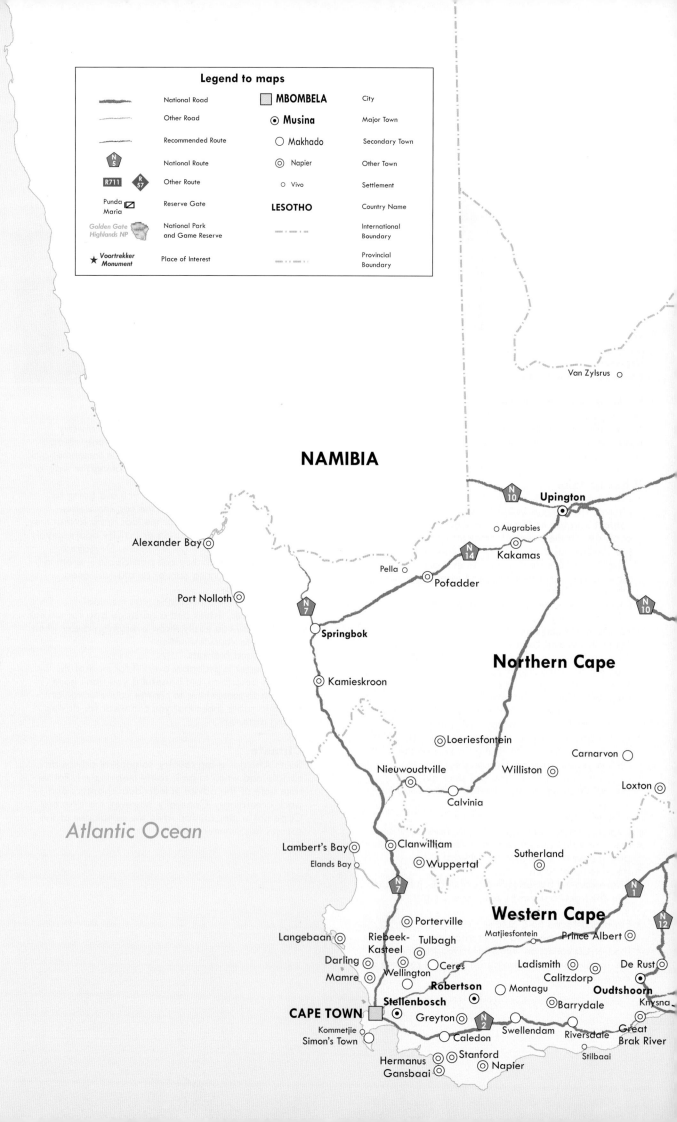

Legend to maps

National Road	
Other Road	
Recommended Route	
National Route	
Other Route	
Reserve Gate	
National Park and Game Reserve	
Place of Interest	

National Road

Other Road

Recommended Route

National Route

Other Route

Punda Maria Reserve Gate

Golden Gate Highlands NP National Park and Game Reserve

★ *Voortrekker Monument* Place of Interest

MBOMBELA City

Musina Major Town

Makhado Secondary Town

Napier Other Town

Vivo Settlement

LESOTHO Country Name

International Boundary

Provincial Boundary

NAMIBIA

Van Zylsrus

N10 Upington

Augrabies

N14 Kakamas

Pella

Pofadder

Alexander Bay

Port Nolloth

N7 Springbok

Northern Cape

N10

Kamieskroon

Loeriesfontein

Carnarvon

Williston

Loxton

Nieuwoudtville

Calvinia

Sutherland

Atlantic Ocean

Lambert's Bay

Clanwilliam

Elands Bay

Wuppertal

N7

N1

Porterville

Western Cape

N12

Langebaan

Matjiesfontein

Prince Albert

Riebeek-Kasteel

Tulbagh

Darling

Wellington

Ceres

Ladismith

De Rust

Mamre

Montagu

Calitzdorp

Oudtshoorn

Robertson

Barrydale

Knysna

CAPE TOWN

Stellenbosch

Greyton

N2

Kommetjie

Swellendam

Great Brak River

Simon's Town

Caledon

Riversdale

Stilbaai

Hermanus

Stanford

Gansbaai

Napier

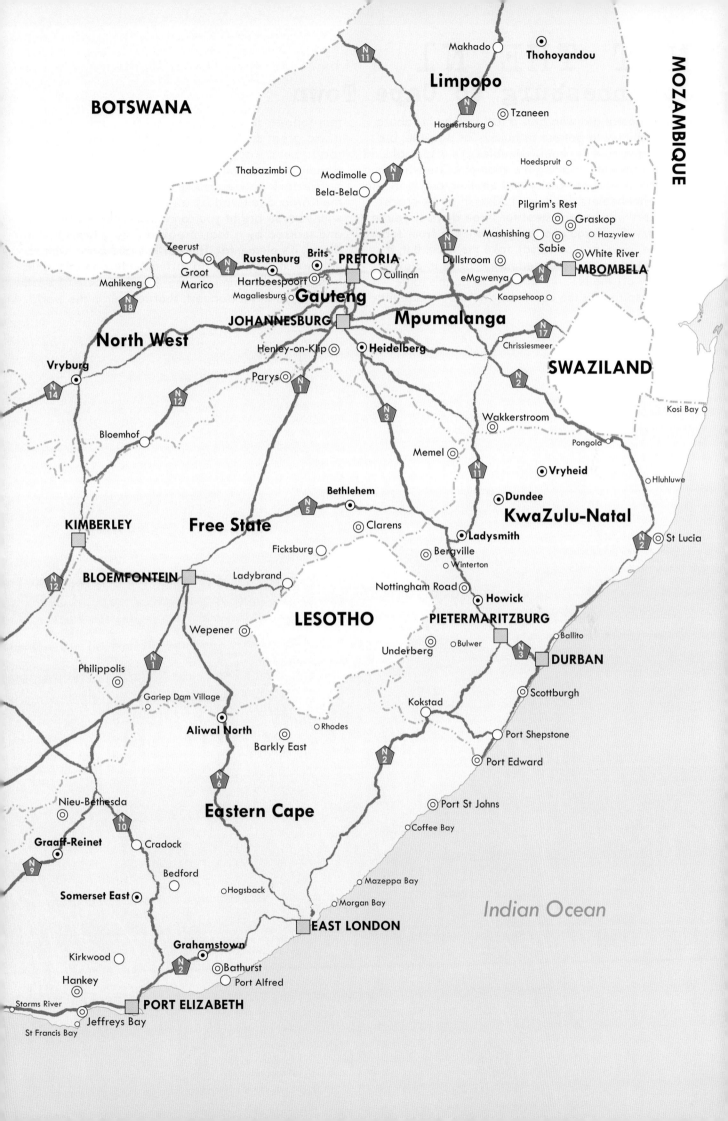

NOT THE N1
Johannesburg to Cape Town

I am a coastal girl who gets a tad twitchy in Joburg so I usually try to get out as quickly as possible, but the N1 gives me the heebie-jeebies. It's a special kind of hell — blearily counting the kilometres between one bland ultra-stop-petro-city and another, and dodging eighteen-wheelers driven at 160km/h by tik-crazed teenagers who haven't slept for three days. If you're in a hurry, fly. If you need to get your car from Joburg to Cape Town (or vice versa), take the train. But, if you want to enjoy the experience — drive it. Slowly. And stay off the N1. My decision to do this route was partly inspired by the car I was driving — a cute little tent-topped Jimny I'd borrowed from Bobo Campers. It was great on the gravel and fine on the tarred back roads, but it was really not ideal for racing eighteen-wheelers on the long, straight stretches of the Karoo, or overtaking sheep trucks on the steep uphills. I love the Karoo. Sheltered by a velvet black sky studded with stars so bright you can almost read by them, and scarred by a tear-streaked history drenched in blood, it's elemental. The earth is laid bare, with no lush green vegetation to soften the harsh outlines. Its beauty is in its simplicity, the sheer expanse of earth and sky, and the cleanest, sharpest air in the world.

Total Distance about 2,000km
Driving Time 24–30hrs

Section ❶
Joburg to Clarens
Distance 300–360km
Driving Time 3–4hrs
Highlights:
Suikerbosrand
Golden Gate
Clarens
SEE PAGE 12

Section ❷
Clarens to Bloemfontein
Distance 280km
Driving Time 4hrs
Highlights:
St Augustine's Priory
The Long March to Freedom
Onze Rust
Women's War Memorial
SEE PAGES 13–14

Section ❸
Bloemfontein to Graaff-Reinet
Distance 600km
Driving Time 8hrs
Highlights:
Philippolis
Bethulie
Gariep Dam
Nieu-Bethesda
Cradock
Samara Private Nature Reserve
Graaff-Reinet
Karoo landscape
SEE PAGES 15–17

Section ❹
Graaff-Reinet to Sutherland
Distance 470km
Driving Time 7hrs
Highlights:
Die Kweperlaan
SA Astronomical Observatory
SEE PAGES 18–19

Section ❺
Sutherland to Stellenbosch
Distance 320km
Driving Time 3–6hrs
Highlights:
Matjiesfontein
Cape Fold Mountains
Klondyke Cherry Farm
Transport Riders' Museum
Fynbos, wine and fruit
SEE PAGE 20

NOT THE N1
Johannesburg to Cape Town

Road tripper:
Jennifer Stern

In a nutshell:
A long, winding peregrina-
tion through the moun-
tainous eastern Free
State and the moody,
contemplative wide-open
spaces of the Karoo.

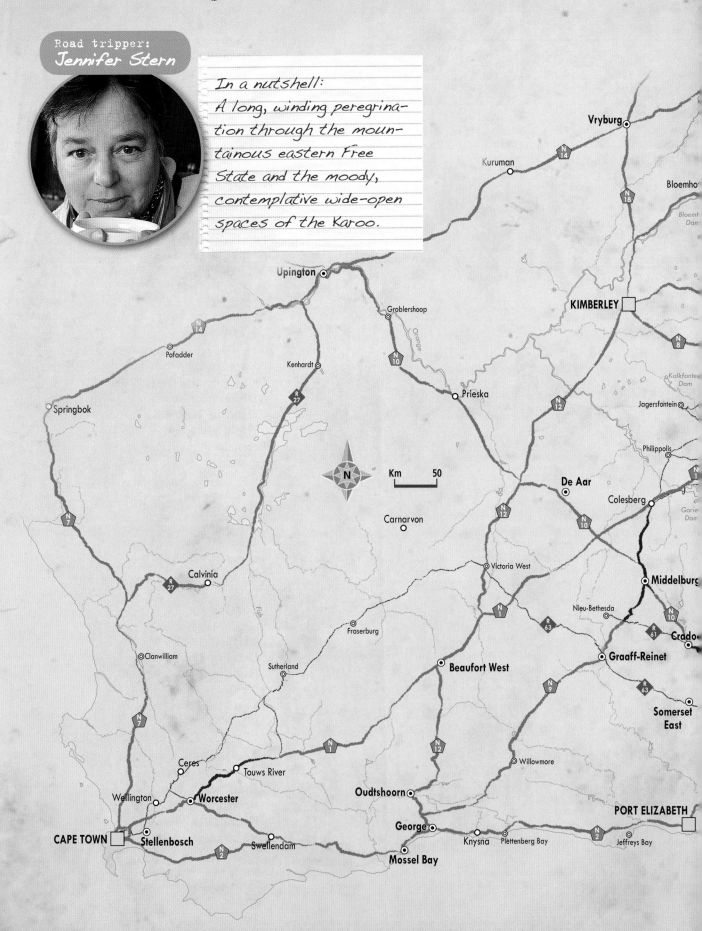

JOHANNESBURG

Klerksdorp

Standerton

Vaal Dam

Kroonstad

Welkom

Bethlehem

Harrismith

Clarens

Woodstock Dam

EMFONTEIN

Ficksburg

Katse Dam

MASERU

Caledon

LESOTHO

Kokstad

Aliwal North

MTHATHA

Queenstown

Butterworth

King William's Town

EAST LONDON

hamstown

Port Alfred

Logistics

This is a linear route ostensibly between Joburg and Cape Town but the surroundings of any big city are somewhat nebulous. There are a million different ways to get out of Joburg and, once you are anywhere near Cape Town, there are so many fabulous destinations and alternative routes that you could get totally sidetracked and never actually get to gaze up at Table Mountain. So I've concentrated on the heart of the route – from Clarens to Ceres.

Driving conditions

Variable – from super-smooth dual carriageways to dodgy gravel roads. But what most of the roads have in common is a relative (or absolute) lack of eighteen-wheelers. There are toll roads between Villiers and Warden on the N3. The alternative route, R103, is a good, fast road with almost no eighteen-wheelers.

Pet-friendly rating ★ ★ ★ ☆ ☆

1 = least suited 5 = most suited

Child-friendly rating ★ ★ ★ ☆ ☆

1 = least suited 5 = most suited

Low-slung vehicle-friendly rating ★ ★ ☆ ☆ ☆

1 = high clearance 5 = lowest slung

Don't miss

- Golden Gate
- Clarens
- Philippolis
- Bethulie
- Graaff-Reinet
- Owl House
- Stars at Sutherland

Emergency service numbers

Emergency (from a landline) 10111
Emergency (from a cellphone) 112
AA roadside assistance 086 100 0234 or 083 843 22 (24 hours)

Best time

None. (Or all.) A few events that may sway your choice include the Craft Beer Festival in Clarens in February, the Clocolan Vintage Tractor Fair in March, the Philippolis Witblits Festival (which involves a lot more than witblits) in April, and, in October in Bloemfontein, both the Rose Festival and the Macufe (Mangaung African Cultural Festival).

SUMMER			AUTUMN			WINTER			SPRING		
D	J	F	M	A	M	J	J	A	S	O	N

Background reading

The Plains of Camdeboo by Eve Palmer describes life on a farm near Graaff-Reinet.
Story of an African Farm by Olive Schreiner is the classic Karoo farm story. There's a movie, too.
Jakhalsdans, the movie, is set in Loxton, and so is *Die Laaste Tango*. Anything by Laurens van der Post – Philippolis's literary son.
The brunt of the war, and where it fell by Emily Hobhouse is the seminal work on the South African War. She was, along with war correspondent Edith Dickenson whom Hobhouse quotes extensively, one of the first writers to concentrate on the humanitarian cost of war as opposed to the glory or the political and financial implications.
Wuthering Heights, the poem by Sylvia Plath, so perfectly describes the Karoo, it's hard to believe she was writing about England.

NOT THE N1
Johannesburg to Cape Town

Section ❶
Joburg to Clarens
Distance 300–360km
Driving Time 3–4hrs
Highlights Suikerbosrand, Golden Gate, Clarens

I usually try to get some distance from Joburg quickly, but there is no easy way out. The N3 and N12 are almost as bad as the N1, and I've got lost every time I've tried the minor roads through the encircling industrial sprawl. So I just bear with the N3 or N12 for a while and then duck off. But you could stop at **Suikerbosrand**, a mere 60-odd kilometres from Joburg, and chill for a day or two and maybe go for a short hike before heading south. It's also a great place to see what the whole Highveld was probably like two centuries ago.

From there you could brave the N3, or head off to the Vaal Dam via Vereeniging or by leaving the N3 at Heidelberg. From there (or from the N3 at Villiers) you could hit the R26 and head to Clarens through Frankfort, Tweeling, Reitz and Bethlehem. I haven't travelled this route and don't know it, but I have discovered from my meanderings further south that even the most unprepossessing little town usually has lots to offer if you take the time to look for the gems.

Try to time it so you drive through **Golden Gate** in the early morning or late afternoon and you will see how it got the name. I went through in winter and the grass and the trees glowed an even more impressive gold than the beautiful cave sandstone. The Glen Reenen Rest Camp is a typical, comfortable SANParks camp with self-catering chalets, camping, a restaurant, a small shop and petrol. There is also a hotel. Golden Gate is worth a stay of a couple of days to go hiking or horse riding and maybe check out the rock art.

Clarens is possibly the prettiest town I have ever seen, but maybe that's because I drove in just before sunset, and all those sandstone houses were glowing a deep gold. People were strolling down the middle of the road with their dogs and children, and artistic second-careerists pedalled past on their ancient gearless bicycles. I breathed a sigh of relief, felt my shoulder muscles unravel, and found a great little guesthouse/deli/restaurant called 278 on Main. A typically Clarens place, it was so obviously the work of the resident artist/owner who in this case created beautiful mosaics. But Clarens is loaded with (somewhat self-consciously) charming emporia. The general dealer is a perfect blend of time-warp old SA and chic deli, and there are furniture shops, art galleries, a knife maker and even a windmill centre. I did the usual necessary research and decided that Highland Coffee is the only coffee shop in the town that has a real barista (as opposed to someone who has read the instructions on the espresso machine). Clarens is really close to Golden Gate, there is great rock art nearby, and the Ash River offers fantastic whitewater rafting.

Windmill Centre, Clarens

Section ❷
Clarens to Bloemfontein
Distance 280km
Driving Time 4hrs
Highlights St Augustine's Priory, The Long March to Freedom, Onze Rust, Women's War Memorial

Head out of Clarens on the R711 to Ficksburg and skirt the town to join the R26 towards Ladybrand. About 2km outside Ficksburg is the Constantia Cherry Farm Stall, where you can buy all manner of cherry things – liqueur, nougat, chocolates, jam, etc. But, more unusually, you can also buy a range of warm, soft, cuddly hand-knitted garments made from locally farmed angora rabbit wool. Head into Clocolan and turn right onto the gravel road opposite the first petrol station. It's then about 5km or so to the Highland Essential Oil farm, where you can see, smell and buy a range of locally distilled essential oils and lots of cool stuff made from them. Get back onto the R26 and carry on to The Cabin on the right-hand side of the road. It's an ensemble of craft shops and restaurants with a really funky kids' playground.

About 10km before Ladybrand is the turn-off to **St Augustine's Priory**, the Cave Church and Mantsopa's grave and spring. This place of pilgrimage is holy to the Basotho, who regard Mantsopa as a prophet and intercessor, and the rock art indicates that it was a place of deep spiritual significance to the San, too. So it's not surprising that the Anglicans chose this spot to build their mission – first worshipping in a cave and only later constructing the church and other buildings. You can tour the site but, if you want a guided tour, you need to book at least two days in advance, and the same for accommodation.

Ladybrand, which was named for the mother of J H Brand, the fourth president of the Orange Free State, displays an intriguing mix of languages. I stayed in a great little B&B called Top House. The building once housed the town's greatest (and really only) industrial giant, Norwood Coaker, who started a huge pharmaceutical and cosmetics factory here in 1886. It closed down in 1990.

St Augustine's Cave Church

Living Life, situated at the old station, is a wonderfully peaceful, slow, gentle restaurant, coffee shop and craft centre in a pretty garden setting. On Piet Retief Street is the Wagenhuis, which is not to be missed. It's an almost unchanged Voortrekker wagon house and stable that is used as an antiques shop and very low-key coffee shop.

Ladybrand is conveniently close to Maseru, so it is a popular destination for people who do business in the Lesotho capital. Sunflower Tours offers guided excursions to all the attractions around Ladybrand and also into Lesotho.

Leave Ladybrand on the N8 towards Bloemfontein. Mud Studio pottery is about 12km from Ladybrand, but it is not very well signposted. I hear it's great but I must have blinked as I drove past because I didn't see the turn-off.

ON THE SIDE >> Mile-high club
Bloemfontein is 1,400m above sea level, which is just under a mile high. So, when you see a Boeing 737 parked in a field next to the road, it's tempting to embark and see what transpires. Seriously, it is a real (but decommissioned) 737 that was dismantled, brought to the site and reassembled. When I saw it, it had just 'landed' and was in the process of being turned into a cocktail bar and restaurant. It's at Emoya – a rather fantastical game farm, restaurant, hotel and conference centre. It's a great place for kids – farmyard animals like pot-bellied pigs and fluffy-legged chickens wander around freely with giraffes, llamas, eland and other animals. It's not far from the dreaded N1 on the south side of town, and is a comfortable and convenient place to overnight – especially if you're travelling with kids.

Bloemfontein is a surprisingly rewarding destination. The Oliewenhuis Art Museum is one of the best I have ever seen. As well as the expected great paintings, the museum has a wonderful carousel of African animals and a marvellous collection of sculptures called **The Long March to Freedom**. It's a spectacular procession of life-sized bronze statues of leading lights in South Africa's history, all striding across the bright green lawns towards the gallery.

Bottles of cherry liqueur

NOT THE N1
Johannesburg to Cape Town

There is so much history in and around this city. About 25km south from the city is **Onze Rust**, the home of the last president of the Orange Free State, Marthinus Theunis Steyn. The farm is owned and run by Steyn's great-grandson, Colin Steyn, and his wife Jackie. It's worth visiting just to see the beautiful buildings, but it's also a conference and wedding venue with a range of accommodation options, and Colin has an impressive collection of SA War memorabilia. The farm is divided into two distinct sections. The original farmhouse is a tranquil country home, but a short drive from the main farmyard takes you right through the rabbit hole and the looking glass into a bizarre universe that feels like a movie set. Actually, it is a movie set, but it's more than that. Colin does battle re-enactments and has an extensive collection of authentic weaponry and uniforms relating to the SA War and to the Afrika Corps during the Second World War, and he has re-created a gold rush-era saloon that is authentically South African but looks a bit like the set of a Western movie — as long as you don't notice the (working) Russian tanks parked a few hundred metres up the hill.

For me, though, the most impressive part of town is the **Women's War Memorial**. It's a rather poignant symbol of what war is really about. It's not about tough men doing honourable battle and emerging covered in glory. It's about devastated farms and families, and skeletal horses carrying equally skeletal, embittered, disillusioned men to homes that no longer exist. The attached museum was closed for renovation when I was there, but I'm sure it's worth a visit, and the sculptures by Danie de Jongh and Anton van Wouw are great.

Waaihoek Cooling Towers, Bloemfontein

Most of Bloemfontein's public buildings are in President Brand Street, which is a treasure-trove of late Victorian/Edwardian/Neoclassical architecture. It helps if you have someone to point you in the right direction and offer some interpretation. I wandered around town with Bush Junkies Safaris' Tony Horn, who is completely in love with his adopted city, and found there is a lot more to this underrated destination than I thought.

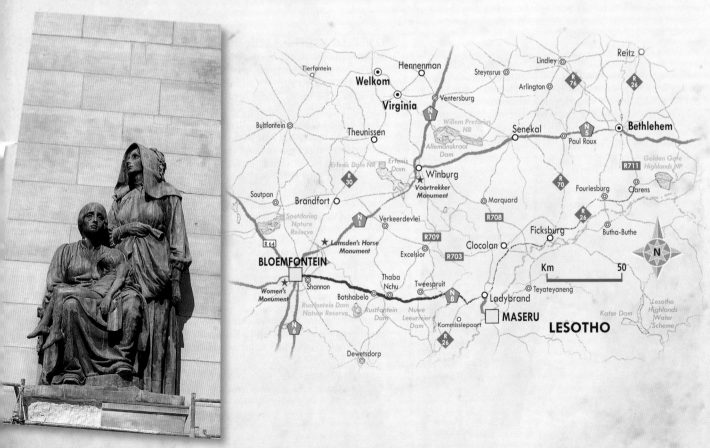

Section ③
Bloemfontein to Graaff-Reinet
Distance 600km
Driving Time 8hrs
Highlights Philippolis, Bethulie, Gariep Dam, Nieu-Bethesda, Cradock, Samara Private Nature Reserve, Graaff-Reinet, Karoo landscape

From Bloemfontein you do have to go on the N1 for a short while. I skived off after a few kilometres to explore Jagersfontein, but you can continue on the N1 for about another 70km and take the Edenburg turn-off for a shorter route to **Philippolis**. Jagersfontein Diamond Mine is the biggest human-dug hole in the world. Yes, not Kimberley. The mine was closed in 1969, leaving huge mine dumps that, because they are as rich in diamonds as many actual mines, are now being reworked, bringing some employment to this rather depressed little town. You can check out the hole if you like, and there is a tiny museum, but there's not much else there.

There is a (supposedly good) gravel road between Jagersfontein and Philippolis, but I couldn't find it so I headed back on the R704 towards Trompsburg, and then turned down the R717 to Philippolis. I missed Trompsburg, but I've since heard that there is an excellent artisanal bakery in the town. Oh well.

Founded as a mission station in 1822, Philippolis was the first settlement north of the Orange River. The Griqua leader, Adam Kok, lived here for a while, and Laurens van der Post was born in the town, but probably Philippolis's most notable former resident is Emily Hobhouse. She started a spinning and weaving school for desperate and destitute women here in the early 20th century, long before the term social entrepreneurism had been coined. It's not nearly as twee as Clarens, but the town is a treasure-trove of gorgeous old buildings, museums and interesting emporia.

Oom Japie se Huis is a guesthouse, art gallery, bar, restaurant and very serious bookshop dealing in collectibles and rare books. It's just one of the surprises of this little town. When I was there I sat down with the proprietor, Richard, and a passing biker drinking superb cardamom-spiced coffee, and chatting about life, the universe and everything. It was so hard to leave.

From Philippolis, take the gravel road to Springfontein and cross over the N1, watching carefully for speeding eighteen-wheelers. There's a small farm stall, Kuil-fontein, on the Springfontein side of the N1.

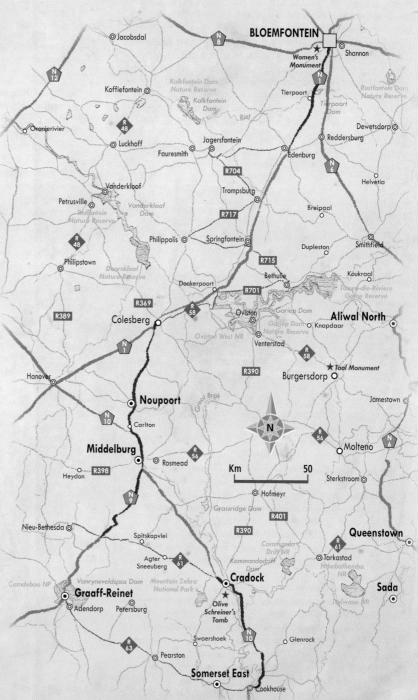

15

NOT THE N1
Johannesburg to Cape Town

It's then about 40km to **Bethulie**, the site of the very worst of all the South African War concentration camps. There is a monument at the site of the concentration camp, and a small museum housed in one of the oldest buildings in the Free State, the former home of French missionary Jean Pierre Pellissier. The town is on the banks of the **Gariep Dam**, and it's worth driving out of town to watch the sun set over the dam from the bridge over the Orange River. If you're into that sort of thing, it is, according to the locals, the longest combined road and rail bridge in the southern hemisphere. Whether that's true or not, it's an impressive arched structure of over a kilometre. The social and tourist life of the town is dominated by the Royal Hotel, which dates back to the 1880s and is haunted by numerous historical figures, all of whom behave very politely — well, politely for ghosts. You can meet them on a ghost tour of the town run from the hotel.

Small country towns often conceal hidden gems in the form of creative people who have opted out of big-city living but who continue to create in the space and quiet of their new homes. Bethulie has its fair share of visual artists, but also boasts a concert pianist, Ben Fourie, who does informal performances in his home if he is given enough warning. It's best to contact him through the Royal Hotel.

Owl House, Nieu-Bethesda

After 20km on the Nieu-Bethesda road, you will pass the turn-off to Ganora Guest Farm, which offers great farm accommodation as well as fossil tours, rock-art tours, stargazing and lots more — even sheep-shearing demonstrations.

Nieu-Bethesda is best known for the Owl House, which was the home of South Africa's foremost out-sider artist, Helen Martins. The garden of statues and the vividly bright and sparkly interior of her home are a poignant illustration of how she brightened up the outside of her life to try to ameliorate the darkness within. It didn't work, and Martins committed suicide, but her legacy brings joy to many, and has contributed to the revival of the town. Once a dour little dorpie, it is now a fashionable artists' retreat and tourist destination of note — with its own artisanal coffee roaster and microbrewery *nogal*. Sneeuberg Brewery and 2 Goats Deli roasts and serves organic coffees to complement the plough-man's platter they put together from locally made goat's-milk cheese, pickles and bread. Oh — and beer, of course.

Sun setting over Gariep Dam

From Bethulie, take the R701 along the northern shore of the dam and the resort town of Gariep Dam. Cross over the Orange River on a somewhat scary, narrow one-vehicle-width bridge and then continue on the R58 towards Colesberg. Head through Colesberg to avoid the N1, but you do have to travel on it for about a kilometre before you can turn onto the N9. The landscape starts changing subtly. The endless plains are now bounded by bizarre, spiny-ridged mountains resembling the prehistoric beasts that once roamed this area when it was hot, moist and marshy. You bypass Noupoort and Middelburg and then you have a choice: either head right on the gravel road to Nieu-Bethesda and continue on a tarred road that rejoins the N9 about 27km before Graaff-Reinet, or turn left onto the R61 to Cradock and the N10 to Somerset East.

WELCOME TO
LAKE
!GARIEP
ROUTE

EASTERN CAPE TOURISM

Cradock was the home of Olive Schreiner. There is a museum in her former home, or you could trudge up to her grave on a nearby farm, but it is quite a long walk so wear proper shoes. The nearby Mountain Zebra National Park is a great game and hiking destination. If you want some time out, park off at the Angler & Antelope near Somerset East and try to lure a fat trout onto your line. It's a bit of a detour but it's very therapeutic.

Then take the R63 to Graaff-Reinet. En route you will pass **Samara Private Nature Reserve**, which is well worth a couple of days of me-time. It's a bit indulgent, but the quiet of the Karoo, the superb food and characterful historical accommodation will soothe your soul. The Karoo has a low carrying capacity, so the game viewing is not an endless procession of big animals like it is in the Lowveld. It's more low-key, more about birds and plants and spotting unusual animals like aardvark and bat-eared fox, or animals not seen in the more classical game destinations, such as gemsbok and black wildebeest. There's even a spa if you want to indulge completely.

Mountain Zebra National Park

ON THE SIDE >> Extinction is forever
The Karoo was once a hot, teeming, lushly green environment where mammal-like reptiles called therapsids frolicked in shallow lakes and metaphorically thumbed their noses at the rapidly dying-out dinosaurs. Well, the therapsids also died out — or at least evolved into far more cuddly creatures: mammals. But their remains can still be found in the sedimentary Karoo rocks, which are also a rich source of dinosaur fossils with an unbroken sequence spanning 50 million years. Check out the fossil collection at the Old Library Museum in Graaff-Reinet.

Graaff-Reinet is one of my favourite towns. It has a fascinating history, and you'll find more museums than you can visit in a day within about one square kilometre. As well as the usual beautiful old historical buildings, you may see South Africa's oldest grapevine, the grave of Robert Sobukwe, and exhibits relating to the SA War and Karoo reptile fossils. For a place to chill and have a cup of coffee, try the Blue Magnolia Nursery, or Polka Café, which is also a bakery and one of the few restaurants open at night. Another interesting one is The Homestead Mohair and Coffee Shop, where you can buy all manner of things hand-knitted or hand-woven from angora (goat, not rabbit) wool. The town is full of wonderful old buildings, many of which have been consolidated into De Kothuize collection of beautiful, characterful and very comfortable self-catering cottages and houses. They are all in the town and within easy walking distance of all the museums and restaurants, and pretty close to the Spar, where you can stock up on self-catering necessities. Best of all, they are super pet-friendly. Some of the cottages have very large gardens, and they will arrange to accommodate all sorts of pets — from cats and parrots to pythons.

Bobo camper

NOT THE N1
Johannesburg to Cape Town

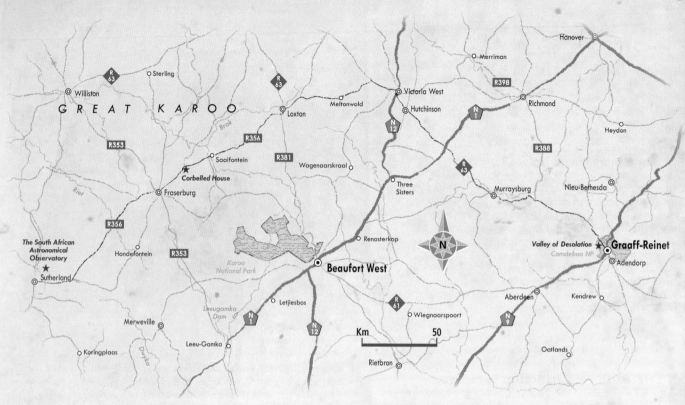

Section 4
Graaff-Reinet to Sutherland
Distance 470km
Driving Time 7hrs
Highlights Die Kweperlaan, SA Astronomical Observatory

From Graaff-Reinet, head out on the R63 to Murraysburg and stop at **Die Kweperlaan** for coffee or lunch, or to buy wonderful local crafts made from merino wool, mohair or goose down. Or spend the night in the attached one-room guesthouse and even have a facial at the on-site mini day spa. Or do a Karoo Cuisine cooking course where mostly fresh local ingredients are used. Pop in to Kay's Café to see photos of the town taken in 1890 and 1990.

From Murraysburg, continue on the R63, over the N1 to Victoria West. Victoria West is a really quiet little town, especially considering it is on the N12. It's best known for the Apollo Theatre, the only remaining Art Deco cinema left in South Africa. There was a great film festival run here for a few years, but it sort of died. However, plans are afoot to revive it in 2014. Let's hope. I found a fabulous, welcoming, pet-friendly little guesthouse here called Die Pophuis Hoekie, which is a collection of cute but very well-appointed self-catering cottages around a central garden. They also offer an excellent breakfast. Pop in to the museum, which has a good display explaining the Karoo fossils, even though there aren't many actual fossils. There's

BEAUFORT-WES
HUTCHINSON
RICHMOND
BRITSTOWN
CAPE TOWN
KAAPSTAD

also a good section on the history of the town and a collection of old guns, ranging from those first experimental ones — they could shoot a whole fifteen rounds a day and were more dangerous to the guys holding them than anyone else — to guns that could actually hit a target about 100m away. Seriously — an impressive collection all lined up in chronological order.

Wagenaarskraal

From Victoria West, continue on the R63 towards Loxton (or detour to Wagenaarskraal). This is a good gravel road, although like all gravel roads it goes through phases. It was a tad corrugated when I drove it. Head through Fraserburg, where you can see an example of a corbelled house right in the middle of the town on the left-hand side. It's another 80km or so to Sutherland — it's the coldest place in South Africa, so pack your woolly socks and beanie, or maybe you should have stocked up on bunny wool mittens. About 14km before the town you'll find SALT and the **SA Astronomical Observatory**. You can do guided day and/or night tours but you must book in advance. Expand your horizons.

I nearly froze my toes off in Sutherland standing outside in the dark looking at stars through a telescope on a guided star tour with Jurg from Kambrokind Guest House. It was worth it, though. And I do just love all the star-themed puns in the town. Jurg's coffee shop is called 'Halley sê kom eet'.

ON THE SIDE >> Guns and going postal
If you're really interested in guns, you may want to do a detour to Wagenaarskraal where you can see an even more extensive collection of historical weapons. For ages this farm was also a post office and shop, so you can peruse the old accounts books and have a look at the last letter mailed there in the 1970s.

ON THE SIDE >> Rocks and stars
You may notice that in the Karoo nothing grows higher than the hearts of sheep (to misquote Sylvia Plath), so early settlers built houses entirely out of stone, including the roof. And because the sky is so clear — and settlements so small, few and far between — the Karoo offers some of the best stargazing on the planet. That's why the Southern African Large Telescope (SALT) was built at Sutherland and the Square Kilometre Array (SKA) is being built at Carnarvon. If you have loads of time, you can go the longer way round through Carnarvon, where you can check out the beginnings of SKA, and you will see lots of great corbelled houses around Williston.

Interior of SALT

NOT THE N1
Johannesburg to Cape Town

Section ❺
Sutherland to Stellenbosch
Distance 320km
Driving Time 3–6hrs
Highlights Matjiesfontein, Cape Fold Mountains, Klondyke Cherry Farm, Transport Riders' Museum, fynbos, wine and fruit

Head out of Sutherland on the R354. After about 75km you need to decide whether you are going to take the gravel road straight to Ceres, or head down to **Matjiesfontein** and drive just over 60km on the N1. In spring, opt for the gravel road because the flowers are beautiful, but on this last trip I gave in and headed towards the N1 because I wanted to explore Matjiesfontein. Well, it's a stunning place with fantastic old Victorian buildings. And I believe there is a tour guide who is quite enthusiastic, but he was on leave. So I had a pretty iffy coffee and milk tart in the coffee shop and then wandered around the almost deserted buildings and museums with no interpretive material and decidedly disinterested locals, so it was a bit of a let-down.

And then I had to deal with the N1, but the distant sight of the **Cape Fold Mountains** kept my spirits up. About 10km after Touws River I escaped the eighteen-wheelers and took the R43 to Ceres. En route you pass the turn-off to Matroosberg, the Western Cape's most dependable and accessible snow destination, and **Klondyke Cherry Farm**, where you can pick your own cherries in summer, as well as picnic and camp. The **Transport Riders' Museum** in the town is undergoing a huge refurbishment so I expect more info soon about the hardy souls who regularly drove the main route from Cape Town to the diamond fields in the 19th century, but I did enjoy the collection of old horse-drawn wagons and carts.

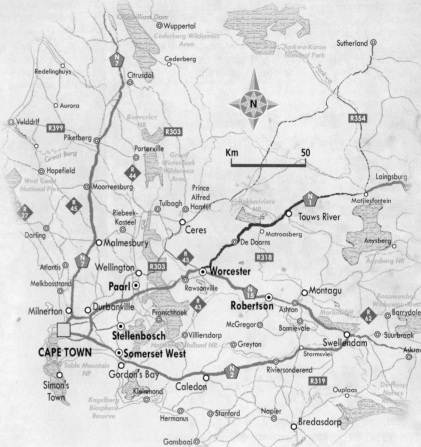

From Ceres, take the rugged, steep and scenic Michell's and Bain's Kloof passes to Wellington and then to Stellenbosch to join up with the Winelands Route (see pages 42–49). Or head to Worcester to join up with Route 62 (see pages 50–61). Another alternative is to take the Gydo Pass from Ceres via Prince Alfred Hamlet and Op-die-Berg to Citrusdal and join up with the West Coast route (see pages 32–41). And it's a short drive to Cape Town from any of these fun detours.

Entering the Winelands

NOT THE N1 Contact details

278 on Main
082 556 5208
www.278onmain.co.za
Angler & Antelope
042 243 3440
wildflyfishinginthekaroo.co.za
Blue Magnolia
049 891 0792
Bobo Campers
011 395 6900
www.bobocampers.com
Bush Junkies
082 953 0737
www.bushjunkies.co.za
Constantia Cherry Farm Stall
051 943 7180
De Kothuize
082 571 6539
www.dekothuize.co.za
Die Kweperlaan
082 509 3120
Die Pophuis Hoekie
053 621 1243, 082 496 4390
diepophuis@telkomsa.net
Die Wagenhuis
083 441 5587
Emoya
051 436 8471
www.emoya.co.za
Ganora
049 841 1302
www.ganora.co.za
Golden Gate Highlands National Park
058 255 1000
www.sanparks.org
Highland Coffee Roastery
058 256 1136
www.highlandcoffeeroastery.co.za
Highland Essential Oils
051 943 0317
www.highlandessentialoils.co.za
Kambrokind Guest House and star tours
023 571 1405, 082 556 9589
www.sutherlandinfo.co.za
Karoo Cuisine
082 944 0499
Klondyke Cherry Farm
023 312 1521
www.cherryfarm.co.za
Kuilfontein
073 407 9324, 072 653 9567
Living Life & Station Café
051 924 2834
www.livinglifesa.co.za
Lord Milner Hotel
023 561 3011
www.matjiesfontein.com
Matroosberg Private Nature Reserve
023 312 2282, 073 194 0885
www.matroosberg.com
Mountain Zebra National Park
048 881 2211
www.sanparks.org

Oliewenhuis Art Museum
051 447 9609
Onze Rust
082 577 7323
Oom Japie se Huis
051 773 0050, 051 773 0486
oomjapiesehuis@gmail.com
Outrageous Adventures (Ash River rafting)
083 485 9654
www.outrageousadventures.co.za
Polka Café
087 550 1363
www.polkacafe.co.za
Royal Hotel
071 683 7767
www.bethulie.net
SA Astronomical Observatory
023 571 1205
www.saao.ac.za
Samara Private Nature Reserve
023 626 6113
www.samara.co.za
Schreiner House Museum & Grave
048 881 5251, 072 173 9906
Sneeuberg Brewery and 2 Goats Deli
049 841 1602, 076 512 9026
www.nieubethesda.co.za/brewery
St Augustine's B&B and Conference Centre
051 924 3318
www.saintaugustines.co.za
Sunflower Tours
082 690 2489
The Cabin
082 707 2894, 073 584 5524
www.the-cabin.co.za
Top House B&B
051 924 2085
www.thetophouse.co.za
Transport Riders' Museum
023 312 2045
www.ceresmuseum.co.za
Victoria West Regional Museum
053 621 0413
Wagenaarskraal
053 004 0030
Women's Memorial and War Museum
051 447 3447, 051 447 0079
www.angloboer.co.za

Regional info
www.bloemfontein.co.za
www.ceres.org.za
www.clarens.co.za
www.ecpt.co.za
www.graaffreinet.co.za
www.ilovefreestate.co.za
www.malotidrakensbergroute.com
www.nieubethesda.co.za
www.philippolis.co.za
www.somerseteast.co.za
www.tourismcapetown.co.za
www.visiteasterncape.org.za
www.visitvictoriawest.com

CEDERBERG
Round trip from Ceres via central Cederberg, Clanwilliam and Wuppertal

Less than three hours from Cape Town, the rugged Cederberg, one of the eight protected areas that comprise the Cape Floral Region World Heritage Site, is one of my favourite escapes. Its dramatic peaks, precipitous cliffs, deep rock pools, intriguing rock art, star-studded skies, subtle blanket of spring daisies and, above all, its magnificent and bizarre rock formations enthral me on every visit.

I've traversed the wilderness area on foot and mountain bike, climbed the imposing orange wall of the Wolfberg and hiked to the top of Tafelberg, Krakadouw, Sneeuberg and numerous other iconic peaks, looking for rare cedars and snow proteas. I've overnighted in the mission villages, taken community-run guided tours of the rock-art sites and enjoyed the hedonistic delights of wine tasting at the country's highest vineyard and the spoils of the luxurious Bushmans Kloof Wilderness Reserve & Wellness Retreat. The Cederberg is compact and very, very special — perfect for a leisurely road trip.

Total Distance 481km
Driving Time about 9hrs

Section ❶
Ceres to Sanddrif Holiday Resort
Distance 125km
Driving Time 2hrs 20mins
Highlights:
Magnificent rock bands of Swartruggens
Stadsaal Caves
Hike to Wolfberg Cracks/Arch
Cederberg Private Cellar
SEE PAGES 26–27

Section ❷
Sanddrif to Traveller's Rest/Bushmans Kloof
Distance 93km
Driving Time 1hr 45mins
Highlights:
Views of Tafelberg
Leipoldt's grave
Sevilla Rock Art Trail
Flowers in season
SEE PAGES 27–29

Section ❸
Traveller's Rest/Bushmans Kloof to
Heuningvlei/Wuppertal
Distance 31km
Driving Time 1hr
Highlights:
View of Biedouw Valley
Seasonal wildflowers
Wuppertal
SEE PAGE 30

Section ❹
Wuppertal/Heuningvlei to Ceres
Distance 232km
Driving Time 4hrs
Highlights:
Clanwilliam Dam
Middelberg Pass
SEE PAGE 30

CEDERBERG
Round trip from Ceres via central Cederberg, Clanwilliam and Wuppertal

In a nutshell:
A circular route through the dramatic wilderness of the Cederberg, famous for its spectacular rock formations, rock art and wildflowers.

Logistics

This is written as a circular trip, but you can link into various other routes covered in the book, such as Route 62 (see pages 50–61), Not the N1 (see pages 8–21) and the West Coast (see pages 32–41). The nearest airport is Cape Town, a 90min drive from Ceres.

Driving conditions

The dirt road through the central Cederberg is generally good but those to Wuppertal and Heuningvlei are stony and rough, so not advisable in a very low vehicle. Parts of the route are in the mountains where the weather can be extreme, so check ahead if heavy rain or snow is forecast.

Pet-friendly rating ★ ☆ ☆ ☆ ☆

1 = least suited 5 = most suited

No dogs are allowed in any of the Cederberg Wilderness areas.

Child-friendly rating ★ ★ ★ ★ ☆

1 = least suited 5 = most suited

This is a great route for kids as distances are fairly short and there are lots of opportunities to get out the car and explore.

Low-slung vehicle-friendly rating ★ ★ ☆ ☆ ☆

1 = high clearance 5 = lowest slung

Don't miss

- Cederberg Private Cellar
- Sevilla Rock Art Trail
- Wolfberg Cracks
- Middelberg Pass

Emergency service numbers

NOTE THAT THERE IS LITTLE CELLPHONE RECEPTION OTHER THAN IN CLANWILLIAM

Emergency (from a landline) 10111
Emergency (from a cellphone) 112
AA roadside assistance 086 100 0234 or 083 843 22 (24 hours)

Best time

Spring (August to October) is wonderful as the weather is at its most predictable and the flowers are at their best. Autumn (April/May) is also a good time. Summers are hot and dry. The Cape experiences winter rainfall so it can be very wet, and cold, during June and July.

SUMMER			AUTUMN			WINTER			SPRING		
D	J	F	M	A	M	J	J	A	S	O	N

Background reading

www.cedheroute.co.za
www.nightjartravel.com
www.slingsbymaps.com (Peter Slingsby's 'the map' of the Cederberg)
South African Wildflower Guide 10: Cederberg, Clanwilliam and Biedouw Valley by Gretel van Rooyen and Hester Steyn

TIP

Drive at dawn or dusk to appreciate the orange rocks and dramatic peaks in their best light.

CEDERBERG
Round trip from Ceres via central Cederberg, Clanwilliam and Wuppertal

Section ❶
Ceres to Sanddrif Holiday Resort
Distance 125km
Driving Time 2hrs 20mins
Highlights Magnificent rock bands of Swartruggens, Stadsaal Caves, hike to Wolfberg Cracks/Arch, Cederberg Private Cellar

The Cederberg lies some 200km north of Cape Town and encompasses 71,000ha of rugged, mountainous terrain. The quickest way there is to head up the N7 from Cape Town then, 26km beyond Citrusdal, to take the turn-off to Algeria. And this is a fine route, which you shouldn't immediately write off. The mountains rise suddenly and steeply from the coastal plain, and the outline of the 2,027m-high Sneeuberg — 'snow mountain', the Cederberg's highest peak — dominates the view as you follow the lush Olifants River Valley towards the turn-off. But an even more spectacular entrance is via Ceres — accessed from Cape Town via the dramatic Du Toitskloof Pass (see page 54) — or the even more dramatic Bain's Kloof Pass — and then up Michell's Pass.

From Ceres, take the R303 through Prince Alfred Hamlet and up the sweeping bends of the narrow Gydo Pass. The view from the lookout near the top is very photogenic, the orderly patchwork of colourful orchards, fields and dams contrasting with the rugged mountainous backdrop. The journey continues past the sign to the Agter Witzenberg Valley — an interesting road that leads to an unexpectedly lush, hidden valley of orchards completely surrounded by stark grey rock. It's a dead end, so once you've had a peek (and perhaps, like I did when I first discovered this oasis, promised to come back and explore), return to the main drag then turn right towards the Cederberg at Op-die-Berg.

Tar gives way to gravel as you journey through the Koue Bokkeveld past the turn-off to Kagga Kamma. 'Cold goat country' it certainly is and in winter you'll usually see snow on the distinctive Koue Bokkeveld Tafelberg (not to be confused with the Cederberg peak of the same name) and Sneeukop peaks that loom large on the left.

The next section, over the Blinkberg and Grootrivier passes, is one of my all-time favourite drives. The **magnificent rock bands of Swartruggens** dominate the view to the right, and as you crest each rise the gravel road snakes out before you, cutting a scar through the otherwise desolate landscape. Up and down the steep hills you go, past the lush oasis of Mount Ceder, to the turn-off to Nuwerust, a fantastic resort with grassy camp sites, chalets, great hiking and on-site sport and traditional rock-climbing routes. The owners are incredibly friendly and attentive; there's even Wi-Fi for those who just can't switch off and, since it's the only place with DStv, the bar hums if there's a rugby match on.

You climb again past the Cederberg Oasis and you pass the back road to Kromrivier (which also leads to Truitjieskraal, a top sport-climbing area) before dropping again to Matjiesrivier.

The entrance to the **Stadsaal Caves**, one of the most accessible of the Cederberg's many rock-art sites, is on your left 4km further on. If you want to visit on your way through, pull in to Nuwerust or Mount Ceder to arrange a permit.

ON THE SIDE >> Stadsaal Caves
Beautiful paintings of elephants that once roamed the area grace the walls of the closest site to the entrance gate. In contrast, the walls of the main chamber, the vast 'Town Hall Cave', are inscribed with the names of several members of the National Party, including that of D F Malan, the first National Party Prime Minister of South Africa. A popular theory is that the Nats met here to plan their 1948 victory, which heralded the start of the apartheid era.

Wolfberg Arch

Continue, carefully, on the gravel road to Sanddrif Holiday Resort, in my view the best base from which to really enjoy the Cederberg. Grassy camp sites and chalets flank the river (which is deep enough to swim in and has a lovely beach), there are mountain-bike trails, stiff hikes to the region's most iconic landforms – the **Wolfberg Cracks**, **Wolfberg Arch** and Maltese Cross – and rock-climbing routes aplenty. The farm is also home to the **Cederberg Private Cellar**, the highest winery in the country, famous for its reds (particularly its award-winning Shiraz), and one of the region's most attractive rock pools, Malgat. Given all this, and the dramatic setting, it's hard to move on, so plan to stay at least a couple of days!

ON THE SIDE >> Rock art

The Cederberg offers hundreds of rocky overhangs and caves with fine examples of rock art. Those at Stadsaal, Bushmans Kloof and on the Sevilla Rock Art Trail are well-known, but one of the beauties of the Cederberg Wilderness Area is that you can go off into the wilderness and explore one of the lesser-known sites on your own.

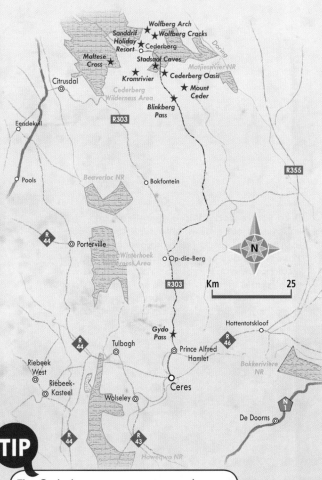

TIP

The Cederberg stars are spectacular since the surrounding high peaks cut out most of the light pollution from settlements outside the valley. If you're in Sanddrif on a Saturday night (other than at full moon when the night sky is lit up), pay a visit to the observatory where local astronomy buffs lay on a short, informative slide show before opening up the telescopes to public viewing.

Section ❷
Sanddrif to Traveller's Rest/Bushmans Kloof
Distance 93km
Driving Time 1hr 45mins
Highlights View of Tafelberg, Leipoldt's grave, Sevilla Rock Art Trail, flowers in season

Leaving the lush oasis of Sanddrif, you drive past orderly vineyards and the grand old Cape Dutch farm building back into rugged landscapes. The area around the farm, and on the left of the road as you drive out, suffered devastating damage in a fire in late December 2012. The bad news is that the hike to the famous Maltese Cross and many of the mountain-biking trails will be closed for some time. But when they reopen we're in for a treat as bulbous plants (geophytes) are always at their most impressive after fire. When the burned area regenerates, look out for a mass of red *Brunsvigia* and *Babiana* poking out from under rocks.

Big protea bushes cover the stony slopes to the left of the road, while if you look over the wetland to the right, **Tafelberg**, with it's distinctive 'spout', comes into **view**. Just after the picnic spot under the trees on your left you pass the rough road that leads to Driehoek camp site and chalets, and the trail head for the very strenuous hike to the summit of Tafelberg. The weird and wonderful landforms on the top of the summit plateau include a much-photographed spacecraft.

Then comes the steep descent down the Uitkyk Pass, most of it on a paved road, which makes a welcome respite from bumpy gravel! You'll see the route of the old wagon trail on your right, and some secluded CapeNature cottages on the lower slopes. Watch out for a sign indicating water about 250m down on the left – this is a good place to fill empty bottles from the fresh mountain stream. The road reverts to gravel before another short paved section past Algeria, the local HQ of CapeNature, with its large camp site shaded by gum trees. Cast your eyes heavenwards at the amphitheatre and the waterfalls in the deep cleft on the right as you approach. Much of this land was forested, but fire damage and large-scale clearance is allow-ing the fynbos to regenerate.

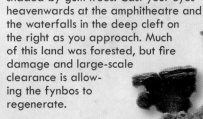

CEDERBERG
Round trip from Ceres via central Cederberg, Clanwilliam and Wuppertal

Where the road splits just past Algeria, take the Clanwilliam road down and over the bridge (the high road to the left takes you over the Nieuwoudt Pass to the N7, which, although longer, is actually the quicker route to Clanwilliam). The shake, rattle and roll journey on the rather poor, winding 'direct' road takes you along the river valley, past the Jamaka Organic Farm, citrus orchards and various places offering accommodation until, around 20km from Algeria, you glimpse the southern end of the Clanwilliam Dam and the valley opens out.

A right turn at the T-junction takes you along the side of the very scenic dam, a popular playground particularly for powerboaters and water-skiing enthusiasts, to the back entrance of Clanwilliam, an attractive market town. You can buy a pair of handmade leather shoes at the Strassberger's shoe factory on the road in, and the main street has a lovely church, old jail, some good cafés, and a Spar — the last decent food shop on your route — to detain you.

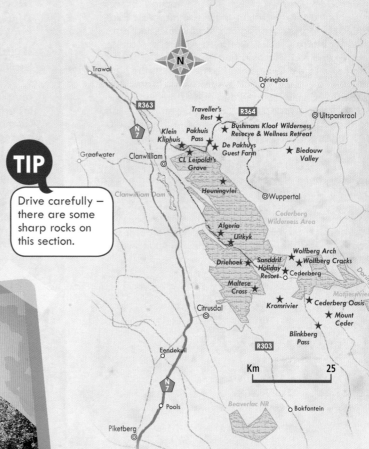

TIP

Drive carefully — there are some sharp rocks on this section.

Clanwilliam Church

Once you've stocked up on supplies — and fuel — turn right out of town onto the R364, a good tar road, and begin the climb over the Pakhuis Pass. Make any urgent calls before you leave — your phone won't work until you return this way in a couple of days. This is a spectacular drive through magnificent rocky landscapes, much loved by hikers and rock climbers. Rocklands is

ON THE SIDE >> Of rock art and rooibos
• The community-run Clanwilliam Living Landscape Project offers fascinating rock-art tours and has a lovely art-and-craft shop.
• Learn more about rooibos (*Aspalathus linearis*) at the Rooibos Tea House, at NetMar, in town, or take a tour of one of the nearby rooibos farms. The herb, endemic to the Cederberg and Clanwilliam area, is used to make tea and a variety of other nutritional and body products.

Rock art

a world-famous bouldering area (a gymnastic form of climbing on low boulders without ropes) and you'll see signs off to the more famous bouldering sites all the way over the pass and down into the valley beyond.

The **grave** of a famous doctor and poet, **C Louis Leipoldt**, on the left of the road about 25km from town, is worth a short stop. Leipoldt (1880–1947) trained as a doctor and, after specialising in pediatrics, went on to become the first lecturer in the diseases of children at the University of Cape Town. A highly accomplished man, he was also a passionate botanist and cook, but is perhaps best known for his diverse writings which included poetry, drama, travel books, detective stories and books on Cape cookery. He loved the mountains and the three peaks at the top of the pass, 'Faith', 'Hope' and 'Charity', visible from his grave, were named by him.

Stop at the car park on the right at the top of the pass to take in the views and stretch your legs. (Camping and chalets are available at Kliphuis just before the top if you want to overnight.) The gravel road leading through the CapeNature reserve leads to the tiny settlement of Heuningvlei — one of the detours on tomorrow's route. You can hike to Heuning-vlei in about four hours (not much longer than it will take you to drive around!) or arrange a lift there in a traditional donkey cart.

The best time to drive this next section of road is in the flower season. The precise timing varies from year to year but generally from late July to September, the roadsides are a blaze of colour as tiny orange, white and purple daisies smile at the sun.

If you're into rock art, stop at the Khoisan Kitchen, on the right just before the Brandwyn River, and get a map and permit for the **Sevilla Rock Art Trail** — a short, interpretive walk along the river on which you can visit nine different caves with remarkably well-preserved and easy-to-locate rock paintings. A swimming hole between sites four and five makes a good detour on a hot day.

Donkey cart transport in Heuningvlei

There are a couple of accommodation options nearby, including the self-catering cottages at Traveller's Rest, which are decorated with San-style murals, and the ultra-secluded Bushmans Kloof Wilderness Reserve & Wellness Retreat, the turn-off for which is 800m further on. This luxurious Relais & Châteaux property has been rehabilitated through the re-introduction of indigenous flora and fauna, and boasts superb accommodation, sublime food, guided walks to see rock art and **spring flowers**, and all manner of spa treatments to help you unwind. There are no dangerous predators, so you can wander freely, admiring some of the 130 rock-art sites, the wonderful tortoises and plains game and taking in the dramatic scenery. A complete spoil worth saving your pennies for!

ON THE SIDE >> San rock art
The mountainous areas in and around the Cederberg have some of the richest rock-art sites in the world, most of which record animal scenes, and are associated with important symbolism.
  Humans are also commonly depicted, often in procession, hunting or out gathering food. Other types of paintings show therianthropes (half-animal, half-human figures) and trance scenes.

ON THE SIDE >> Save the cedar
The Clanwilliam cedar tree is a conifer species endemic to the Cederberg Wilderness, one of 630 cedars worldwide, of which only nine occur in southern Africa. It's listed in the South African Red Data Book as Vulnerable and has also been shortlisted by the IUCN as a species worthy of protection.

PADKOS
I'm a grazer, so I always pack plenty of food to eat at scenic viewpoints along the way. My favourite quick bite is spicy hot cross buns with hummus. I'm always seduced by the smell of fresh bread, so one of my regular stops is the Bodega de Vinho deli at Rooiberg Winery on Route 62, which has a wonderful selection of savoury breads straight from the oven.

CEDERBERG
Round trip from Ceres via central Cederberg, Clanwilliam and Wuppertal

Section ❸
Traveller's Rest/Bushmans Kloof to Heuningvlei/Wuppertal
Distance 31km
Driving Time 1hr
Highlights View of Biedouw Valley, seasonal wildflowers, Wuppertal

The turning on to the gravel road that leads to Wuppertal/Biedouw Valley is on the right only a few kilometres beyond the turn-off to Bushmans Kloof. On the corner you'll see a clump of trees shading the 'Englishman's Grave'. A local historian has kindly left some information on this unlucky fellow, and there's more on this, and other local lore, in the museum in Clanwilliam, which you'll pass through again on the return trip. You are now heading south and should recognise the familiar profile of Tafelberg in the distance. After about 8km you reach Hoek se Berg, where the plateau ends and the road begins its steep, winding descent down to the flat valley floor.

A detour into the **Biedouw Valley** is an absolute must in **flower season** when the normally rather drab veld is covered by a colourful carpet of wildflowers. But the pet- and child-friendly Enjo Nature Farm halfway along the valley is a wonderful place to escape to at any time of year. There are fantastic walks and pools and, if conditions are right, the farm owner, Moritz, a qualified pilot, might be persuaded to take you for a flip in his plane.

It's another steep climb out of the valley through a rugged, eroded 'Badlands'-type landscape and after 13km you'll come to the turn-off to Heuningvlei on your right. There's a surprisingly good backpacker's lodge in this quaint little village of whitewashed buildings, and donkey-cart rides can be arranged, but the main attraction is that it lies at the foot of the mighty Krakadouw. So if you're a hiker you might like to detour for a day or two up the sandy road. Otherwise, continue down the steep, winding Kouberg Pass to **Wuppertal**, the largest mission settlement in the area, founded in the early 19th century. The remote village has remained largely untouched by the 21st century so is a wonderful place to slow down and soak in the atmosphere. Accommodation is in self-catering chalets, there's a lovely tearoom with a small gift shop, and you can visit the famous 'veldskoene' shoe factory, attractive old Moravian Church and museum.

The condition of both roads varies, so it's worth checking the status quo before leaving Clanwilliam. But even when they've been recently graded they are rough, so take your time and enjoy the scenery.

Section ❹
Wuppertal/Heuningvlei to Ceres
Distance 232km
Driving Time 4hrs
Highlights Clanwilliam Dam, Middelberg Pass

Retrace your journey back to Clanwilliam. You can either speed back to Cape Town on the N7 or head out again towards the Clanwilliam Dam then take the back road to Citrusdal.

Seven kilometres out of Clanwilliam you'll reach the turn-off to Algeria (the road you drove in on). Ignore it and keep right onto Bain's Old Road, which follows the eastern bank of the **Clanwilliam Dam**. This is a lovely stretch with great views, beautiful old bridges with great rock slabs as barriers, and well-tended orchards. And if you're overheating you can always stop by the side of the road and swim!

The gravel road stays more or less parallel with the N7, on the eastern bank of the Olifants River, until you hit tar again 16km outside the scruffy town of Citrusdal. Turn left here onto the R303, which takes you on a gravel road over the magnificent **Middelberg Pass** and down to Op-die-Berg to complete the circle.

It's a glorious finale. The road snakes uphill in a series of zigzags revealing a 'hidden' valley on the right, while on the left are the backs of the jagged peaks of the central Cederberg you passed as you drove along the Blinkwater and Grootrivier passes on your way in. The landscape changes as you leave the rugged wilderness and enter the more refined Cape Winelands district; fields of proteas, onions and wheat replace the maze of weathered boulders and uniform orchards.

From Op-die-Berg you're on familiar territory heading down towards the Gydo Pass. Stop at the top of the pass again to admire the patchwork of dams, orchards and arable fields of the Ceres Valley – a very different scene from the spectacular rock gardens that you've left behind.

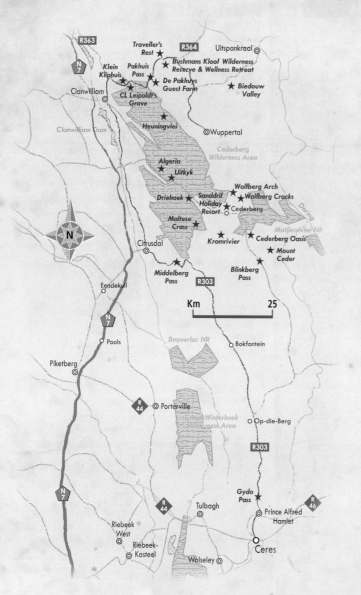

CEDERBERG Contact details

Bushmans Kloof Wilderness Reserve & Wellness Retreat
021 437 9278
www.bushmanskloof.co.za
CapeNature
086 122 7362, 021 483 0190
www.capenature.co.za
Cederberg African Travel
027 482 2444
www.cedheroute.co.za
Clanwilliam Info
027 482 2024
www.clanwilliam.info
Enjo Nature Farm
027 482 2869
www.soulcountry.info
Heuningvlei Backpacker's Lodge
027 492 3070
Nuwerust
027 482 2813
www.cederbergexperience.co.za
Sanddrif Holiday Resort/Cederberg Private Cellar
027 482 2827
www.cederbergwine.co.za
Traveller's Rest/Sevilla Rock Art Trail
027 482 1824
www.travellersrest.co.za
Wuppertal Information Office
027 492 3410

Gydo Pass

WEST COAST
Fossils and Fisherfolk –
Riebeek-Kasteel to Lambert's Bay

I first began exploring the West Coast when I moved down to Cape Town in 1993 to join CapeNature Conservation as the luckiest photographer in the world. I spent a lot of time exploring and photographing the Cederberg and, rather than drive on the N7, I used to head up the coastal route on the R27 to Lambert's Bay and then cut across to Clanwilliam. Not exactly the shortest route, but a beautiful journey that's etched in my travel log and one I still repeat often today. Even getting covered in guano while photographing the gannets at Bird Island never put me off.

The coastline of South Africa stretches for more than 2,500km from its desert border with Namibia on the Atlantic coast, around the tip of Africa and up to the border of Mozambique on the Indian Ocean side.

The cold Benguela current sweeps up from the Antarctic along the Atlantic coast, laden with plankton and providing rich fishing grounds for snoek, lobster, abalone, calamari, octopus, oysters and mussels – all of which comprise traditional West Coast fare.

The Cape West Coast region is vast and varied, comprising the vineyards and olive groves of the Swartland, the fishing villages, colourful characters and fossils of the Cape West Coast Peninsula, the magnificent bird life of the Berg River region, the rocky Cederberg Wilderness Area, and the Matzikama and Hardeveld – both famous for their wildflowers. You could spend weeks exploring – but this three-day trip gives you a good taste of what it's about.

Total Distance 364km
Driving Time 7hrs

Section ❶
Riebeek-Kasteel to Langebaan
(via the West Coast National Park)
Distance 125km
Driving Time 2hrs 15mins
Highlights:
Olive and wine tasting at Riebeek-Kasteel
West Coast National Park
Postberg Nature Reserve
Strandloper Seafood Restaurant
SEE PAGES 36–37

Section ❷
Langebaan to Paternoster
(including Cape Columbine)
Distance 71km
Driving Time 1hr 20mins
Highlights:
West Coast Fossil Park
Fishing boats on the beach at Paternoster
Cape Columbine Lighthouse
SEE PAGE 38

Section ❸
Paternoster to Lambert's Bay
Distance 168km
Driving Time 3hrs 25mins
Highlights:
Paternoster fisherfolk
Pelicans at Velddrif
Bird Island Nature Reserve
Muisbosskerm
SEE PAGES 39–40

Road tripper:
Shaen Adey

In a nutshell:
An iconic South African odyssey that illustrates the fascinating geology, history and contemporary landscape of the Cape West Coast – famous for its fossils, wine, seafood, quaint fishing villages and wildflowers.

Logistics

This is designed as a linear trip but can link in to the Surf Route (see pages 178–191) and Cederberg Route (see pages 22–31). The closest international airport is Cape Town International. It takes 3 hours and 10 minutes from Lambert's Bay to the airport driving on the N7 via Clanwilliam. There is one toll road, from Elands Bay to Lambert's Bay.

Driving conditions

Generally good. Tar until you reach Paternoster, then you hit sections of dirt road en route to Lambert's Bay. The toll road between Elands Bay and Lambert's Bay is often very corrugated, so take it easy. But why rush anyway?

Pet-friendly rating ★ ★ ★ ★

1 = least suited 5 = most suited
Providing you avoid the West Coast National Park and Cape Columbine Nature Reserve, otherwise ★

Child-friendly rating ★ ★ ★ ★ ★

1 = least suited 5 = most suited
Distances are short with plenty of places to stretch the legs en route, and the resorts are child-friendly.

Low-slung vehicle-friendly rating ★ ★ ★ ☆ ☆

1 = high clearance 5 = lowest slung
Though I'd be reluctant to take my sports car along the corrugated toll road between Elands Bay and Lambert's Bay.

Don't miss

- Postberg Nature Reserve
- West Coast National Park
- Cape Columbine Lighthouse
- Paternoster fisherfolk
- Bird Island Nature Reserve
- Muisbosskerm

Emergency service numbers

Emergency (from a landline) 10111
Emergency (from a cellphone) 112
AA roadside assistance 086 100 0234 or 083 843 22 (24 hours)
West Coast National Park 022 707 9902 (duty manager after hours 071 505 7070)
Ambulance 10177

Best time

The West Coast is great all year round but obviously best in spring when the wildflowers bloom. This is also the only time the Postberg Nature Reserve opens its gates to the public (August and September). The Cape gannets leave Bird Island between May and the end of June, so bear this in mind when planning a trip to avoid disappointment.

SUMMER			AUTUMN			WINTER			SPRING		
D	J	F	M	A	M	J	J	A	S	O	N

Background reading

A West Coast Odyssey by Gabriel, Louise and Nikolai Athiros, and Mike Turner
West Coast Cookbook by Ina Paarman

Don't forget

Crayfish and mussel permit, angling gear, hat, sun block, camera, binoculars, plus bird and mammal field guides.

TIP

Paternoster is famous for its West Coast lobsters (*kreef* or crayfish) but you need to have a permit to catch it, available from most post offices for around R100. Crayfish season is usually from November to April, but check the regulations on season, permitted areas and catch (www.sanparks.org/docs/general/marine_rec_brochure.pdf). Do NOT be tempted to buy crayfish from the locals out of season (or unless you have a permit). The police often trap on the road out of Paternoster.

WEST COAST
Fossils and Fisherfolk – Riebeek-Kasteel to Lambert's Bay

Section ❶
Riebeek-Kasteel to Langebaan
(via the West Coast National Park)
Distance 125km
Driving Time 2hrs 15mins
Highlights Olive and wine tasting at Riebeek-Kasteel, West Coast National Park, Postberg Nature Reserve, Strandloper Seafood Restaurant

Riebeek-Kasteel, in the Riebeek Valley, is one of the oldest towns in South Africa and is just 80km from Cape Town. The quirky little town is home to artists and foodie types and has some fun festivals. The annual Olive Festival early in May offers a weekend of **olive and wine tasting** along with entertainment; the Shiraz and Art Weekend is in October, and the MedFest in March.

From Riebeek-Kasteel head out on the R315 to Malmesbury, stopping at Kloovenburg Wine and Olive Estate as you leave town. The estate is well known for its award-winning reds and a Chardonnay that's so good it's now stocked by Harrods in London. In 2008 the estate was awarded the title of Best South African Olive Oil by *Wine Magazine*.

As you leave the estate and head up the Bothmanskloof Pass, the views get better and better, with sweeping vistas back over the valley, vineyards, olive groves, wheat fields and, in the distance, the Winterhoek Mountains. The road winds down and enters Malmesbury, the heart of the Swartland, with several beautiful old historic buildings, including the old Jewish Synagogue, now the Malmesbury Museum.

Follow the R315 to Darling, where you'll find Pieter-Dirk Uys's theatre, Evita se Perron, named after his alter ego. It's a fantastic restaurant/cabaret venue and their Christmas in July is an absolute must. The Duckitt Nursery, the largest orchid nursery in South Africa, is open to the public on the first Saturday of the month. Darling is also famous for its September Wildflower Show.

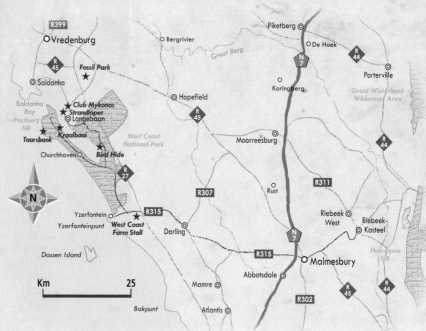

ON THE SIDE >> !Khwa ttu
Before you head north, try to factor in a couple of hours to visit !Khwa ttu, 5km south of the R315/R27 junction, for a fascinating insight into the culture, heritage, knowledge and modern-day life of the San people.

Scenic road between Riebeek-Kasteel and Malmesbury

From Darling it's 16km on the R315 to the Yzerfontein/Darling turn-off on the R27. With its collection of parrots and predators, the West Coast Farm Stall at this junction is an unusual place; if you want to see white tigers, black leopards and white lions close up, this is your chance. Yzerfontein, 7km down the road, is a small place with beautiful sandy beaches including the famous 16-Mile beach, which stretches all the way to the Postberg Nature Reserve. On clear days you can catch a glimpse of Dassen Island, home to 68,000 African penguins, 10km off the coast.

Postberg, above Langebaan Lagoon

From the Yzerfontein/Darling turn-off, head north up the coast on the R27. It's a beautiful stretch of coastline with views over the shrubby coastal vegetation and Atlantic Ocean. The gates of the **West Coast National Park** are 11km up the road. The entrance fee is minimal – and it's free if you have a Wild Card. The speed limit is 50km/h, so slow down and remember that tortoises have the right of way! From the top of the small rise just beyond the gates you get the first views of the turquoise waters of the Langebaan Lagoon and, on a good day, if you stop at the Atlantic viewpoint you can see Table Mountain. Further down the road you pass a turning to Churchhaven, with its picturesque whitewashed fishermen's cottages, but unless you are invited it's closed to non-residents.

A little further on you reach Kraalbaai with its wooden jetty and houseboats – a fantastic spot for a beach picnic. 'Eve's footprints', found here in 1995, are said to be those of a young woman who lived 117,000 years ago. The originals have been moved to the Iziko Museum in Cape Town, but there's a replica at the Geelbek Information Centre in the park.

Continuing on towards Taarsbank you come to the entrance of the **Postberg Nature Reserve**, which sits at the tip of the peninsula. During flower season the fields in this area are transformed by spectacular displays of daisies, and you might also see eland, blue wildebeest, bontebok, springbok, gemsbok, Cape mountain zebra and bat-eared fox.

Continue on to Taarsbank – on a windless day it's another stunning spot for a picnic or braai and a top spot for some whale-watching in season. Every year southern right whales migrate from their icy feeding grounds of Antarctica to our warmer climates, reaching our coastline in June, with sightings peaking in July and August. These majestic giants use the sheltered bays along the West Coast as their breeding grounds, staying for up to five months playing, courting and nursing newborn calves.

Return on the same road but after 24km take a turning to the left that heads to Langebaan. There's a dirt road down to a bird hide a little further along and it's a good place to view species such as curlew sandpiper, sanderling and grey plover. Back on the tar road you soon pass a turning on the right to Duinepos. The beautiful chalets are good value. A little further on there's a turning to the left to the Geelbek restaurant and visitor's centre, where you will find the replica of Eve's footprints.

ON THE SIDE >> Fossils
The West Coast Fossil Park, a national heritage site, is world renowned for its exceptionally well-preserved fossils dating back 5.2 million years. Many of the animals – such as saber-toothed cats, short-necked giraffes, hunting hyenas and African bears – that once roamed the West Coast are now extinct. The fossils were discovered in 1943 when phosphate was mined here, but sadly tons of fossils were destroyed before their value was realised.

Closer to the Langebaan side of the park you come to an area with a few marked mountain-bike trails and then a turning left to Seerberg. The views from here are some of the best in the reserve. From now onwards you'll start seeing kitesurfers zapping across the lagoon and as you exit the Langebaan gates look out for a road heading left; it's near a sharp bend and goes down to one of the hottest kitesurfing spots on the lagoon.

Langebaan is a busy town that boasts up-market accommodation and a choice of restaurants. One of the best places to eat local food is the **Strandloper**, an open-air **seafood restaurant** right on the beach. They serve up local dishes and spoils of the coast, things like *bokkoms* (dried, salted mullet), mussels in wine, and *kreef* (crayfish) – booking is essential. Club Mykonos just up the road is a great place to stay, especially if you have kids.

Spare us a Thought

WEST COAST
Fossils and Fisherfolk –
Riebeek-Kasteel to Lambert's Bay

Section ❷
Langebaan to Paternoster
(including Cape Columbine)
Distance 71km
Driving Time 1hr 20mins
Highlights West Coast Fossil Park, fishing boats on the beach at Paternoster, Cape Columbine Lighthouse

Detouring to the **West Coast Fossil Park** means heading back to the R27 but it's well worth a visit. Otherwise head out of town on the Oosterwal road and look for a signpost left to Laguna Mall and Club Mykonos. A little further you'll come to a T-junction – turn right following signposts to Club Mykonos. Follow this road past the fairly new residential area and soon you start getting views of a massive steel factory on the outskirts of Saldanha Bay. Just beyond the factory the road goes over railway lines where trains up to 2km long can be seen delivering ore from the Northern Cape. Look left and you'll see the terminal where the ore is unloaded and then transported on conveyer belts out to ships. From the town itself you get a better idea of the scale of this loading jetty stretching half a kilometre out to sea.

The two solitary rocks on the hillside above the Saldanha Bay are known as Adam and Eve but if you want stunning views, head to the Hoedjieskop Reserve, a hill in the middle of the town with 360-degree views over the bay and town. Back down in the harbour you'll find the Slipway Waterfront Restaurant, known for its steaks and delicious seafood dishes including mussels and oysters freshly plucked from the bay.

From Saldanha follow the main road out of town. It becomes the R399 and takes you straight into Vredenburg, passing beautiful granite boulders en route. Once in Vredenburg, turn left at the traffic lights onto Hoof Street, signposted to Paternoster. Following this road for 13km will take you to **Paternoster**, a quant little **fishing village** with beautiful whitewashed cottages.

If you want a spoil, check into Abalone House, the village's first five-star boutique guesthouse. Then take a drive to the Cape Colombine Reserve. The Seekombuis, an open-air seafood restaurant, is at the reserve's gates. If budget's an issue, or if you want something rustic, stay at The Beach Camp, situated right on the beach within the reserve. Whilst there do a tour of the **Cape Columbine Lighthouse** – it's definitely worth climbing the spiral staircase to the top for the spectacular views over Tietiesbaai.

Paternoster is a foodie haven, with several top-notch options for eating out. My favourite is Reuben's Restaurant at Abalone House, which has heart-warming dishes as well as a six-course tasting menu. The Gaaitjie Salt Water Restaurant, run by an absolute character, Suzi Holtzhausen, is incredibly popular but is fairly pricey. Based in a fisherman's cottage, the décor's simple yet comfortable, so the emphasis remains on the food – tasty local dishes with a Suzi twist. Try the oven-baked sole with bacon, leeks and roasted vegetables.

The Noisy Oyster is popular and the fairy lights hanging in the trees around the courtyard give the place a very romantic feel. On cold nights aim for a spot close to the fire and choose the Thai seafood curry to warm you up. Blikkie Pizzeria's two claims to fame are its second place in the South African leg of the Global Pizza Challenge and the fact that it's housed in the oldest building in Paternoster. But for location the Voorstrandt tops the charts: the red-and-green tin cottage is nestled right down on the beach. They have a variety of dishes focusing mainly on seafood and nothing beats a sundowner on their stoep.

Section ❸
Paternoster to Lambert's Bay
Distance 168km
Driving Time 3hrs 25mins
Highlights Paternoster fisherfolk, pelicans at Velddrif, Bird Island Nature Reserve, Muisbosskerm

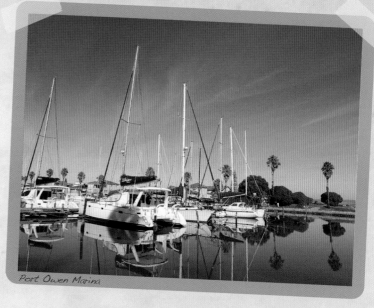

Port Owen Marina

The **fishermen in Paternoster** usually launch their colourful little boats at dawn, so it's worth heading down for a walk along the white sandy beach before breakfast.

Leaving town, turn left onto a dirt road signposted to Stompneusbaai. Just beyond the sports field you'll find the cemetery, the graves adorned with fishing nets and shells. There are many granite outcrops scattered along this route and blue crane are often seen in the fields. At the next intersection, turn left (a right turn would take you back to Vredenburg). You know you're almost at Stompneusbaai when the road drops down towards the sea, affording you great views over the bay and its large boulders protruding out of the water. There are a few fisheries on the water's edge including Lucky Star, a popular South African brand. If you have time on your hands, or feel like a game of golf, turn left on the tar road to Shelley Point and Britannia Bay. Within the estate there's also a large sculpture of Vasco Da Gama, and it's worth strolling to the lighthouse at Shelley Beach.

From Stompneusbaai the road hugs the coastline for a while, an incredibly beautiful drive on a windless day. Just after the Total garage, turn left and head down for a glimpse of the Sandy Point harbour. Continuing along the coastal road you get to St Helena Bay. The Beira Mar restaurant, one of the best restaurants in the area, is a stone's throw from the water's edge.

Continue on this road, leaving the coastline for a while, until you reach a stop sign. Turn left onto the R399 and at the next intersection turn left again

onto the R27. You pass saltpans, often packed with flamingos, before crossing the Berg River into Velddrif. **Velddrif** is famous for its *bokkoms* – to see them turn right at the stop sign and drive for 1.2km until you see Bokkom Lane. This is where the fishermen salt and dry their catch along the banks of the Berg River, so many a hopeful **pelican** will be cruising by. The signs alone are worth photographing: 'Beste Bokkoms Beste Prys', 'Ek en DJY Vissery', 'Calamarie & Tjips', 'Velddrif CBD – Central Bokkoms District'. There are a few small boat operators based on Bokkom Lane that will take you on a bird-spotting trip up the river.

Return in the direction from which you came and continue past Port Owen to Laaiplek. At the T-junction, detour left to the mouth of the Berg River and working harbour. As you enter the harbour, you find Die Vis Vlekhuis where you can get excellent fish and chips and watch the boats coming and going through the incredibly narrow mouth.

Heading back to the junction from Velddrif, go straight and follow the coastline through Dwarskersbos on to Rocherpan Nature Reserve. The 914ha reserve consists largely of a seasonal vlei that's usually dry between March and June. Their four newly refurbished cabins are ideal for birders wanting to stay long enough to tick off the 183 birds listed. White pelicans and greater and lesser flamingos, all listed in the Red Data book as endangered bird species, are often sighted.

At the next T-junction, turn left towards Elands Bay, driving past fields of potatoes and Draaihoek Lodge, with its own private nature reserve along the coastline. The road now runs parallel to the dunes and although you can't see the ocean, it's spitting distance away. Following the road

Paternoster

WEST COAST
Fossils and Fisherfolk – Riebeek-Kasteel to Lambert's Bay

uphill you get awesome views over the surrounding area and soon glimpse the Verlorenvlei wetland, which is rich in bird life. The road drops and winds beside the wetland briefly. At the next intersection, follow the sign to Elands Bay South if you want to pop down to the harbour – a hive of activity when the snoek are running. Following the sign right to Elands Bay North (Elandsbaai Noord) and then, immediately turning left once over the bridge, this road will take you into Elands Bay, a very quiet town and popular surfers' haunt (see pages 178–191, Surf Route). The streets are named after local fish – Stompneus, Bokkoms, Snoek and Kreef to name a few. Getting petrol is a bit of a giggle. There are two pumps in the middle of nowhere, and all you have to do is hoot and someone will emerge from either the bottle store or the hotel to fill your tank! The Wit Mossel Pot restaurant and backpackers has a great vibe, serves delicious seafood and really comes alive when a band's playing.

From Elands Bay, head back under the bridge, turn left onto the dirt road to Lambert's Bay and pay a small fee at the boom. Lambert's Bay isn't far but it's slow going due to corrugations. Although you can't see the ocean, the road literally hugs the dunes all the way to Lambert's Bay and the first thing you notice when you come into town is the smell of the fish processing factories and the sound of gulls. Don't miss a visit to **Bird Island Nature Reserve**, home to 25,000 Cape gannets. Lambert's Bay Boat Charters, based at the entrance to Bird Island, take trips out to view the resident Heaviside's dolphins, endemic to the West Coast and Namibia, and there's a good chance of spotting southern right whales and dusky dolphins. The world's smallest desert (all of 2km²), aptly named 'The Dunes', lies 10km out of town on the Clanwilliam road.

ON THE SIDE >> Sea birds
Bird Island Nature Reserve in Lambert's Bay provides shelter and protection for thousands of sea birds, particularly Cape gannets, various species of cormorants, and penguins. Visiting the island, you are a mere wingspan away from more than 25,000 Cape gannets listed as vulnerable on the IUCN Red Data List. While egg-laying season can happen year-round, it peaks from September to April before the birds migrate.

Isabella's Restaurant is my favourite spot for a bite. As in most coastal towns, they focus on seafood, but it's their position on the waterfront opposite Bird Island that makes the restaurant special. There is also **Muisbosskerm**, voted one of the 'Top Ten Sea Views to Dine For' by National Geographic. Booking is essential.

The quickest way back to Cape Town is to take the R365, then the R366 to the N7.

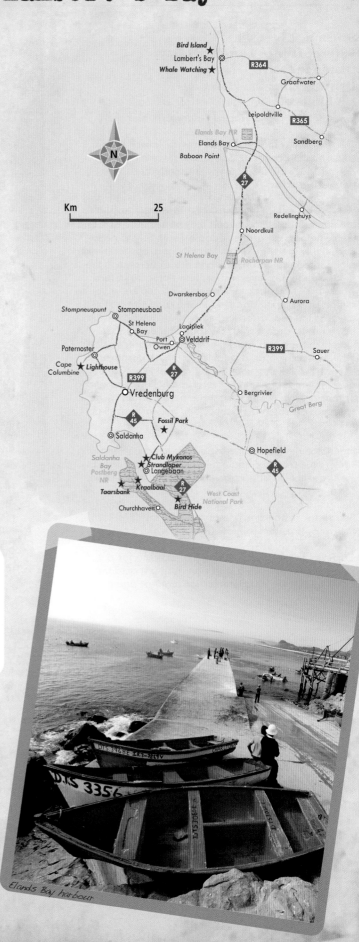

Elands Bay harbour

WEST COAST Contact details

Abalone House
022 752 2044
www.abalonehouse.co.za
Beira Mar Restaurant
022 736 1393
www.beira.co.za
Bird Island
021 483 0190
www.capenature.co.za
Blikkie Pizzeria
022 752 2246
Cape Columbine Lighthouse
021 449 2400 (reservations), 022 752 2705
www.transnetnationalportsauthority.net
Club Mykonos
080 022 6770
www.clubmykonos.co.za
Die Vis Vlekhuis
073 826 5927
Draaihoek Lodge
022 952 1170
www.draaihoek.com
Duinepos Chalets
022 707 9900 or 083 704 7067
www.duinepos.co.za
Flower Line
071 320 7146
Gaaitjie Salt Water Restaurant
022 752 2242
www.saltcoast.co.za
Geelbek Information Centre
022 707 9902/3
www.sanparks.co.za
Isabella's Restaurant
027 432 1177
!Khwa ttu
www.khwattu.org
022 492 2998
Kloovenburg
022 448 1635
www.kloovenburg.com
Lambert's Bay Boat Charter
082 922 4334
www.sadolphins.co.za
Muisbosskerm
027 432 1017
www.muisbosskerm.co.za
Reuben's Restaurant
022 752 2044
www.abalonehouse.co.za
Rocherpan Nature Reserve
021 483 0190
www.capenature.co.za
SANParks central reservations
012 428 9111
www.sanparks.co.za
Seekombuis
072 258 9041
www.seekombuis.co.za
Strandloper Seafood Restaurant
022 772 2490
www.strandloper.com

The Beach Camp
082 926 2267
www.beachcamp.co.za
The Noisy Oyster
022 752 2196
Voorstrandt
022 752 2038
www.voorstrandt.com
West Coast Fossil Park
022 766 1606
www.fossilpark.org.za
West Coast National Park
022 772 2144
www.sanparks.co.za
Wit Mossel Pot
082 496 8931

Regional info
Cape West Coast Tourism
022 433 8505
www.capewestcoast.org
Lambert's Bay Tourism
027 432 1000
www.lambertsbay.co.za
Riebeek Valley Tourism
022 448 1545
www.riebeekvalley.info

Pelican landing

PADKOS

When I'm setting out on a road trip the one thing I can't do without is good coffee. So I always have a jetboil stove with coffee plunger, some strong espresso and a slab of Lindt salt chocolate in the boot. Otherwise my weakness is cheese, so I'll always pull over for cheese tastings or a good deli.

WINELANDS
Cape Town to Somerset West

There is so much more to the Winelands than wine. And, let's face it, wine and driving really don't go together well, so I have concentrated on the more scenic, culinary and cultural aspects — but not leaving out the wine, of course.

Total Distance 184km
Driving Time 3hrs

·······································

Section ❶
Cape Town to Stellenbosch
Distance 60km
Driving Time 1hr
Highlights:
Spring flowers
Stellenbosch Botanical Gardens
Pierneef Station Panels
SEE PAGE 46

·······································

Section ❷
Stellenbosch to Franschhoek
Distance 32km
Driving Time 30mins
Highlights:
Helshoogte Pass
Tokara
Franschhoek Motor Museum
Huguenot Monument
SEE PAGE 47

·······································

Section ❸
Franschhoek to Paarl
Distance 32km
Driving Time 30mins
Highlights:
Afrikaans Taal Monument
Wine Valley Horse Trails
Manor House Alpacas
Spice Route
goat's-milk cheese
SEE PAGES 47–48

·······································

Section ❹
Paarl to Somerset West
Distance 60km
Driving Time 1hr
Highlights:
Jam
pottery
cheese
mountain-bike trails
SEE PAGES 48–49

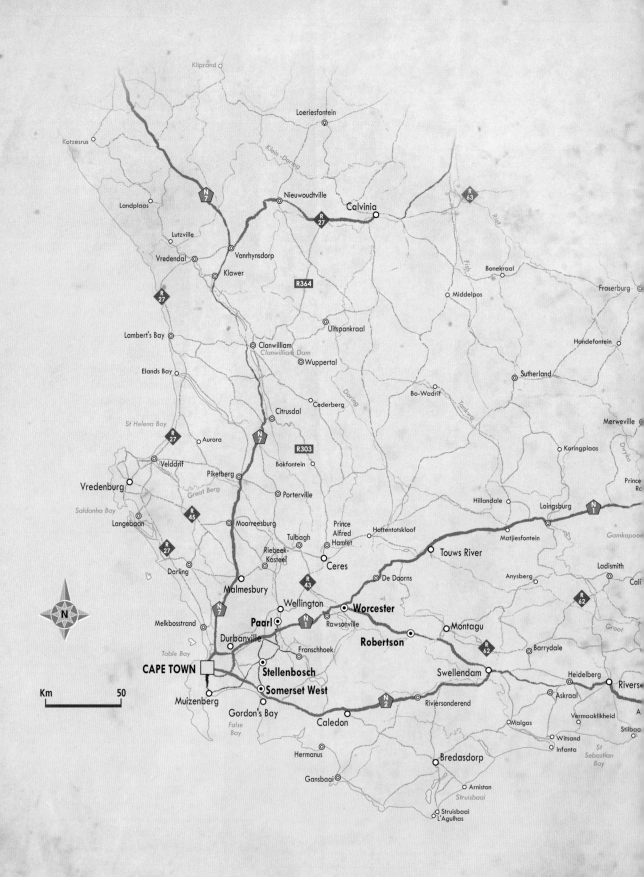

In a nutshell:
A series of marginally overlapping day trips between the main wine-growing centres.

Logistics
The route is laid out as one big loop around Stellenbosch and Paarl, but you could also stay in Stellenbosch, Paarl or Franschhoek and modify the route to form a series of loops. Some backtracking is necessary, but the distances are not huge.

Driving conditions
Good tarred roads but with relatively long gravel driveways. At time of writing, the alpaca farm had an appalling driveway but it is due for upgrading in time for the official opening of the venue at the end of 2013.

Pet-friendly rating ★ ☆ ☆ ☆ ☆
1 = least suited 5 = most suited

Child-friendly rating ★ ★ ★ ★ ☆
1 = least suited 5 = most suited

Low-slung vehicle-friendly rating ★ ★ ★ ★ ☆
1 = high clearance 5 = lowest slung

Don't miss
- Pierneef Station Panels at Rupert Museum
- Nelson Mandela statue
- Paarl Rock
- Taal Monument
- Huguenot Monument and Museum, Franschhoek
- alpacas
- oh – and a million great food and wine options

Emergency service numbers
Emergency (from a landline) 10111
Emergency (from a cellphone) 112
AA roadside assistance 086 100 0234 or 083 843 22 (24 hours)
If you've had too much to drink, call a designated driver to get you and your car home or to your hotel:
Goodfellas 086 143 3552
Scooter Angels 086 146 4663
Smartguyz 086 176 2786

Best time
There is no best time, really. The Winelands are always wonderful. It can be a bit hot in summer, but then it's great to park off in a cool cellar. And, when it's chilly in winter or autumn, there is nothing better than sipping red wine by a log fire. It's best to avoid high holiday seasons and, if you can, you will find everything much quieter during the week, but check for closed days.

SUMMER			AUTUMN			WINTER			SPRING		
D	J	F	M	A	M	J	J	A	S	O	N

Background reading
My Wine Route by Mike Froud (www.mapstudio.co.za) is probably the best available guide to local wine, so it's worth reading to decide which wineries you may like to visit for tasting.

ON THE SIDE >> Drinking and driving
Don't. Really, just don't. Unless you are a very experienced wine taster and skilled expectorator who can hit a spittoon from ten paces, you really need to choose between tasting and driving. And if you can't decide among you who is going to do which, hire a chauffeur or do a guided tour, and leave your car at the hotel. Winelands Experience is one company that offers tailor-made chauffeur-driven wine-tasting trips.

WINELANDS
Cape Town to Somerset West

Section ❶
Cape Town to Stellenbosch
Distance 60km
Driving Time 1hr
Highlights Spring flowers, Stellenbosch Botanical Gardens, Pierneef Station Panels

If you want to visit the Constantia and Cape Point wineries before leaving town, head out on the R310 (Baden Powell Drive). This scenic route hugs the False Bay coast and skirts past Khayelitsha.

ON THE SIDE >> Detour
It doesn't sound particularly glamorous but, if you are a keen birder, turn left into Strandfontein Road, continue for about 4km and turn off to Zeekoevlei and the sewerage works. You can see up to 80 different species on a good summer's morning.

If you've taken the R310, continue over the N2 or, if you've taken the N2, take the R310 towards Stellenbosch. This is the start of the Stellenbosch Wine Route and you will see the first of hundreds (if not thousands) of wine-tasting options. I am not even going to try to tell you where you should stop for wine tasting. It almost doesn't matter as there are no bad wineries, just some that are better, prettier or better value than others. If you're serious about wine, check out *Platter's South African Wines* or the wine route websites. Or spend six months visiting every cellar.

Once in Stellenbosch, there is so much to do other than wine. You could spend hours just walking up Dorp Street admiring the gorgeous buildings and choosing from the plethora of food outlets for a quick or leisurely refuel. The **Stellenbosch Botanical Gardens** are a little secret on the corner of Van Riebeeck and Neethling streets, where you can chill out with a cup of tea or watch the students lounging around on the lawns, snoozing, chatting or quickly catching up on pre-tut reading. There are loads of gorgeous exotic plants, bonsais, a gift shop and a tearoom.

There are so many museums, national monuments and great buildings, but I think the one thing you should not miss is the exhibition of the **Pierneef Station Panels** at the Rupert Museum. Okay, I am a Pierneef fan and may even buy one when I become a best-selling author and outsell Wilbur Smith.

Just before you reach the N2, there is an intermittent sculpture garden where you can view and buy interesting large sculptures from the artist if and when he is there. His main subject seems to be baboons, which he has perfected.

This route traverses the Wolfgat Nature Reserve and is spectacular in **spring**, when there are **flowers** everywhere – including more arum lilies than you ever imagined could exist in one place. And this despite the ongoing illegal picking and selling of these gorgeously graphic plants. The plants aren't endangered, but the cute little orange-footed arum frog, which can live only in them, is. So don't buy arum lilies on the side of the road, tempting as it may be. Don't take this road just after or during a strong southeaster as it is covered in sand and can be quite dangerous – if you don't end up slewing across the road, other vehicles probably will, so rather opt for the N2 in these conditions.

Scenic winelands

Section ❷
Stellenbosch to Franschhoek
Distance 32km
Driving Time 30mins
Highlights Helshoogte Pass, Tokara, Franschhoek Motor Museum, Huguenot Monument

Taal Monument, Paarl

ON THE SIDE >> Me Me Me time
The Hydro at Stellenbosch was South Africa's first hydro and wellness centre, and it is still one of the few that does more than aromatherapy and facials. You can spend a day here just being pampered, a weekend chilling, or a more extended period for a serious de-stress or detox — all in fabulous surroundings.

Heading out of Stellenbosch, continue on the R310, over the **Helshoogte Pass**. There are loads of wineries here, but the one that offers most in the way of other attractions is **Tokara**. It's on the left, and Thelema is on the same road, so you could do them both if you like. As well as great wine, Tokara makes fantastic olive oil. Do a tasting at the Olive Shed and then buy some oil or other yummy things from the deli, which also serves excellent coffee and great deli-style meals. There is also a more formal restaurant. Most impressive, though, is probably the view. You can see forever from up there, so take a stroll around.

From Tokara, continue towards Franschhoek. Slow down after passing Zorgvliet because the turn-off to Hillcrest Berry Orchard sneaks up on you pretty suddenly. Here you can get the best scones (with a choice of truly yummy jams). And, of course, there's a small deli and gift shop.

Slow down as you drive through the village of Pniel. People live here, children walk to school and dogs may well wander across the road.

Turn right onto the R45 towards Franschhoek, and pop into L'Ormarins to check out the huge collection of vintage cars and other transport memorabilia at the **Franschhoek Motor Museum**. And taste the wine, too, of course.

There is so much to do in Franschhoek, you will probably want to stay a week. It's a sophisticated food venue, the wineries are fantastic and there is a strong Gallic influence. Find out more at the **Huguenot Monument** and Museum, which commemorates the French protestant refugees who were so influential in developing South Africa's wine industry. For a relaxed tour of the town, hop on the Wine Tram, and hop off if you would like to spend more time somewhere.

Section ❸
Franschhoek to Paarl
Distance 32km
Driving Time 30mins
Highlights Afrikaans Taal Monument, Wine Valley Horse Trails, Manor House Alpacas, Spice Route, goat's-milk cheese

Take the main road (R45) from Franschhoek to Paarl, which is unlike any other main road you have ever seen. Keep a beady eye out for the sign to the **Afrikaans Taal Monument** as it is easily missed. You turn left, and then need to follow the tiny little brown signs that only display the monument symbol. After a few twists and turns you are on the road that takes you directly up Paarl Mountain and to the monument. It's an interesting place, with a fantastic view. There's a small shop and take-away and it's a great place for a picnic. You can walk all the way up Paarl Mountain from here. If you want to continue the theme, pop in to the Afrikaans Language Museum in the town.

ON THE SIDE >> Short detour to freedom
About 5km before the N1 on the R301, turn in to Groot Drakenstein Prison. If you plan ahead you can visit the house in which Nelson Mandela spent his last days as a prisoner, but you can have a look at the wonderful Jean Doyle bronze of him at the gate without any prior booking. Take a while to study the plinth and ponder the symbolism of the Malmesbury shale, the prison bars and the broken barbed wire. The statue stands on the very spot that Mandela took his first steps as a free man.

Return to the Main Road, from where the route describes an anti-clockwise circle around Paarl Mountain. Continue with the Main Road, skirting the CBD. As you leave town, the road wiggles a bit and then splits, with the Main Road going left and the R45 heading right. Follow the Main Road then turn left into Rhebokskloof. This is the home of **Wine Valley Horse Trails**, which offers horse-wagon tours through the vineyards, and quad-bike tours and horse rides around the farm or up Paarl Mountain.

WINELANDS
Cape Town to Somerset West

After leaving Wine Valley Horse Trails, turn left onto the R44 towards Stellenbosch and look out for Olywenbosch on your left-hand side. Do an olive oil tasting and maybe buy some of their balsamic vinegar. A little further on, you can detour off to the right to visit Vesuvio, another great olive farm.

Turn left into the Suid Agter Paarl Road. After about a kilometre you'll find **Manor House Alpacas** on the left. I was there in May 2013, and they weren't quite ready for mainstream tourists yet, and I was really pleased I was driving the little 4x4 I had borrowed from Bobo Campers for my Not the N1 trip because the road was – well – challenging and I really would not have liked to take my cute little hatchback on it. I spent a while chatting to the owner, looking at the half-finished building, cuddling the alpacas, and admiring the beautiful alpaca wool products. The plan is that, by early 2014, the road will be usable by all vehicles, the coffee shop and wool shop will be completed and there will be a special alpaca cuddling section. These animals are just so adorable that spending five minutes with them is virtually guaranteed to put a smile on your face for the rest of the day.

After the alpacas, continue for a couple of kilometres and turn left into **Spice Route**. This is an amazing destination that offers so much more than the expected wine tasting and huge restaurant. You can watch glass blowing at the Red Hot Glass Studio and admire and/or buy a range of beautiful decorative or utilitarian glass works of art. And then there are the other wonderfully apt food and drink pairing options that may appeal to different members of your party. A beer and biltong tasting makes sense, as does coffee and handmade chocolate. And perhaps end it all with pizza and grappa. An awesome place that can keep you occupied (and extremely well fed) for ages.

Virtually next door is Fairview, with its great wine and renowned range of **goat's-milk** (and cow's-milk) **cheeses**. You can marvel at the goat tower, taste a range of cheeses and buy all kinds of yummy things in the deli. In summer, they have wonderful children's programmes, including a cheese-making workshop.

Section 4
Paarl to Somerset West
Distance 60km
Driving Time 1hr
Highlights Jam, pottery, cheese, mountain-bike trails

Continue on the Suid Agter Paarl Road under the N1, onto the R101 and then take the R45 back towards Franschhoek. After about 5 or 6km, turn right into the Simondium/Klapmuts Road (still the R45). After a few kilometres, the **Jam Jar** is on your right-hand side. It's a tiny little place that makes a superb range of jams. I rather fancied the roasted chilli jam and the lavender jelly. They don't take credit cards, so make sure you have cash. On the left, a bit further on, is **Nico Liebenberg's pottery studio**. He does a beautiful range of stoneware, ovenware, hand basins and other wonderful objects.

After another few kilometres **Dalewood Cheeses** is on the left. Here you can taste a range of great cheeses including, if you're lucky, South Africa's champion cheese, Huguenot. Unfortunately, it is made in relatively small quantities and is often out of stock. I was there just a week before the new batch was due to mature.

> **ON THE SIDE >> Take a flutter**
> It's worth turning right and going across the N1 to visit Butterfly World – especially if you are travelling with children. It's a huge greenhouse-type thing with luxuriant plants and thousands of free-flying butterflies.

Turn left onto the R44 towards Stellenbosch. Warwick Wine Estate on the right-hand side of the road offers a Big Five wine safari, weather permitting. It's a steep and scenic drive in an open safari-style vehicle through the vineyards to the top of the mountain, showing the Big Five wine varieties: Cabernet Sauvignon, Sauvignon Blanc, Pinotage, Merlot and Cabernet Franc. They do great picnics in summer and, in winter, tapas in front of a log fire.

A little further on is the multi-purpose wine-and-everything venue Delvera. There's an on-site potter, a jeweller who works almost exclusively in used spoons, mountain-bike hire, great **MTB trails**, horse rides, donkeys and a kiddies' boot camp that should keep the little ones out of your hair for a while. Chrisna's Olives has a range of great olives as well as olive oil and some other deli products. They offer moonlight walks, and trail runners can scamper around the farm on a designated trail.

Muratie is about a kilometre from the R44 on the road to Delheim. I have always loved Muratie as much for its great wine and superb port as the look and feel. It's one of South Africa's oldest wineries and it has undergone minimal structural and decorative changes over the years. In fact, until the 1980s it looked much as it must have for the previous two centuries. It has recently been expanded to include a restaurant and a low-key gallery, but it has retained its character and still feels like a cellar with rough walls and unfinished cement floors. They've added a few threadbare rugs and some paintings, but they haven't desecrated the ancient walls with paint. I noticed some of the old cobwebs have been sacrificed, but there is a new crop forming so it should be back up to speed in a decade or so. Try the handmade nougat.

Mooiberge Strawberry Farm

Here you can turn back towards the N1 or continue with the R44 through Stellenbosch towards Somerset West. En route you will pass the Mooiberge Farm Stall and Strawberry Farm. Even if you don't stop for the yummy deli goods or to pick your own strawberries in season, you can't help but notice the wonderfully inventive scarecrows. They change regularly, but are always entertaining. Continue to Somerset West, and take the N2 back to Cape Town or join up with the Overberg Route (see pages 62–69). If you decide to head back towards the N1, skive off on the R304, pass the turn-off to the R101 and take the next right to Joostenberg Deli & Bistro to refuel or stock up before you head off on your next adventure.

WINELANDS Contact details

Afrikaans Language Museum
021 872 3441
www.taalmuseum.co.za
Botanical Gardens
021 808 2330
www.sun.ac.za/botanicalgarden
Dalewood Fromage
021 875 5725
www.dalewood.co.za
Delvera
021 884 4352
www.delvera.co.za
Fairview
021 863 2450
www.fairview.co.za
Franschhoek Motor Museum
021 874 9000
www.fmm.co.za
Franschhoek Wine Tram
021 300 0338
www.winetram.co.za
Groot Drakenstein Prison
021 483 9715, 021 483 9727
Hillcrest Berry Orchards
021 885 1629
www.hillcrestberries.co.za
Huguenot Memorial Museum
021 876 2532
www.museum.co.za
Huguenot Monument
021 876 3649
www.hugenoot.org.za
Jam Jar
084 549 9925
Joostenberg Deli & Bistro
021 884 4141
www.joostenberg.co.za
Manor House Alpacas
084 425 5535 or 084 793 3666
www.alpacas.co.za

Mooiberge Farm Stall and Strawberry Farm
021 881 3222
www.mooiberge.co.za
Muratie
021 865 2330/6
www.muratie.co.za
Olywenbosch
021 869 8035
www.olywenbosch.co.za
Pottery by Nico Liebenberg
083 564 5350
www.nicoliebenbergpottery.co.za
Rupert Museum
021 880 1344
www.rupertmusuem.org
Spice Route
021 863 5200
www.spiceroute.co.za
Taal Monument
021 863 4809
www.taalmonument.co.za
Tokara
021 808 5900
www.tokara.co.za
Warwick Wine Estate
021 884 3144
www.warwickwine.com
Winelands Experience
021 876 4042
www.winelands.travel
Wine Valley Horse Trails
083 226 8735
www.horsetrails-sa.co.za

Regional info
www.franschhoek.org.za
www.paarlonline.com
www.somersetwestinfo.co.za
www.stellenbosch.travel
www.wineroute.co.za

ROUTE 62, THE PASSES AND BEYOND
Cape Town to Oudtshoorn

There are few drives in South Africa more scenic than Route 62, particularly if you detour off the main drag and take the spectacular passes as described below. The landscape is dominated by tortured orange rocks, folded by tectonic forces then weathered by the elements, providing a dramatic contrast to the orderly rows of vines and orchards. Marketed as the longest wine route in the world, the route is also a botanist's dream, taking you from Cape fynbos, through the succulent Karoo, past the pristine Bosmansbos Wilderness (one of eight protected areas that comprise the Cape Floral Region World Heritage Site) and through the heart of another, the Swartberg Nature Reserve.

The route, modelled on Route 66 in the USA, takes in the small towns of the Langkloof, the Breede River and the Klein Karoo and is a quieter and more attractive drive than the busy N2 highway. The arts and crafts, hot springs, fine wines and ports, quirky towns, plethora of trendy coffee shops and quaint guesthouses, and the chance to open up and speed down the straight Karoo roads on a motorbike are what draw most travellers to the route. But my pilgrimages are of a different sort. I take this road because I love rocks. I can barely keep my eyes on the road as I pass one great folded range after the other. The steep faces and deeply incised kloofs just beg to be explored. So it's no surprise that the R62 is the gateway to some of the country's best wilderness-hiking and rock-climbing areas: Montagu, the Mecca of rock climbing in the Western Cape; Towerkop, scaled on the first recorded rock climb in South Africa; Seweweekspoort Peak, the highest top in the Western Cape, and Oudtshoorn, the only limestone crag in the country.

Total Distance 600km
Driving Time 8hrs 42mins

Section ❶
Cape Town to Barrydale
Distance 273km
Driving Time 3hrs 45mins
Highlights:
Springfield Wine Estate
Sheilam Cactus and Succulent Garden
Cogman's Kloof
Blue cranes dancing in the fields
Barrydale
SEE PAGES 54–56

Section ❷
Barrydale to Prince Albert
Distance 216km
Driving Time 3hrs 30mins
Highlights:
Seweweekspoort
Groenfontein Valley
Swartberg Pass
Die Hel
SEE PAGES 56–58

Section ❸
Prince Albert to Oudtshoorn
Distance 111km
Driving Time 1hr 27mins
Highlights:
Meiringspoort
A meal at Kalinka
Cango Wildlife Ranch
SEE PAGES 59–60

ROUTE 62, THE PASSES AND BEYOND
Cape Town to Oudtshoorn

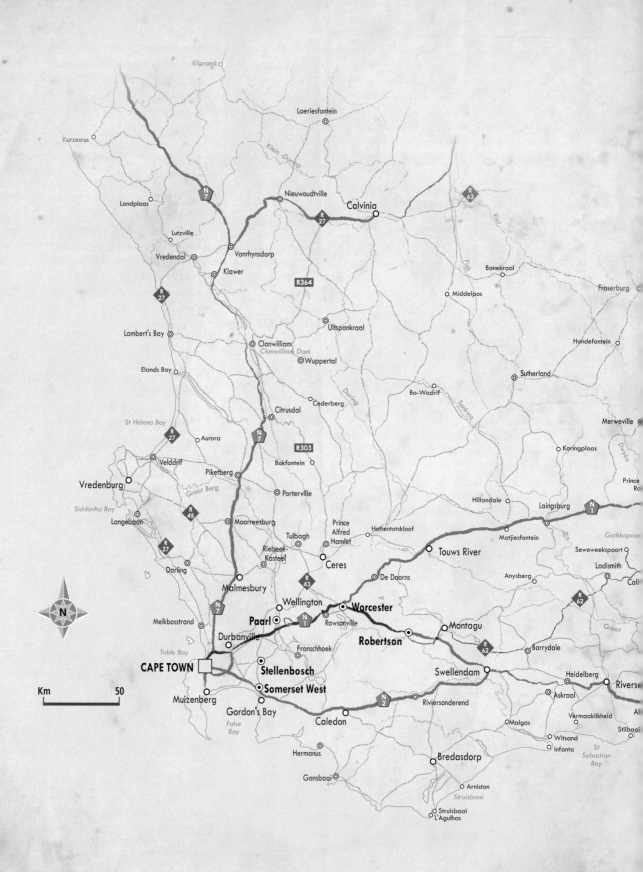

In a nutshell:

A scenic journey along the longest wine route in the world, from the Cape Winelands to the rocky poorts and passes of the Karoo.

Logistics
Cape Town is the logical starting point and there are also airports at Port Elizabeth and George. From Oudtshoorn you can zap down to George to join the Garden Route (see pages 70–81), continue on the R62 to PE and link into the Frontier Country route (see pages 82–89) or head north to link up with the Not the N1 route (see pages 8–21).

Driving conditions
Be prepared for serious mountain weather on the Swartberg Pass and check the condition of the Groenfontein road before setting out. The optional detours to Die Hel and through Anysberg are on extremely rough roads, which you need to drive VERY carefully if you are in a sedan.

Pet-friendly rating ★★★☆☆
1 = least suited 5 = most suited

Child-friendly rating ★★★★☆
1 = least suited 5 = most suited
This is a route that you can take slowly, stopping often to smell the flowers, to walk and to check out interesting fauna like ostriches, meerkats and even crocodiles, so it's a good route for kids.

Low-slung vehicle-friendly rating ★★★★☆
1 = high clearance 5 = lowest slung
Other than the optional detours to Die Hel and back through Anysberg, the roads are good.

Don't miss
- A tasting, or two, at one of the Robertson Valley wine farms
- The Seweweekspoort, Swartberg and Meiringspoort passes

Emergency service numbers
Emergency (from a landline) 10111
Emergency (from a cellphone) 112
AA roadside assistance 086 100 0234 or 083 843 22 (24 hours)

Best time
The Karoo experiences extreme temperatures, so late spring (September to November) and autumn (April and May) are the best months.

SUMMER			AUTUMN			WINTER			SPRING		
D	J	F	M	A	M	J	J	A	S	O	N

Background reading
Karoo Keepsakes by Chris Marais & Julienne du Toit. A fantastic resource and an entertaining insight into the people and stories of the Karoo.
Platter's South African Wines
Bird and flower field guides

Don't forget
Binoculars

ROUTE 62, THE PASSES AND BEYOND
Cape Town to Oudtshoorn

Section ❶
Cape Town to Barrydale
Distance 273km
Driving Time 3hrs 45mins
Highlights Springfield Wine Estate, Sheilam Cactus and Succulent Garden, Cogman's Kloof, blue cranes dancing in the fields, Barrydale

Google the R62 and you'll get a bewildering array of starting points with a number of towns jumping onto the marketing bandwagon. The R62 regional road actually starts in Ashton and ends in Humansdorp near Port Elizabeth, but most people start their journey in Cape Town, choosing this inland route to PE over the busier N2.

Despite being on the N1, a major highway, the drive out of Cape Town is very pretty. The great granite mounds of Paarl Rock rise out of the vine-covered plains to the left, while the Simonsberg and Fransch-hoek mountains dominate the view to the right. It's hard to resist detouring to sample some of the fine wines on the picturesque back roads of the Fransch-hoek and Stellenbosch regions but fear not, there are plenty of little-known wine farms on your journey.

You're on a passes route, so just before the Huguenot Toll Tunnel turn off left and take the R101 over the Du Toitskloof Pass. It's a bit longer than the alternative toll tunnel, but the views are stupendous and there are lots of picnic spots where you can soak in the views of Paarl, the Berg River, Table Bay and the sprawling city of Cape Town. Once down in Du Toitskloof you re-join the N1 to Worcester then turn right onto the R60.

The R60 runs through the valley of the Breede River, one of the largest navigable rivers in the country. Numerous rafting companies offer fun paddling trips, often with wine tasting thrown in, should you need diversion. Other distractions include numerous farm stalls, the best of which are The Country Pumpkin and Rooiberg Winery, home to the Bodega de Vinho bakery and delicatessen. The BYO picnic garden makes this a convivial stop, and kids (and big kids) can scale their famous landmark, the biggest chair in the country.

The centre of the Robertson Valley wine area, Robertson is an obvious starting point for a Route 62 journey 'proper'. The valley offers four major wine festivals and produces some of the best white wines in the country.

Boasting several provincial heritage sites, the jacaranda-lined town is also home to Reuben's, owned by celebrity chef Reuben Riffel. Just on the edge of town, the Dassieshoek Nature Reserve has some stunning hikes, including one of the most spectacular overnight hikes in the country, the Arangieskop hiking trail.

The biggest chair in the country

ON THE SIDE >> Longer detours
Unless you're in a rush, factor in some extra time to explore the Robertson Valley. A drift down the Breede River sipping wine and nibbling deli delights, a walk in the Vrolikheid Nature Reserve, a stop in arty McGregor and tastings at the boutique wine farms of Bonnievale can be woven into a short semicircular route between Robertson and Ashton.

TIP

The Karoo Botanical Garden, at the entrance to Worcester, is a great spot to stretch your legs or to picnic on the well-kept lawns surrounded by birds and prickly succulents.

Once you're through Robertson, deviate briefly from the R62 by taking the R317 towards Bonnievale and swing off 3km later at **Springfield Wine Estate** to sample my favourite wine, 'Life from Stone'. This gorgeous estate offers free tastings and the opportunity to bring your own picnic to enjoy at the tables out by the dam.

From Springfield, continue along the R317, enjoying the striking cannas and rows of vines, before turning left at Bon Courage to rejoin the R62 towards Ashton. This is a beautiful road lined with wonderful bougainvillea, squat palm trees and colourfully painted Wellington boots! Someone at the quirky Klaasvoogds Post Office-cum-general store-cum-wine and petrol sales shop clearly has a sense of humour. And as you cross the railway tracks look out for quaintly dressed 'patient passengers' sitting on a bench.

Detour briefly (again!) by turning left onto the R60, then, as you hit the hill, take a right onto the Klaasvoogds West Road. The Klaasvoogds Meander is one of the R62's best-kept secrets — the Constantia of Robertson if you like — with some stunning wine farms, restaurants and guesthouses like Mo and Rose and Fraai Uitzicht 1798, as well as the **Sheilam Cactus and Succulent Garden**. Walking into this operating nursery feels as if you've just stepped out of Dr Who's Tardis in Mexico! Vast, and I mean VAST, cacti pierce the blue sky and there is row upon row of prickly 'Golden barrels of Mexico' — a type of *Echinocactus* (otherwise known as Mother-in-law's chair) — as well as fascinating little stone plants and other treasures indoors.

There's no avoiding scruffy Ashton. The most remarkable thing about the town is its mountainous setting, though Platform 62, behind the historic steam locomotive, has a good selection of local produce, including wines at cellar prices, and a good café, The Shed Restaurant.

But the next section, through **Cogman's Kloof**, is as scenic as it gets. The pass, along the Kingna River, was surveyed by Thomas Bain who, with his father, Andrew Geddes Bain, was responsible for surveying many of the passes in the southern Cape in the second half of the 19th century. Just before you approach the tunnel (often described as 'the window into the Karoo'), look at the cliffs on your right. Montagu is the mecca of rock climbing in the Cape and you'll often see climbers on the Legoland crags.

With its dramatic setting, beautiful architecture, quaint B&Bs, arts and crafts route, wonderful restaurants and laid-back vibe, Montagu is my favourite town on Route 62. If you want to pamper yourself, you can wallow in the hot springs, stop off at the Montagu Cellars to sip the region's famous Muscadel or treat yourself to dinner in the courtyard or cozy dining room at Jessica's Restaurant. But for the ultimate spoil, book a wine-tasting and sightseeing trip in the Montagu Country Hotel's vintage Cadillac.

And if active pursuits are more your thing, pull into De Bos camping and chalets to mingle with the climbing and mountain-biking fraternity, or head out on the 16km Bloupunt Hiking Trail from Die Ou Meul (The Old Mill) information centre in the Montagu Mountain Reserve.

A stunning drive past yet more folded orange cliffs brings you to the Montagu Guano Cave, 8km out of town. The holiday resort has various attractions including an adventurous trip to a cave system nestled in one of the deep kloofs. The cave is home to thousands of bats, the second biggest colony in South Africa.

TIP

Keep your eyes peeled and you'll often spot a typical Overberg inhabitant, the **blue crane**, on the next section of the drive.

You're now on the Klein Karoo Wine Route, the country's easternmost wine-producing region. Stretching from Montagu to the Langkloof, it is drier than most other wine regions but enjoys a diverse terroir. The scenery changes to more typically Karoo as you pass Sanbona Wildlife Reserve (another wonderful spoil if you have time to linger), climb up the Op de Tradouw Pass then begin the steep descent down the other side into Barrydale.

Sheilam Cactus and Succulent Garden

ROUTE 62

ROUTE 62, THE PASSES AND BEYOND
Cape Town to Oudtshoorn

If you have time for a detour, or are heading to Swellendam/the N2, take a drive over the historic Tradouw Pass, stopping to enjoy the spectacular views, swimming holes and waterfalls that cascade off the cliffs. This inspired route – another of Thomas Bain's masterpieces – is stunning at any time of year but is particularly impressive in its spring colours and in late autumn when the pass is a blaze of magnificent red aloes, many of which, along with indigenous trees, were planted when the pass was rebuilt, widened and tarred before reopening in 1980.

ON THE SIDE >> Thomas Bain
Thomas Bain, 'the man with the theodolite eye', was a master builder who, when surveying, would travel the region on horseback with his compass and theodolite, eyeing up river courses and sketching what he thought looked like the best line to build a pass.

Surrounded by orchards and wine farms, **Barrydale** enjoys a beautiful setting at the foot of the Langeberg Mountains and has developed as one of the major stopping-off points on the R62, with lots of funky cafés, restaurants and quirky shops. Most are on the R62 itself, which actually bypasses the town, but it's worth seeking out some of the less prominent gems such as The Blue Cow, a great brunch spot at the Waterfront, and the wonderfully fresh Mediterranean fare at Mez on Van Riebeeck Street. And if you want bragging rights, invest in a piece of artwork from Magpie Collective's gallery. Two of their chandeliers, made from recycled plastic, hang in the White House, a nod to President Obama's taste in modern art.

Section ❷
Barrydale to Prince Albert
Distance 216km
Driving Time 3hrs 30mins
Highlights Seweweekspoort, Groenfontein Valley, Swartberg Pass, Die Hel

The high peaks of the Bosmansbos wilderness area dominate the view to the right as you continue east through orchards and great tilted slabs of shale into more open country. A stop at Ronnies Sex Shop, one of the icons of the R62, is almost mandatory. Ronnie originally intended opening a farm stall, and painted 'Ronnies Shop' on the wall, but his friends changed the name as a joke – an unintended, but brilliant, piece of marketing that has ensured the popularity of this roadside pub, particularly with bikers. Since there are braai facilities, and braai packs and salad for sale as well as a small menu, it makes a good pit stop.

ON THE SIDE >> The sock is the proof
Towerkop's place in mountain lore was assured when, in 1885, a local farmer, Gustaf Nefdt, scrambled up its reputably unscaleable cliffs to the summit, thereby notching up South Africa's first recorded rock-climbing route. When his claim to have conquered the peak was refuted, he roped up some witnesses and, from under a summit rock, produced one of his socks as proof!

An interesting detour is to take the gravel road out of Ladismith (towards Knuyswagensdrift) past the Ladismith Elandsberg water-seepage tunnel. There's not much to see other than an old crane and evidence of excavations, but a signboard explains the significance of this unique underground tunnel that delivers pure mountain water to the Ladismith community.

About 2.5km along this road is the trail head for the hike to Stanley's Light, a somewhat controversial local attraction. In 1963 Stanley de Wit, a keen mountaineer, harnessed the energy of water from a perennial stream to power a light that could be seen from town. Be warned, the 14km round trip is a stern undertaking that will take the best part of a day.

WELCOME TO OUR COUNTRY PUMPKIN

The road continues through the verdant apricot orchards of the picturesque Hoeko Valley back to the R62, and then on through a pretty kloof to the turn-off to Seweweekspoort (the R323), coined by C Louis Leipoldt, the famous doctor and poet, 'one of the seven wonders of the Cape'. It's a good gravel road that becomes increasingly narrow as the drama unfolds. Everywhere you look are great walls of folded rock with aloes and other brave plants clinging to the cliffs. The road crosses the river several times and a short walk from one of the many picnic sites shaded by a rock overhang reveals cooling pools and fountains.

Once through **Seweweekspoort** you have choices. A right turn will take you to the Gamkapoort Dam, a dead end but fun place to chill in one of the basic cottages belonging to the charismatic Fox Lederboer. Alternatively you can head back to Cape Town on the R323 through Vleiland and pick up the N1 at Laingsburg (or return via the Anysberg Nature Reserve — see page 59).

But if you are continuing east, drive back through the poort — no great hardship since there are very different views — and follow the R62 for 27km and over the Huisrivier Pass to Calitzdorp.

Seweweekspoort

Amalienstein church

Nestled in the foothills of the Swartberg, the sleepy town of Calitzdorp is renowned as the port capital of South Africa. And a tour of the cellars, or a visit to the annual port festival in June, should be high on your list of must-do's. But, with its classic Karoo façades, historical homesteads, galleries, studios and eclectic eateries — including Lorenzo's pizzeria and deli, Die Handelshuis and the Red Coffee Pot — not to mention eccentric locals, the Klein Karoo enclave has more than just fortified wine to detain the traveller.

TIP
Swing by the Dutch Reformed Church (a national monument) at 18:00 to listen to a recital on its magnificent organ.

ON THE SIDE >> The train station
The old train station, on the edge of town, has been converted into a camp ground/backpackers' lodge, so makes an unusual place to lay your head.

The R328 (the Groenfontein road) from Calitzdorp towards Prince Albert is one of the prettiest roads in the country — another wonderfully scenic trip on an undulating gravel road that offers superb mountain views.

The **Groenfontein Valley** route has flourished in recent years and you'll pass boutique wine farms such as Du'SwaRoo and Peter Bayly wine farms, and a number of studios including Clementine's pottery studio, De Oude Poskantoor Gallery & Coffee Shop, and woodworker and photographer Roger Young's gallery, housed in a renovated school building in Kruisrivier. Light lunches, teas and coffees are served on the verandah of the gallery, making this a very rewarding stop when in need of a short break. Alternatively, stop for a swim or picnic at the Calitzdorp Dam. The surrounding slopes are covered with spekboom, an evergreen succulent that is popular due to its propensity to absorb greenhouse gases.

TIP
Take a peek at the lovely old church at the former Amalienstein Mission, down the dirt road almost opposite the Seweweekspoort turn-off.

ON THE SIDE >> Red Hills
The bright red outcrops of the Red Hills (Rooikoppe) to the east of Calitzdorp were formed millions of years ago by tectonic action along the Kango Fault and are reminiscent of Uluru in Australia. Isolated koppies, made of iron-rich sediments, which have oxidised into the distinctive red, are found in a line all the way from Calitzdorp to De Rust.

A couple of unusual relic species that have lived on in these ancient sediments include a cycad, *Encephalatos horridus*, and an ancient fish that is still found in the streams that run off the Swartberg foothills.

TIP
Bikers love to open up on this road — take care!

ROUTE 62, THE PASSES AND BEYOND
Cape Town to Oudtshoorn

ON THE SIDE >> Succulents
The area boasts around 500 species of indigenous succulent, 200 of which are endemic.

TIP

Gravel roads can be a challenge during and after heavy rain, so call the tourism office, or any of the establishments along the route, for updates on road conditions.

The turn-off to Prince Albert is 55km from Calitzdorp. Continuing on the R328 would bring you round, past the Cango Caves, and down into Oudtshoorn to rejoin the R62, but taking the direct route would deprive you of driving one of the most spectacular mountain passes in the world, the Swartberg Pass. The author Lawrence Green declared, 'I have travelled only one road in my lifetime more dramatic, and that was the fifteen thousand foot pass beyond Darjeeling that leads into Tibet.' The pass, built in 1888 by – you guessed it – Thomas Bain, was declared a South African National Monument in its centenary year and is a provincial heritage site.

A good gravel road takes you to Die Top where you can stretch your legs and enjoy the incredible views. A little way down the other side of the pass you'll see the huts at Ou Tol, one of the overnight stops on the Swartberg hiking trail. There are a couple of short, circular hiking trails here on which you can enjoy the magnificent fynbos of this range, one of the protected areas that make up the Cape Floral Region World Heritage Site.

ON THE SIDE >> Vegetation
The Swartberg Mountains support a diverse range of different vegetation types including renosterveld, fynbos, Karoo veld, spekboom veld (a form of succulent thicket), numerous lilies and other geophyte species, and wonderful lichens. Although most plants flower in spring, there is colour throughout the year, and in early autumn flowering protea and erica species attract large numbers of sugarbirds and sunbirds. Apparently some 680 plant species occur within 100m of the **Swartberg Pass** – so while you're catching your breath, take a wander or get down on your haunches and smell the flowers!

Prince Albert, at the northern foot of the Swartberg Pass, is a gem. A pretty town surrounded by orchards and wheat fields, it is somewhere to unwind and take in the vastness, stark beauty and quirkiness of the Karoo. Get your bearings and book accommodation at the Lazy Lizard café and curio shop then settle down for an evening of Karoo lamb, warm hospitality and star-studded night skies.

ON THE SIDE >> Detour to Die Hel
As you descend towards Prince Albert you'll see the famous Otto du Plessis road that leads into the hidden valley of Gamkaskloof, or **Die Hel** as it's also known. A rough and steep gravel road, it's not for the faint-hearted, though it can be driven (very carefully) in a sedan. In the 1800s the animals of a party of trekboers disappeared into the kloof. The trekboers followed them into a well-watered valley and decided to settle there. This was the beginning of the small community, which had virtually no contact with the outside world – the only way into the valley was on foot and provisions were brought in on the backs of donkeys. The Road to Hell, the gravel road from the Swartberg Pass, was constructed in 1962 and named after Dr Otto du Plessis, the Administrator of the Cape at that time. Far from encouraging the inhabitants of the valley to stay and enjoy the benefits of the new link with the outside world, the road precipitated a mass exodus, leaving the beautiful clay brick houses to decay. In 1997 Gamkaskloof was declared a national heritage site and the traditional dwellings were gradually restored and now provide attractive accommodation for tourists.

Cycling the Swartberg Pass

Section ③
Prince Albert to Oudtshoorn
Distance 111km
Driving Time 1hr 27mins
Highlights Meiringspoort, a meal at Kalinka, Cango Wildlife Ranch

Ostriches

Again, from Prince Albert, you have choices. Driving back over the Swartberg Pass gives you the chance to really appreciate this phenomenal feat of engineering. Alternatively, you could keep driving north to join the N1 (and then back to Cape Town or on to Joburg on the Not the N1 route, see pages 8–21). Another scenic, but rugged, alternative route back to the Mother City is to swing off left at Laingsburg, over Rooinek and onto the (very) rough dirt road that heads west through the magnificent Anysberg Nature Reserve.

But the best round trip is to head out of Prince Albert on the R407 east towards the N12. At Klaarstroom (47km from Prince Albert) the tarred national road heads south through **Meiringspoort**.

Stop at the Waterfall Information Centre for insight into this incredible road, which crosses the Groot River some 25 times on a series of drifts. Originally a bridle path, plotted by J P Meiring, after whom the poort is named, it was recced by Sir John Molteno and our heroes, the engineers Andrew and Thomas Bain. The folded rock bands reflect the power of the tectonic forces and you don't need to be a geologist to recognise the hard and soft sedimentary layers in the exposed cliffs.

It's just a short drive to Oudtshoorn, so linger in this magical kloof, enjoying a picnic at one of the well-maintained rest spots, watching rainbows in the cascades and marvelling at the changing hues of the orange rock.

Herrie se Klip (Herrie's Stone) next to Herrie se Drif is a popular stop. Afrikaans poet and author C J Langenhoven carved the name of a fictional elephant from his novels on a stone here in 1929. The site is now a national monument. How times change!

If, like me, geology is your soul food, then you will be in raptures by the time you emerge back into typical Karoo country at De Rust. Not that the purple elephant outside the town's Herrie se Plek supermarket and eatery is 'typical' – again, it is a humorous reference to Langenhoven's imaginary tusker!

You'll pass The Feather Palace guesthouse, a national monument built in 1908, on the road from De Rust to Oudtshoorn. Oudtshoorn, the largest town in the Little Karoo, enjoyed a feather boom at the start of the 20th century in response to European demand for ostrich feathers to decorate ladies' hats and as other fashion accessories. Many of the famously opulent 'feather palaces' constructed in that time survive today, and the J H J le Roux house, at the C P Nel Museum in town, provides a fascinating insight into the lives of the feather barons.

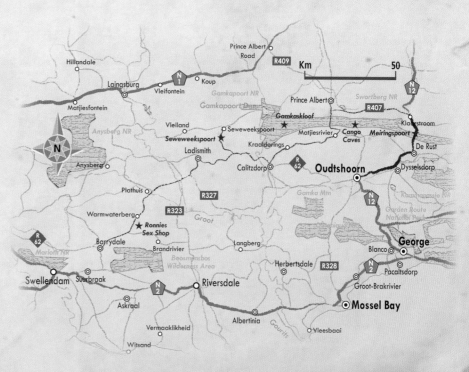

Given this history, **Kalinka** is perhaps the appropriate place to end your tour. The food at this chic, somewhat eccentric restaurant is fantastic, and chef Olga and her staff make you feel very rich and important! Headlines is a top spot for sampling ostrich (in every shape and form) and other traditional dishes, while Café Brulé and Café Soleil are the places to head for good coffee (for something different try an amazing rooibos-flavoured red cappuccino at Café Soleil), yummy cakes and light meals.

The surrounding area is still home to the world's largest ostrich population, so if the big birds and ostrich-back racing interest you, take a trip to the Highgate Ostrich or Safari show farms. Other famous attractions include the **Cango Wildlife Ranch**, where you can do a croc-cage dive, and the spectacular chambers of the Cango Caves near the turn-off to the Swartberg Pass. De Hoek Mountain Resort, nearby in the foothills of the Swartberg Mountains, is a great base if you want to hike or climb. The only limestone crag in the whole country is at its entrance gate.

ON THE SIDE >> Langenhoven
Oudtshoorn's most famous inhabitant was Cornelis Jacobus (C J) Langenhoven, the famous Afrikaans writer who penned the original South African anthem, 'Die Stem' ('The Call'). Meiringspoort, one of his favourite writing haunts, is believed to have inspired the evocative words in the anthem 'when the echoing crags resound'.

TIP
Take a pre-dawn trip out from Oudtshoorn to see the cute little meerkats that live in the surrounding area.

Epilogue
The R62 regional road continues until it meets the N2 near Humansdorp (just west of Port Elizabeth), a pretty journey that takes you back through De Rust, and on to Uniondale, the gateway to the ruggedly beautiful Baviaanskloof, and the small but interesting towns of Joubertinia and Kareedouw.

If by now you've developed a passion for passes, there are plenty more to explore. You can zap south over the Outeniqua Pass on the N12 from Oudtshoorn to George (where you can link up with the Garden Route, see pages 70–81), though if you're not in a rush, the magnificent old Montagu Pass is the more scenic route over the Outeniqua Mountains. Or your Grand Finale could be another of Thomas Bain's masterpieces, the spectacular Prince Alfred Pass from Avontuur, near Uniondale, to Knysna.

Karoo scenery

ROUTE 62 Contact details

Vineyards between Ashton and Robertson

Aquatrails Rafting
021 782 7982
www.aquatrails.co.za
Café Brulé
044 279 2412
Café Soleil
044 272 7383
Calitzdorp Port Festival
www.portwinefestival.co.za
Calitzdorp Station
044 213 3587
www.oudtshoorninfo.com/accommodation.php?id=350
Cango Caves
044 272 7410
www.cangocaves.co.za
Cango Wildlife Ranch
044 272 5593
www.cango.co.za
Clementine's
082 925 0871
De Bos Guest Farm
023 614 2532
www.debos.co.za
De Hoek Mountain Resort
044 272 8214
www.dehoekmountainresort.co.za
De Oude Poskantoor
083 285 4751
www.oudepostkantoor.co.za
Die Handelshuis
044 213 3172
Fraai Uitzicht 1798
023 626 6156
www.fraaiuitzicht.com
Headlines Restaurant
044 272 3434
Jessica's Restaurant
023 614 1805
www.jessicasrestaurant.co.za
Kalinka
044 279 2596
www.kalinka.co.za
Lazy Lizard
023 541 1379
www.lazylizardprincealbert.co.za
Living Waters Mountain Estate/Donkey Trail
083 628 9394
www.karooair.com
Lorenzo's
044 213 3939
Magpie Collective
028 572 1997
www.magpieartcollective.com
Meerkat Adventures
084 772 9678
www.meerkatadventures.co.za
Mez
082 0775980

Mo and Rose
023 626 4134
www.moandrose.co.za
Montagu Guano Cave
084 553 4187
www.montaguguanocave.co.za
Robertson Small Hotel
023 626 7200
www.therobertsonsmallhotel.co.za
Roger Young Gallery
044 213 3100
Sheilam Cactus and Succulent Garden
023 626 4133
www.sheilamnursery.com
The Red Coffee Pot
082 571 2433
The Retreat at Groenfontein
044 213 3880
www.groenfontein.com

Regional info
www.nightjartravel.com
www.oudtshoorn.com
www.robertsonwinevalley.com
www.route62.co.za

OVERBERG
Somerset West to Riversdale

My ma was 'n van Dyk van Gansbaai. Seriously, my mom was born in what was then a tiny, isolated fishing village that her ancestors settled literally centuries ago. We holidayed there when I was a kid, and I still have family there, so it's a kind of home from home. Hermanus has become somewhat urban, Stanford is a fashionable rural 'des res' of note, and Kleinbaai (previously Van Dyksbaai) is the shark-diving capital of the universe, but the rest of the Overberg and Overstrand has retained its sleepy rural demeanour. Tripping here is all about flowers, whales, sharks and gorgeous rural scenery.

Total Distance about 392km
Driving Time 6hrs

Section ❶
Somerset West to Hermanus
Distance 82km
Driving Time 1hr
Highlights:
Wine
Yummy farm stalls
Olive oil
Whale-watching
SEE PAGE 66

Section ❷
Hermanus to Riversdale via Gansbaai
and Malgas
Distance 310km
Driving Time 5hrs
Highlights:
Whales and sharks
Baardskeerdersbos
Elim
Cape Agulhas
Bredasdorp Shipwreck Museum
The pont at Malgas
Blue cranes
SEE PAGES 67–68

Section ❸
Hermanus to Riversdale via
Hemel en Aarde and N2
Distance 230km
Driving Time 3hrs
Highlights:
Hemel en Aarde Valley
Swellendam's Cape Dutch buildings
Fairy Sanctuary
SEE PAGES 68–69

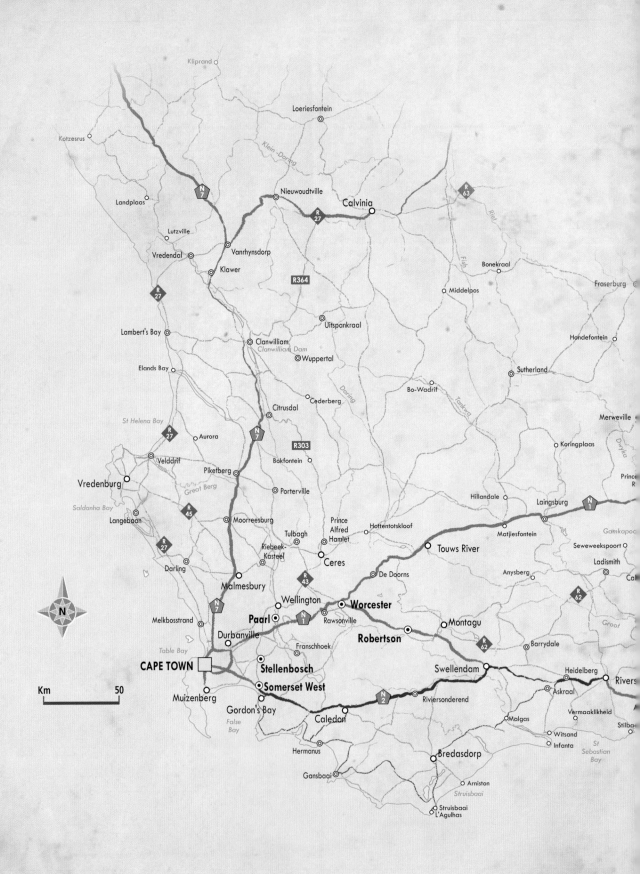

Road tripper:
Jennifer Stern

In a nutshell:
A real country ramble
through farmlands,
rural idylls and quaint
coastal villages.

Beaufort West
Letjiesbos
R61
...fontein
Rietbron
N12
Seekoegat
Volstruisleegte
Prince Albert
Willowmore
Klaarstroom
Matjiesrivier
De Rust
Dysselsdorp
Oudtshoorn
Uniondale
N12
Haarlem
R62
George
The Crags
Blanco
N2
Pacaltsdorp
Knysna
Plettenberg Bay
Groot-Brakrivier
Mossel Bay
...sbaai

Logistics

There are so many options – you can just drive round and round for ages, but I prefer doing the whole route as per Sections 1 and 2. For Section 1, you can choose to go round the mountain along the sea, but we have covered this option in In Deep Water (see pages 200–207). Section 3 is an interesting alternative to Section 2, and is not included in the total kilometres. But, if you're doing this as a there-and-back trip, you could do either Section 2 or 3 backwards. This route can link up to the Winelands route (see pages 42–49), the Garden Route (see pages 70–81) or Route 62 (see pages 50–61).

Driving conditions

Much of the route is on excellent tarred roads and some on good gravel. The N2 is a bit featureless, so be careful of nodding off. The speed limits around Riversdale are draconian and strictly monitored, and note the 80km/h limit as you bypass Swellendam.

Pet-friendly rating ★ ★ ☆ ☆ ☆

1 = least suited 5 = most suited

Child-friendly rating ★ ★ ★ ★ ☆

1 = least suited 5 = most suited

Low-slung vehicle-friendly rating ★ ★ ☆ ☆ ☆

1 = high clearance 5 = lowest slung

Don't miss

- Whales
- Shark cage-diving
- The pont at Malgas
- Blue cranes
- Platbos Forest
- The southernmost point of Africa

Emergency service numbers

Emergency (from a landline) 10111
Emergency (from a cellphone) 112
AA roadside assistance 086 100 0234 or 083 843 22 (24 hours)
Hermanus NSRI Emergency 082 990 5967

Best time

It can be somewhat rainy and cold in winter, but it's the best time for shark cage-diving and whale-watching. Spring is awesome for flowers, and summer is real beach holiday time. And autumn – aaah – balmy days and crisp nights, red wine and open fires. September is the busy time with the Hermanus Whale Festival, the Flower and Eco Festival and the Stanford Bird Festival. The Baardskeerdersbos Art Route happens twice a year, usually over a weekend in early April and September. The whales are still around in September and the shark diving is almost as good as a few months earlier. So September is the month of choice – if you can find accommodation. Oh, and in September Gansbaai also holds the Fees van die Gans – whatever that is.

SUMMER			AUTUMN			WINTER			SPRING		
D	J	F	M	A	M	J	J	A	S	O	N

Background reading

Try to watch *Sharkman*, the documentary by the Foster Brothers. It's about local Kleinbaai lad, Mike Rutzen, who hypnotises sharks. You can also try looking for the out-of-print *A Deathless Story or the 'Birkenhead' and its Heroes, Being the Only Full and Authentic Account of the Famous Shipwreck Extant, Founded on Collected Official, Documentary, and Personal Evidence, and Containing the Narratives and Lives of Actors in the Most Glorious Ocean Tragedy in History* – now that's a mouthful!

OVERBERG
Somerset West to Riversdale

Section ❶
Somerset West to Hermanus
Distance 82km
Driving Time 1hr
Highlights Wine, yummy farm stalls, olive oil, whale-watching

You have two choices as you leave Somerset West – you can continue on the N2 or turn off onto the R44 and take the scenic coastal road past Pringle Bay, Betty's Bay and Kleinmond. I usually do one out and the other on the way back, but I will describe the route over the berg, because the area we are discussing is the Overberg and also because the coastal route is described in In Deep Water (see pages 200–207). Sir Lowry's Pass is an easy two-lane road, so you shouldn't get stuck behind slow trucks as they haul themselves up the steep incline. Do stop at the viewpoint at the top to look back at Cape Town and False Bay, but keep your windows closed because the baboons have been known to climb through them into cars – not much fun.

This area is apple and **wine** country, and there are loads of great little **farm stalls**. Peregrine Farm Stall opposite the Grabouw turn-off has an on-site restaurant, nursery, gift shop, info office and estate agent. A bit further on, on the left, is Tri-Active Lodge, a pet-friendly multi-activity adventure centre, conference and team-building facility and guesthouse. Comfy and casual, it's a great place to kick off your shoes, let your hair down and just chill – or go mountain biking or hiking or indulge in a host of family-friendly adventures. Accommodation is in simple but comfortable en-suite cabins or permanent tents.

If you want something a tad grander and definitely a bit unusual, Old Mac Daddy is a trailer park without the trash. Gorgeous designer-decorated Airstream caravans are set up on a mountainside overlooking the apple orchards of Elgin. It's a full-on hotel with

Clarence Drive, en route to the Overberg

superb food, so don't expect dodgy gas stoves in your trailer suite. Caravanning was never like this when I was a kid. And just before the last long uphill is Houwhoek Farm Stall, conveniently situated between the two passes.

Once over Houwhoek, take the R43 to Hermanus. A couple of kilometres after leaving the N2 you'll find Bakenshoogte olive farm that offers tastings of their two fab **olive oils**. Make sure you have cash as they don't do credit cards. You'll pass the Bot River Lagoon on your right and then the small towns of Hawston and Vermont before entering Hermanus.

Hermanus markets itself as the best land-based **whale-watching** venue in the world and, in season, the official whale crier keeps tourists informed of the best viewing spots. The Old Harbour Museum in the old fishing harbour – where my ancestors used to park their boats – is well worth a visit for its whale and fishing memorabilia, and old photos of the area.

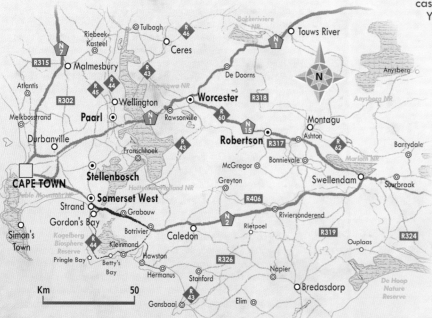

Agulhas Lighthouse

Section ❷
Hermanus to Riversdale via Gansbaai and Malgas
Distance 310km
Driving Time 5hrs
Highlights Whales and sharks, Baardskeerdersbos, Elim, Cape Agulhas, Bredasdorp Shipwreck Museum, the pont at Malgas

With the Hermanus Lagoon on your right and beautiful mountains on your left, leave town and travel 23km to the very fashionable rural artists' retreat of Stanford. Check out the local craft shops and maybe do some beer tasting at Birkenhead Brewery. Klein River Cheese, just down the road from the brewery, has fantastic cheese and they do a great picnic in summer. Another 20km further on is the little fishing village of Gansbaai, but there are two really interesting floral destinations before you get there. Platbos is the most southerly natural forest in South Africa. It's a little hidden gem with walks, accommodation, a labyrinth and the opportunity to contribute to reforestation. Grootbos, which is 13km past Stanford, is a treasure-trove of coastal fynbos, with an indigenous plant nursery that trains local youth to become horticulturalists. Gansbaai is 7km beyond Grootbos.

Go through Gansbaai and turn right to Kleinbaai for **whale-watching** and **shark cage-diving**. Both these activities are best in winter, when the southern right whales are in residence, and the sharks congregate in Shark Alley, just off Dyer Island. If you do this, check out the jetty on Dyer Island – my grandfather built it. There are loads of shark cage operators, but Marine Dynamics is a one-stop shop, with shark cage-diving, a licensed whale-watching boat and the Great White House guesthouse, restaurant and bar.

From Kleinbaai, turn right on to the R43 and, after about 5km, turn left towards **Baardskeerdersbos**, which is about 18km further on. This road is partly tarred and partly gravel, but it feels more like a time machine than a road, because you are about to enter another reality. It's a tiny village populated by artists and rat-race refugees who paint, sculpt, cook and cater their way into what are usually second or third careers. For one weekend in spring and one in autumn, the artists throw open their homes and studios to the public for the Baardskeerdersbos Art Route.

Continue with the same road for another 18km to **Elim**. This historical mission station has changed little over the years. Beautiful old buildings, a very slow pace of life that centres round the church, and a cute little restaurant in the Old Mill provide a backdrop for the free-range cows that wander aimlessly through the village. (Or possibly aimfully – who can understand cows?) Carry on for about 35km and then turn right onto the R319, go through Struisbaai to **Cape Agulhas**, look right to the Atlantic Ocean and left to the Indian Ocean. Chances are you won't see any difference.

Head back through Struisbaai along the R319 to **Bredasdorp**, and check out the **Shipwreck Museum**, which details some of the wrecks off the nearby coast. They also have a huge collection of bottles of every shape, colour and size. Continue on the R319 for about 5km and then turn right towards Malgas. This is a good gravel road. After about 40km, you will pass the miniature hamlet of Ouplaas. We always used to stop here for petrol en route to Malgas when I was a kid, but they have built a school in front of the only shop and petrol station, so I promise you will miss it if you blink. I paid great attention on my return route and found the town but, as it was Sunday, it was all locked up and I couldn't access the shop and petrol station because they are locked up inside the school grounds. About 11km further on you will see the Breede River Trading Post, which sells basic supplies, makes pizzas and also sells the fabulous local olive oil from St Sebastian Bay at the mouth of the Breede River. Carry on over the Swellendam-Infanta road and head down the hill to **Malgas** on the banks of the Breede.

67

OVERBERG
Somerset West to Riversdale

The port at Malgas

Cross over the **pont**, which is open from sunrise to sunset and costs R40 for a car, and then carry on towards Heidelberg. About 30km on you will pass through the town of Slangrivier. If you're getting tired of the gravel, turn left and head up to the N2 to travel on the tarred road. Or continue a further 5km on gravel and turn left onto the R322 towards the N2.

ON THE SIDE >> The port and the pont
In the 19th century, Malgas was an important trading port from which wheat was transported down the river by the specially built 158-ton steam-assisted sailing ship, the *SS Kadie*, and then by sea to Cape Town. The sinking of the *Kadie* in 1865, coupled with a few years of drought, ended Malgas's career as a major trading port. Since then the mouth has silted up, and the little town now survives on tourism, not trade. You can rent a houseboat and wander up and down more than 40km of navigable river. That's a fun excursion, but an absolutely mandatory experience for any self-respecting road tripper is to cross the Breede River on the hand-drawn pont at Malgas. It's the only one left in the country. I still have memories of the old ferryman, Moxie Dunn, who pulled the pont for all the years that we holidayed at Malgas in my childhood. Cyclists and pedestrians travel for free on the pont.

ON THE SIDE >> Detour to Witsand
You could also head towards the coast on the R322. It's about 30km on a good tarred road. If you're really into gravel, you could have turned right quite a bit earlier and wended your way to Witsand along some good dirt roads, but this route is the easiest on vehicle and driver. Witsand has awesome land-based whale-watching in winter, and it's where the world's record Zambezi shark was caught (and released – it's still there). But before you panic, there have been no recorded incidents with Zambezis in the Breede other than a certain amount of 'taxation' of anglers' catches.

Once you're on the N2, head off towards Riversdale. I almost always stop at the Blue Crane farm stall for coffee and/or breakfast, or a little treat. They sell a great range of local preserves. It's about another 3km to Heidelberg, where the Garden Route (see pages 70–81) takes over.

ON THE SIDE >> Quest
I've heard a rumour there is an organic restaurant and a day spa at Slangrivier (it really is a one-horse town, so this is interesting news). Anyhow – I tried to get more info, only to be told they were closed for the winter. So, is it true? Is there a fabulous organic restaurant in this exceedingly unprepossessing town? You find out, and let me know if you hunt it down.

Section ❸
Hermanus to Riversdale via Hemel en Aarde and N2
Distance 230km
Driving Time 3hrs
Highlights Hemel en Aarde Valley, blue cranes, Swellendam's Cape Dutch buildings, Fairy Sanctuary

Head back through Hermanus and then turn right onto the R320 through the **Hemel en Aarde Valley**, where you will find the bulk of the wine farms of the Walker Bay region. There is good tasting to be had, so choose who's going to drive. Continue to Caledon and then turn right onto the N2.

The road is long, straight and undulating with seemingly endless fields of wheat or canola on either side. It may sound a bit boring, but this is what the Overberg is all about, so you really should see at least some monoculture.

Beautiful blue crane

ON THE SIDE >> Blue cranes
The beautiful and elegant **blue crane** is South Africa's national bird, and it's most easily seen in the wheat fields of the Overberg. It's vulnerable, partly through habitat destruction but mostly through poisoning. (Hmm, since it forages in wheat fields that should concern us.) Anyhow – it's a beautiful bird.

Another 50km gets you to Riviersonderend. Most people just zip through this relatively unremarkable town, perhaps stopping for petrol, but take a moment to pop in to the Oumeul Bakery on the Main Road (on the right-hand side heading towards Cape Town). They do the best spinach pies I have ever tasted, and I hear the meaty ones are just as good. They also serve pretty good coffee and a range of pastries. And check out the local cheeses and other delicious delights.

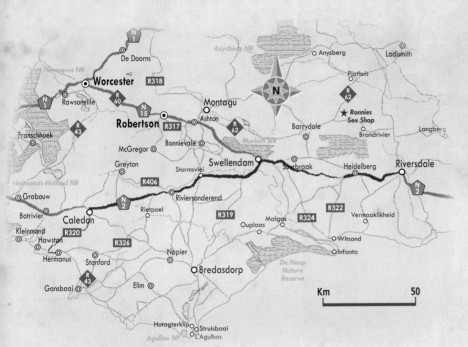

From Riviersonderend, it's about 20km to the turn-off to Stormsvlei — an absolutely tiny little village. But there is a great little restaurant there that is so much more relaxing for a meal and a break than the MacWimpsters at the ultra-stop-petro-cities. They also sell a huge range of preserved flowers — not dried flowers, preserved flowers. They look real and feel almost real. It's hard to explain. You have to see and touch.

Another 37km gets you to **Swellendam**, with its gorgeous old **Cape Dutch buildings**. My favourite spot here is the **Fairy Sanctuary**. Yes, it's a sanctuary for fairies — no hunting of fairies allowed. It sounds weird but it really is charming. It's also a sanctuary for frazzled drivers, but please leave your cynicism in the car. Heidelberg is 50km further on, and then you continue as per Section 2, but backwards.

TIP

The N2 bypasses Swellendam, but the speed limit for a few kilometres on either side of the town is 80km/h and they don't have cameras — they have real live traffic officers.

OVERBERG Contact details

Baardskeerdersbos Art Route
www.baardskeerdersbosartroute.com
Bakenshoogte Olive Oil
028 284 9149
www.bakenshoogte.co.za
Birkenhead Brewery
028 341 0013
www.walkerbayestate.com
Blue Crane Farm Stall
028 722 2651
Fairy Sanctuary
028 514 1786
www.swellendamsfairysanctuary.
blogspot.com
Grootbos Private Nature Reserve
028 384 8000
www.grootbos.com
Houwhoek Farm Stall
028 284 9015
www.houwhoekfarmstall.co.za
Klein River Cheese
028 341 0693
www.kleinrivercheese.co.za
Malagas Hotel and Conference Centre
028 542 1049
www.malagashotel.co.za
Marine Dynamics
079 930 9694
www.sharkwatchsa.com
Old Harbour Museum
028 312 1475
www.old-harbour-museum.co.za
Old Mac Daddy
021 844 0241
www.oldmacdaddy.co.za
Oumeul Bakery
028 261 1568
www.oumeul.co.za
Peregrine Farm Stall
021 848 9011
www.peregrinefarmstall.co.za
Platbos Forest
082 411 0448
www.platbos.co.za
Shipwreck Museum
028 424 1240
Stormsvlei Farm Stall and Restaurant
028 261 1167
www.stormsvlei.co.za
The Great White House
082 895 2736
www.greatwhitehouse.co.za
Tri-Active Lodge
021 844 0975
www.triactive.co.za
Wine tasting
www.hermanuswineroute.com

Regional info
www.overberg.co.za

GARDEN ROUTE
Riversdale to Port Elizabeth

The stretch of road between Cape Town and PE is one I have travelled so many times for so many reasons, but I never get bored with it – especially the section from Mossel Bay onwards. There is so much to do here that you can get stuck forever. Actually, once I did. I was driving through on my way back to Cape Town and, before I quite knew what I was doing, I had bought a home and moved to Plett. Of course, after experiencing one Christmas holiday in Plett the charm wore off. But the Garden Route has that effect on you, so be warned.

Total Distance about 500km
Driving Time 5hrs 30mins

Section ❶
Riversdale to George
Distance 150km
Driving Time 2hrs
Highlights:
Aloes
Oystercatcher Trail
Bartolomeu Dias Museum
Outeniqua Hop
SEE PAGES 74–75

Section ❷
George to Knysna Seven Passes
Distance 83km
Driving Time 2hrs
Highlights:
Beautiful bridges
The Big Tree
Totties Shop
Millwood Museum
Spookasem
SEE PAGE 76

Section ❸
George to Knysna N2
Distance 63km
Driving Time 1hr
Highlights:
Kaaimans River Gorge
Wilderness
Wild Oats Community Farmers' Market
Buffelsbaai horse riding
Knysna Lagoon
SEE PAGES 77–78

Section ❹
Knysna to Port Elizabeth
Distance 260km
Driving Time 3hrs
Highlights:
Mountain-bike trails
Farm stalls
Plett dolphin and whale trips
Keurbooms River
Bloukrans Bungee
Storms River
Hiking
Treetop canopy tour
SEE PAGES 78–80

GARDEN ROUTE
Riversdale to Port Elizabeth

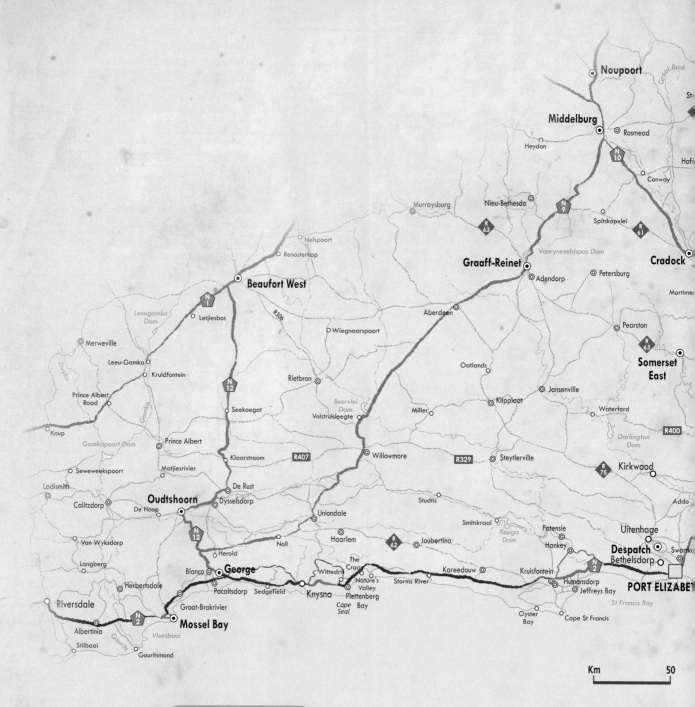

Road tripper:
Jennifer Stern

In a nutshell:
A linear route along the gorgeous beaches, forests and streams of South Africa's prettiest and most accessible coastal route.

Logistics

In theory this is a linear route but I have given you two different options for the heart of the Garden Route — the N2 and the Seven Passes Road. It's not so much a difference in geography as it is in time. You will travel back 50 years by taking the Seven Passes Road.

Driving conditions

Most of this route is on tar, but there are a few good gravel sections on the Seven Passes Road, and there are some short gravel sections around the Crags, too.

Toll roads: The N2 through the Tsitsikamma.

Pet-friendly rating ★ ★ ★ ☆ ☆

1 = least suited 5 = most suited

Child-friendly rating ★ ★ ★ ★ ★

1 = least suited 5 = most suited

Low-slung vehicle-friendly rating ★ ★ ★ ☆ ☆

1 = high clearance 5 = lowest slung

Don't miss

- Aiden's cheesecake
- Bloukrans Bungee
- Dolphins and whales
- Featherbed Nature Reserve
- Horse riding on the beach
- Ebb and Flow at Wilderness
- Fab slackpacking hikes
- Storms River Mouth and Village

Emergency service numbers

Emergency (from a landline) 10111
Emergency (from a cellphone) 112
AA roadside assistance 086 100 0234 or 083 843 22 (24 hours)
Mossel Bay NSRI Emergency 044 604 6271
Port Elizabeth NSRI Emergency 041 507 1911

Best time

The Garden Route is always gorgeous. Summer is beach time, in spring there are flowers and fantastic weather, crisp autumn days are bracing and beautiful, and winter brings whales and the Oyster Festival. If you want to see whales, humpback whales pass through between July and November, which is serendipitously when the southern rights are in residence — mating, calving and generally having some quality family time. The only times I would avoid are the school holidays when the beaches are packed with nuclear (as in about to go critical) families, and Plett is to be avoided at the beginning of December when about five million matriculants in full breeding plumage descend on the town.

SUMMER			AUTUMN			WINTER			SPRING		
D	J	F	M	A	M	J	J	A	S	O	N

Background reading

Dalene Mathee gets across the feel of the Knysna Forest like no one else. Obviously best in the original Afrikaans, but only if you *lees die taal goed*, which I don't really; otherwise stick to the excellent translations. In order I would suggest *Kringe in 'n bos* (*Circles in a Forest*), *Fiela se Kind* (*Fiela's Child*) and *Moerbeibos* (*The Mulberry Forest*). She also wrote a fourth forest book, *Toorbos* (*Dream Forest*), which I haven't read. *Fiela se Kind* was made into an excellent Afrikaans movie, and *Circles in a Forest* was filmed in English with Arnold Vosloo at his peak when he looked like a young Marlon Brando playing a Greek god.

GARDEN ROUTE
Riversdale to Port Elizabeth

Section ❶
Riversdale to George
Distance 150km
Driving Time 2hrs
Highlights Aloes, Oystercatcher Trail, Bartolomeu
Dias Museum, Outeniqua Hop

Where the Garden Route begins and ends depends
pretty much on who you ask. I'm a bit of a purist, so
I think it starts at Mossel Bay, but I am starting this
chapter at Riversdale to include Albertinia about
40km further on. Very few people ever actually
venture into the town, so I thought I would explore.
I turned off between the two petrol stations and
carried on over the railway line and discovered a
little country gem. Skinkikofi is a stange little coffee
shop run by the friendly Lettie Pretorius. As well as
simple meals, tea, coffee and sugary confections, she
sells vintage clothing, some antiques, furniture made
by her husband, and bright handmade garments
including can-can-style aprons. It's not stylish, it's not
fashionable, but it is delightful.

ON THE SIDE >> Aloe aloe aloe
You've probably heard of *Aloe vera*, which is cultivated in
many parts of the world and quite aggressively marketed.
Well, here in South Africa, *Aloe ferox* grows wild. *Aloe ferox*
has as many, if not more, therapeutic benefits as does *Aloe
vera*. Try to get this straight, though. It's the gel from the plant
that is used in wound dressing and cosmetics, and they are two
different plants. If I had ten rand for every time I heard someone say that *Aloe ferox* contains *Aloe vera* I could probably
buy a new car. That's like saying pine trees contain oak trees.
They're different. And ours is better. So check out one or both
of the **aloe** factories near Albertinia on the N2.

ON THE SIDE >> Detour
Another 8km further is the turn-off to Gouritsmond, which is
the westernmost point of the Oystercatcher Trail. You can't
cross the river here by car but, if you're cycling, you may be
able to persuade someone to row you and your bike across.

You'll see two bridges if you look left as you cross the
Gourits River on the N2. One is the railway bridge,
and the other a disused road bridge, which was
until relatively recently used
for bungee jumping and
bridge swinging. That's all
over now so, if you want to
jump off a bridge, you'll have
to head further east to the
Bloukrans Bridge discussed in
Section 4.

About 20km after the bridge is the turn-off to
Boggemsbaai, where you can park off for a few days
and do absolutely nothing (Sandpiper Cottages offer
a whole lot of self-catering cottages to choose from).
Or fish or walk. It's another stop on the **Oystercatcher
Trail**. In fact, this whole coast, from here to Mossel
Bay, is Oystercatcher Trail country. So don't drive it,
walk it. And I guess that means we stay on the N2 for
the drive.

You'll pass the sci-fi-looking PetroSA plant (previously
MossGas) on your left. The road is wide and inviting
but the speed limit is 100km/h and the local traffic
authorities are quite alert. Keep straight to go to
Mossel Bay but, if you want to carry on with the N2,
keep your wits about you and skive off to the left
after the One Stop.

Mossel Bay is a very popular beach destination,
especially in summer, and the diving and surfing
are both great, but it has much more to offer than
sun, sand and sea. The **Bartolomeu Dias Museum**
complex is fascinating. There is a full-size replica of a
Portuguese caravel that actually sailed from Lisbon to
Mossel Bay in 1988 to mark the 500th anniversary of
the landing of Bartolomeu Dias on the beach in front
of the museum. And there are loads of wonderful old
stone buildings in the town. The stroll along the cliffs
from Cape St Blaize offers fantastic views of the sea
– often with dolphins surfing in the waves – and also
the chance to view an archaeologically significant, but
not particularly well-preserved cave in which people
lived many thousands of years ago. This and other
caves along the coast are threatened by runoff from
developments, a situation that has wrought ongoing
conflict over the last few years.

I love the natural tidal pool in front of the Point Hotel,
just below Cape St Blaize – it's ooh, I dunno, about
100m long and you can swim lengths in it. Long lengths.

Oystercatcher Trail

Boggemsbaai

The N2 from Mossel Bay to George is a wide, scenic, gently curving dual carriageway that can inspire fast driving, so watch that your right foot doesn't start to droop. George is the biggest town in the Garden Route, with the only airport, so it's the place to do serious shopping, get your car fixed and all those boring urban things. But it's famous for two things — beer and golf. They sort of go together, I guess.

Seriously, George is the centre of the South African hop-growing industry, and the outskirts are so much more rural and picturesque than you would imagine. You can't miss the hop farms, with the very visible hop plants trailing along high trellises, but there are also loads of strawberry farms, dairies and cheese-makers, so pick up an **Outeniqua Hop** brochure and follow the route from farm to coffee shop to craft studio. My very favourite restaurant in George is Leila's Arms on a farm in Blanco. Time slows down here — the food is slow-cooked, the décor is decidedly eclectic and it's generally a laid-back kind of place.

If you're into trains you will love the Outeniqua Transport Heritage Museum. It's just a pity that it is no longer a terminus for the fabulous Outeniqua Choo-Tjoe steam train that used to transport people from this museum to the Bartolomeu Dias Museum in Mossel Bay. Maybe it will be revived one day.

PADKOS

I am a minimalist sort of padkos girl. I take a cucumber, a hunk of good cheddar cheese, some nuts, a few raw carrots, apples and oranges, and just munch on them when I feel peckish. This can keep me going for a week or more, and the cheese will keep in one of those miniature cooler bags. If I have time to plan ahead, I make roast veggie wraps but that only works for a day or so after you leave home. So there are two types of padkos really — the planned and the unplanned. My absolute favourite is freshly squeezed veggie juice, but that also only works for the day you leave home, so it's not practical for a long road trip.

My favourite padkos stops are: Blue Crane near Heidelberg, because it has become a habit — they know me there and I love the rose garden. The food's good, too. Then there's Stormsvlei Farm Stall and Restaurant, Oumeul Bakery in Riviersonderend for the spinach pies, the village shop in Hoekwil (for the cheesecake), Spookasem in Rheenendal, because it has the best vibe and great melktert, and Nature's Way in Nature's Valley for the yummy home-made ice cream donated by the Jersey cows grazing peacefully in the field.

GARDEN ROUTE
Riversdale to Port Elizabeth

Section ❷
George to Knysna Seven Passes
Distance 83km
Driving Time 2hrs
Highlights Beautiful bridges, the Big Tree, Totties Shop, Millwood Museum, Spookasem

The Garden Route I visited on holidays with my parents when I was two bricks and a tickey high was a place of narrow roads, steep, forested hills, funny little towns with funny little shops, and incredible scenery. Now it's a place of highways, sushi restaurants, five-star guesthouses, private landing strips and polo fields. But, if you know where to look, you can still find that old Garden Route magic. It's on the Seven Passes Road.

From the centre of George, head towards the N2 on Courtenay Street and turn left into the Saasveld Road about a kilometre from town. The road is part tar, part gravel, but all in very good shape. It's narrow and twisty, though, so be careful. I travelled this road one morning (when I knew the N2 was *vrot* with speeding cars) and I saw three runners, two horse

riders and I think about five mountain bikers — but no cars. You cross two **beautiful bridges** over the Kaaimans and Touw rivers before you hit the 'villagette' of Hoekwil. Stop here for coffee and cheesecake at the Village Shop. Seriously, they serve Aidan's cheesecake, which is officially the best in South Africa, and possibly the best in the world. They also do other food.

You can head down to Wilderness and the N2 or you can continue, but let's stick to one route at a time and continue with the Seven Passes Road.

After a few kilometres on your left is the turn-off to the **Big Tree**, and a nice little picnic spot. It's a very peaceful and quiet (or lonely and isolated) spot, so you probably want to go there with a medium-sized group, especially during the week. But there is another tree further on.

As you continue towards Knysna, the scenery changes and the tangled forest and deep river gorges give over to more open space. You'll pass Karatara, which is in the early stages of changing character from somewhat dreary forestry town to vibrant arty community. A bit further on is Rheenendal. At Rheenendal is an amazing little petrol station and general dealer. **Totties Shop** is like a flashback to the 1950s. Then, on your left, is the turn-off to the **Millwood Museum** and Tea Garden, the Big Tree and the Dalene Mathee Memorial. You can do a short, gentle amble around the old goldfields and even, if you're feeling brave, enter an old mine shaft. The Homtini MTB route starts nearby and, if you're feeling tree-huggish and missed out on the one near Hoekwil, there is another huge tree here. This one is 31m high and 9m in circumference, so you will need about four or five friends to help you hug it. In theory, anyway. Fondling of the trees is discouraged. There are gorgeous rock pools, lovely walks, fantastic trees and generally it's a great place to hang out for a while. Dalene Mathee's ashes are scattered in the forest here, and there is a memorial to her near the tree.

And a bit further along is **Spookasem**, which is the cutest little eclectic tearoom/coffee shop/craft shop. Stop for a while, browse the gorgeous handmade rag dolls, and sit in the lovely garden with a view of the forest, sipping tea or coffee and munching on milk tart. It's a little piece of heaven. Then continue another 8km or so to rejoin the N2 just west of the Knysna Lagoon.

Big Tree

Section ❸
George to Knysna N2
Distance 63km
Driving Time 1hr
Highlights Kaaimans River Gorge, Wilderness, Wild Oats Community Farmers' Market, Buffelsbaai horse riding, Knysna Lagoon

Just outside George you go past the turn-off to Victoria Bay (Surfing Road Trip, see pages 178–191) and then start heading down into the **Kaaimans River Gorge**. This road is littered with speed cameras, so stick to the speed limit and (unless you're driving a truck) stay in the right lane. The forest closes in around you until, at the bottom, you look right across the beautiful river to the houses of the few lucky souls who get to stay there. At the top of the next hill you curve left into **Wilderness**. In front of you is the ocean, with dolphins surfing in the waves and quite likely paragliders overhead pretending to be Jonathan Livingstone Seagull. Wilderness has some of the best paragliding in the country, and you can do a tandem paraglider flight or even a whole paragliding course with Cloudbase Paragliding.

Once through the town, you can turn off to the SANParks camp Ebb and Flow, where you could spend days lounging around, walking, fishing, paddling or just getting to know your family. Here you'll find loads of great hiking, kloofing, mountain biking and paddling trails run by Eden Adventures. From here you can drive up to Hoekwil on a good but steep tarred road for cheesecake if you do not intend doing the Seven Passes Road. After Wilderness you pass the beautiful Swartvlei on your left and Groenvlei on your right before travelling through Sedgefield – South Africa's first official slow town.

Ready to bungee

Soon after you crest a gradual hill, you are greeted with a view of a bright green idyllically bucolic little valley, at the end of which is the turn-off to **Buffelsbaai**. This is a gem. The surf is great, there is a wonderful 6km walk along the beach to Brenton-on-Sea and – best of all – a lovely gentle horse trail. **Riding a horse** on a beach is on everyone's bucket list. (Or should be.)

Then you cross the Knysna River and wend your way into the town on the edge of the lagoon. Before you head into the town, swing left and then go right under the N2 towards Belvidere where you can check out the beautiful tiny stone church built in 1851 from local stone and local wood in the Norman style. You can visit any day except Sundays when there are services. The road continues to the gorgeous settlement of Brenton-on-Sea, with its long, lovely beach that stretches all the way to Buffelsbaai. Return to the N2 and either continue into Knysna or cross over the N2 and drive up Phantom Pass to Rheenendal if you want to see some of the Seven Passes Road and didn't follow that route as described in Section 2.

TIP

Slow down here: the speed limit is 60km/h.

ON THE SIDE >> Farmers' Markets
The Saturday morning **Wild Oats Community Farmers' Market** just on the George side of Sedgefield was one of the first of the now very popular farmers' markets springing up all over the country. Actually I think it may have been the very first. Anyhow, it's still one of the best, with genuine artisanal food producers and farmed produce, much of which is organic. And, of course, you can get Aidan's cheesecake there – and his wonderful goat's-milk cheese. And between Knysna and Plett, at Harkerville, is the Harvest Time Market, also on Saturday mornings. It's smaller than Wild Oats but it's also a great little market. You can't buy Aidan's cheesecake there, but Cloud Cottage goat's-milk cheese is possibly one of the best in the country and you can get that there. There is also a Friday night market in Knysna and one in Wilderness. A newly started Saturday morning 'farmers' market' outside George is, to my mind, a bit of a disappointment. It's more like a fast-food mall than a farmers' market, but I guess it's a good place to have breakfast and meet friends if you are in the area.

GARDEN ROUTE
Riversdale to Port Elizabeth

The small village of **Knysna** that I remember from those long-ago family holidays has disappeared, but it's been replaced with a very stylish, very chic, very tourist-friendly town that works surprisingly well. The only thing that doesn't work is the fact that all traffic between Sedgefield and Plett goes through the town. All traffic. Every eighteen-wheeler, every family towing a ginormous caravan, and every car carrying Garden Route holiday-makers. In December it is a nightmare and the few kilometres through town can take you a couple of hours. But it's a delight at any other time.

It all happens at the Knysna Waterfront, a surprisingly pleasant collection of shops, restaurants and hotels on Thesen Island. Some are newly built and some are renovated industrial buildings, like the fantastic Turbine Hotel situated in what was once a power station. Do the self-guided tour, reading the plaques that give some of the history.

You can go for a wonderful sail on the **lagoon** or out through the Heads with Springtide Charters, or hop on the weird little ferry boat that takes you across to the Featherbed Nature Reserve on the Western Head for an uphill open-vehicle tour, a downhill stroll and lunch. Not long ago I spent a weekend on a houseboat here with a group of friends and highly recommend it as possibly the best of all possible ways to enjoy the lagoon. You get your accommodation and entertainment all wrapped up in one package, and you don't need any experience because they're really easy to drive and you learn all you need to know in the quick orientation. That's assuming you can drive a car, but if you're reading this book you probably can drive a car.

Section ❹
Knysna to Port Elizabeth
Distance 260km
Driving Time 3hrs
Highlights Mountain-bike trails, farm stalls, Plett dolphin and whale trips, Keurbooms River, Bloukrans Bungee, Storms River, hiking, treetop canopy tour

As you leave Knysna, you can turn off to the right to The Heads, carry on about 4km and turn left to Diepwalle/Uniondale on the R339, or continue on towards Plett via Harkerville and the Garden of Eden.

At Diepwalle there are three great day-walks marked with elephants. This is also great **mountain-biking** territory. There are a number of circular trails leaving from the Garden of Eden and also the gorgeous linear Petrus se Brand between the Garden of Eden and Diepwalle. I prefer to do it from Diepwalle as there are more downhills that way and the last 6km before the Garden of Eden is one of the best easy singletrack sections ever. The ground is soft and springy, it's fast, not too technical and beautiful as it twists through the trees. If you didn't bring a bike, you can rent one from Outeniqua Biking Hire in the forest across the N2 from the Garden of Eden.

There are so many cute little **farm stalls** and gift shops I won't even try listing them, so just choose whichever one appeals to you most. You will go past the site of the Harvest Time Market — if it's a Saturday, it's worth stopping.

ON THE SIDE >> Alternative to the N2
From Diepwalle, you can return to the N2 or continue on the R339 through the forest and then turn right onto the R340 and head down to rejoin the N2 just east of Plett. This is a good gravel road, but it can be pretty dodgy after rain. You will bypass the small town of Wittedrif on your right and then, before you get to the N2, you will see the Bitou River. You hit the N2 between the Bitou and Keurbooms rivers that join together just downstream to form a huge, beautiful lagoon before entering the sea. Turn right to Plett or left towards Port Elizabeth — but I strongly suggest you turn right as I wouldn't bypass Plett.

Knysna

Diepwalle

Plettenberg Bay is an awesome little town that has also grown beyond all recognition to become the playground of the Garden Route, so it has more fabulous guesthouses, restaurants and coffee shops than you can possibly even see in a week, let alone patronise.

Plett is the only launch site along the whole South African coast with two licensed boat-based **whale-watching** operators – Ocean Blue Adventures and Ocean Safaris. This is partly historical but also largely due to the fact that this bay is one of the best boat-based marine mammal watching destinations in the world, with guests seeing up to seven species of marine mammal in one trip. Seals are guaranteed, as they hang out at Robberg; bottlenose **dolphins** are so regularly seen they can almost be depended on and, in season, southern right whales are hard to avoid, and humpback whales are easily spotted as they loll about. Common dolphins are not quite as common as the bottlenoses but they are quite regularly seen, and the shy humpback dolphins are also regularly spotted although they don't usually hang around the boats. Bryde's whales are in residence all year round and are spotted quite frequently but not as often as the others and – very occasionally – you may see an orca, a minke or even a sperm whale. And you'll also see loads of sea birds and general great scenery. For a slightly more energetic ocean experience, you could go sea kayaking with Dolphin Adventures. You won't see as many animals but you will earn an extra croissant with breakfast. You can also do a scenic flight over the bay with African Ramble, which is awesome in whale season, or do a tandem parachute jump with Skydive Plett.

It's the Robberg Peninsula that defines the beautiful bay that gives Plett its character, and Robberg is also great for its own sake. There are three concentric circular walks. The long one takes you right to the end of the peninsula and must be done on low tide. The others are very manageable. It's also worth checking out Nelson Bay Cave, a fab little field museum in a cave that was inhabited by our ancestors hundreds of thousands of years ago.

As you leave Plett on the N2, you will cross first the Bitou River and then the **Keurbooms River**. Turn left to the CapeNature offices where you can rent a canoe to explore the river. Even better, book ahead and reserve the Whiskey Creek cabin for a few nights. It's a gentle paddle of about 6km – up the flat, dark, mysterious river with its overhanging forests, tiny little beaches and loads of birds – to the cabin. Once there, you are alone with the people you have chosen to take with you. Paradise.

About 15km from Plett is The Crags, which seems to have become *the* animal rescue centre of the Garden Route, if not the country. Birds of Eden, Monkeyland and the Elephant Sanctuary are all within a kilometre of each other. Monkeyland is a huge enclosure with rescued primates, including lemurs, monkeys and apes, living in a natural forest in a big space. It's not the wilds, but it's a reasonable facsimile thereof. Birds of Eden is the biggest free-flying aviary in the world, measuring two hectares and cunningly built over a natural river gorge in the forest. Yes, it's a cage, but what a cage! You can walk in among the birds, most of which are free to fly all around the enclosure. The Elephant Sanctuary is home to a small herd of rescued orphan elephants who earn their keep by interacting with tourists. It's a great way to find out more about these amazing animals and you can even go for a short ride. Although they are close together, it is almost impossible to do all three of these in one day. Monkeyland and Birds of Eden have a special offer if you do both, so I would save the elephants for the next day.

As you near the border between the Western Cape and Eastern Cape you can decide whether you are brave enough to 'Face Adrenalin' and do the 216m-high **Bloukrans Bungee**. It's the highest bridge bungee in the world and it's a real scream machine – but safe. In order to do this, you will need to do at least half of the toll road section.

GARDEN ROUTE
Riversdale to Port Elizabeth

The first toll plaza is about 20km from Plett. Here you can turn off onto the R102 and drive down a beautifully forested road to Nature's Valley, which is the end point of the Otter Trail and an all-round gorgeous little coastal settlement. There's not much there — one restaurant, one small shop, a sprinkling of guesthouses, a SANParks camp site and lots of lovely walks. But that's the attraction.

From Nature's Valley you continue on the R102 and can either turn onto the N2 and pay a toll or carry on with the R102 and drive the beautiful, steep, twisty-turny, forested Bloukrans Pass. But then you can't do the bungee. Or, if you want scenery and screams, do the Bloukrans Pass and then turn back towards Plett on the N2, do the bungee and return to PE. That way you won't have to pay the tolls. But, at time of writing, that's all pretty much academic because the Bloukrans Pass is closed and it will probably be a very long time before it is reopened.

A little further on is the turn-off to **Storms River Mouth**, one of the most beautiful of all the SANParks camps. As well as just parking off, fishing or strolling here, you can do a kayak and lilo tour with Untouched Adventures, exploring the deep, dark, mysterious Storms River Gorge. The Otter Trail is a self-contained independent **hike** that heads west towards Nature's Valley, and the Dolphin Trail is a guided, catered slackpacking trail that heads east. No rustic hiking huts and heavy backpacks on the Dolphin Trail. You sleep in luxury guesthouses, eat fabulous meals that are cooked for you and, when you get to your next over-night stop, magically find your luggage in your room.

Or you could stay in Storms River Village, where you can do South Africa's first **treetop canopy tour**, mountain bike through the forest or go blackwater tubing. When I'm here I always opt to stay at At the Woods.

From Storms River (Village or Mouth) it's just a few kilometres to the petrol station at the bridge on the N2 over the Storms River. You can get a pretty iffy meal here and some very bad coffee, or you could just stock up on chocolate and chips from the shop but, if you're hungry, rather stop about 30km on at Oude-bosch (see below). There is also a small gift shop, but the best is the view of the gorge, so take a walk out onto the bridge. It's one of the few bridges on the N2 that accommodates sightseeing pedestrians. And, if you haven't had enough adrenaline, you can do a zipline slide with Tsitsikamma Falls Adventures nearby.

About 30km from the Storms River Bridge, turn into the Kareedouw Road towards Eerste River (the sea side). At the T-junction a few hundred metres on is Oude-bosch Farm Stall, where you can munch on far better fare than you get at Storms River. They also have a huge protea farm, which you can explore on a guided tour if you like.

Treetop canopy tour

I believe the Garden Route ends at the Storms River Bridge, but that's either because I'm a purist or it's just prejudice. Anyway, from here it's a pretty clear run to PE, but you can hang a left up the R330 to Hankey to see the grave of Saartjie Baartman and perhaps head back to Cape Town through the Baviaanskloof and then join up with Route 62 (see pages 50–61). Or turn off to Jeffreys Bay for a quick surf (see Surfing Road Trip, pages 178–191).

After crossing the Gamtoos River, the R75 is a scenic, bucolic alternative to the hectic N2. From PE, you can fly out, turn around and go home, or connect up with the Frontier Country route (see pages 82–89) or the Wild Coast route (see pages 90–97) a bit further on. A short detour up the N10 will connect you with the Not the N1 route (see pages 8–21) and/or the Great Trek route (see pages 106–119).

Celebrating the beauty of the Garden Route

GARDEN ROUTE Contact details

African Ramble
083 375 6514, 084 359 2929
www.aframble.co.za
At the Woods
042 281 1446, 082 328 2371
www.atthewoods.co.za
Bartolomeu Dias Museum
044 691 1067
www.diasmuseum.co.za
Birds of Eden
044 534 8906
www.birdsofeden.co.za
Blackwater tubing
042 281 1757
www.blackwatertubing.net
Buffalo Bay Horse Rides
073 251 3122
www.buffalobayhorserides.co.za
CapeNature (Robberg and Keurbooms)
021 483 0190
www.capenature.co.za
Cloudbase Paragliding
044 877 1414, 082 777 8474
www.cloudbase-paragliding.co.za
Dolphin Adventures
083 268 8582
www.dolphinadventures.co.za
Dolphin Trail
042 280 3588
www.dolphintrail.co.za
Ebb and Flow
044 877 0046, 044 356 9021
www.sanparks.org/parks/garden_route
Eden Adventures
044 877 0179
www.eden.co.za
Elephant Sanctuary
044 534 8145
www.elephantsanctuary.co.za
Face Adrenalin
042 281 1458, 071 248 5959, 073 124 1373
www.faceadrenalin.com
Featherbed Nature Reserve
044 382 1693
www.knysnafeatherbed.com
Garden Route National Park, Tsitsikamma section
042 281 1607
www.sanparks.org/parks/garden_route
Garden Route National Park, Wilderness section
044 877 0046, 044 356 9021
www.sanparks.org/parks/garden_route
Knysna Houseboats
044 382 2802
www.knysnahouseboats.com
Leila's Arms
044 870 0292
www.leilas.co.za
Millwood Museum and Tea Garden
076 733 9918, 072 254 7470
Monkeyland
044 534 8906
www.monkeyland.co.za

Ocean Blue Adventures
044 533 5083, 083 701 3583
www.oceanadventures.co.za
Ocean Safaris
044 533 4963, 082 784 5729
www.oceansafaris.co.za
Otter Trail
see Garden Route National Park (above)
Oudebosch Farm Stall
042 285 0562
www.oudeboschfarmstall.co.za
Outeniqua Biking Hire
044 532 7644, 083 252 7997
Outeniqua Hop
www.outeniqua-hop-route.co.za
Outeniqua Transport Heritage Museum
044 801 8289
Oystercatcher Trail
044 699 1204
www.oystercatchertrail.co.za
Sandpiper Cottages
044 699 1204
www.sandpiper.co.za
Skinkikofi
072 547 2748
Skydive Plett
082 905 7440
www.skydiveplett.com
Spookasem
072 820 0170
Springtide Charters
082 470 6022, 082 829 2740
www.springtide.co.za
The Village Shop
044 850 1037
Tree Top Canopy Tour
042 281 1836
www.canopytour.co.za
Tsitsikamma Falls Adventures
042 280 3770, 082 578 1090
www.tsitsikammaadventure.co.za
Untouched Adventures
073 130 0689, 076 959 2817
www.untouchedadventures.com

Regional info
www.cruisethecrags.co.za
www.gardenroute.com
www.gartour.co.za
www.georgetourism.org.za
www.gogardenroute.co.za
www.plettenbergbay.co.za
www.visiteasterncape.co.za
www.visitknysna.co.za

FRONTIER COUNTRY
Port Elizabeth to East London

Being able to sleep through the sound of machine-gun fire is a skill that one associates with living in places like Bosnia or Afghanistan, but it's one I learned when I was studying in Grahamstown in 1985. Now that's because the Eastern Cape was a hotbed of resistance all through the 1980s. Actually, that's not much of a change for the area the tourism authorities call Frontier Country, and which I tend to think of as the crucible. It's been a hotbed of resistance for more than two centuries.

It was here that most of the people who make up South Africa's rainbow nation first met, clashed, fought, killed each other and, ultimately, learned to live together. It's a place of deep cultural values and immense beauty. It is infused with history, and almost every street corner, collapsing gatepost or isolated building tells a story. In the short distance between Port Elizabeth and East London you can see a micro-cosm of South Africa, from history and culture to bush and beach. But you need to know where to look.

Total Distance 462km
Driving Time 7.5hrs

Section ❶
Port Elizabeth to Grahamstown
Distance 130km
Driving Time 1.5hrs
Highlights:
Donkin Heritage Trail
Amakhala Game Reserve
New Sidbury Club
Lots of museums and monuments in
Grahamstown
SEE PAGE 86

Section ❷
Grahamstown to Port Alfred
Distance 60km
Driving Time 1hr
Highlights:
Bathurst Agricultural Museum
Toposcope
Pig and Whistle
Kowie History Museum
1820 Settlers Church
SEE PAGE 87

Section ❸
Port Alfred to Grahamstown via Salem
Distance 56km
Driving Time 1.5hrs
Highlights:
Kariega Game Reserve
Salem
SEE PAGE 87

Section ❹
Grahamstown to Fort Beaufort
Distance 82km
Driving Time 1.5hrs
Highlights:
Bain memorial on Ecca Pass
Fort Brown
Martello tower
War of the Axe site
SEE PAGE 88

Section ❺
Fort Beaufort to East London
Distance 134km
Driving Time 2hrs
Highlights:
Fort Hare University
Steve Biko Garden of Remembrance
SEE PAGE 89

FRONTIER COUNTRY
Port Elizabeth to East London

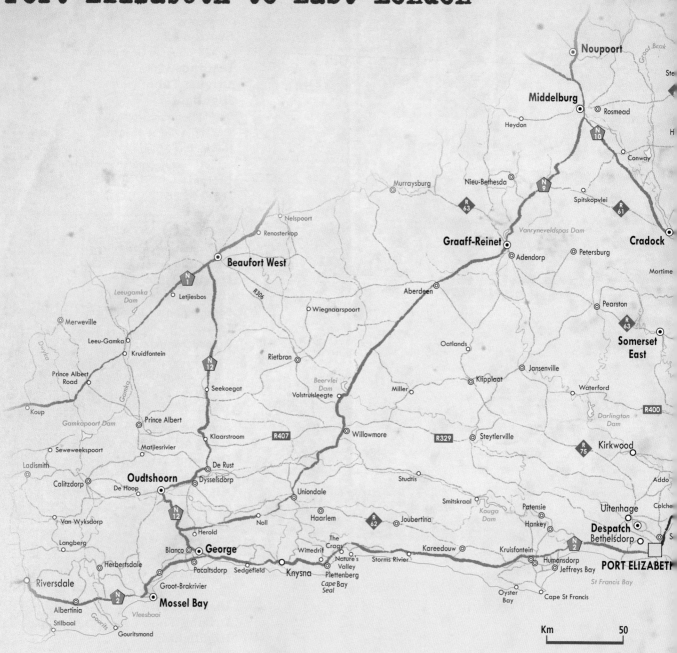

Road tripper:
Jennifer Stern

In a nutshell:
A trip back in time to
explore the conflicts
that shaped the Eastern
Cape and, subsequently,
the whole of South
Africa. It is the crucible
in which our country
was forged.

Logistics

This is written as a linear trip, so you can fly in to PE, rent a car and fly out from East London at the end. It can also be tagged between the Garden Route (see pages 70–81) and the Wild Coast (see pages 90–97) trips, or it can be a sort of sideways extension of Not the N1 (see pages 8–21).

Driving conditions

Most of this route is on good or reasonable tar, with some gravel sections.

Pet-friendly rating ★ ☆ ☆ ☆ ☆

1 = least suited 5 = most suited

Child-friendly rating ★ ★ ☆ ☆ ☆

1 = least suited 5 = most suited

Low-slung vehicle-friendly rating ★ ★ ★ ☆ ☆

1 = high clearance 5 = lowest slung

Don't miss

- Donkin Heritage Trail
- Guided tour reliving the Battle of Grahamstown
- New Sidbury Club
- Toposcope in Bathurst
- Bathurst Agricultural Museum
- Church at Salem

Emergency service numbers

Emergency (from a landline) 10111
Emergency (from a cellphone) 112
AA roadside assistance 0861 000 234 or 083 843 22 (24 hours)

Best time

It's cold in winter and hot in summer, so the shoulder seasons are always the most comfortable, but there are a few annual events that may be worth planning for. The National Festival of the Arts in Grahamstown is usually round about the first week of July, and the Bathurst Ox Braai is one of the biggest New Year's Eve parties in South Africa.

SUMMER			AUTUMN			WINTER			SPRING		
D	J	F	M	A	M	J	J	A	S	O	N

Background reading

Richard Gush of Salem by Guy Butler is a play, but it's worth reading if you can't see it performed.

ON THE SIDE >> Who were the 1820 Settlers?

When the Europeans from the Cape, both the British and the trekboers, first came to the Eastern Cape they came up against the Xhosa who, not surprisingly, were somewhat disgruntled at the prospect of their land being expropriated and settled. And the disgruntlement segued into a series of frontier wars that lasted about a hundred years from 1779 to 1878. So the British offered vast tracts of fabulous virgin land to penniless urban innocents who thought they were heading out to the Land of Milk and Honey, with the intention that these expendable people would form a living barrier between the Cape Colony and the rest of Africa. Well, they tried to wrest an agricultural living out of the zuurveld but it was hard going. Many gravitated to Grahamstown, which was becoming a big military centre, settled into the area now known as Artificers' Square, and plied their trades. The people made it, but the farms didn't really. The bush said no, so the bush won. And many of the original farms are now game reserves – some still owned by the descendants of the original settlers.

1820 Settlers Monument

FRONTIER COUNTRY
Port Elizabeth to East London

Section ❶
Port Elizabeth to Grahamstown
Distance 130km
Driving Time 1.5hrs
Highlights Donkin Heritage Trail, Amakhala Game Reserve, New Sidbury Club, lots of museums and monuments in Grahamstown

This is a short distance, but you want to leave early as there is a lot to see and do en route. This is where many of the 1820 Settlers landed before heading off in pretty much the same direction you will be taking. I recommend spending half a day in PE, perhaps walking the **Donkin Heritage Trail** and/or visiting the No. 7 Castle Hill Museum. Leave town at about 07:00 to arrive at Nanaga Farm Stall, about 50km from the city at the intersection of the N2, N10 and R72, at 08:00 when they open. They do great breakfasts but, if you're stuck for time, just grab a quick coffee and pick up some preserves and baked goodies to make up a picnic hamper for later.

The Greater Addo Elephant National Park is a bit of a detour but it's worth it if you want to see lots of animals. Game-wise, it's no better or worse than the private nature reserves hugging the route, but it is significantly more affordable.

About 40km further on is **Amakhala Game Reserve**, which consists of a number of old settler farms that have been consolidated into one big game reserve by the present owners, many of whom are direct descendants of the original settlers. On the left is the **New Sidbury Club**, which is well worth a visit to look at the photographs and memorabilia relating to the now deserted village of Sidbury. If you're doing the day trip at Amakhala, visit Sidbury and/or the club first.

From either Amakhala or the New Sidbury Club, it's a short drive to **Grahamstown**, which is so full of history, gorgeous old buildings and interesting academics and writers it's a veritable cultural treasure-trove. A guided tour of the town and re-creation of Egazini, or the Battle of Grahamstown, is one of the best ways of getting a handle on what this whole period in history was about – and you can find out why the municipality is called Makana.

View over Grahamstown

ON THE SIDE >> Detour to Sidbury
The town of Sidbury, which dates back to the early 19th century, was never incorporated as a town so, when the farm on which it stood was sold to Kwantu Game Reserve, the town went too. It's still possible to visit, but there's not much there. Just ask at the reserve gate and say you are going to the churches. A gravel road forms a crescent from the N2 through Sidbury and back to the N2, but the PE side is in much better condition than the Grahamstown side, so it's probably best to backtrack if you visit. You will no doubt learn more from the New Sidbury Club on the N2 than from the town. When the village died, the cricket club moved, and took along all its photos and memorabilia. The club members, many of whom are descended from settler families, cherish and guard their heritage, and willingly share stories with visitors.

While not strictly settler-themed, the Observatory Museum offers a fascinating insight into cutting-edge Victorian technology, including the only existing camera obscura in the southern hemisphere. If you're into South African literature, don't miss the National English Literary Museum.

Port Elizabeth coastline

Section ❷
Grahamstown to Port Alfred
Distance 60km
Driving Time 1hr
Highlights Bathurst Agricultural Museum, Toposcope, Pig and Whistle, Kowie History Museum, 1820 Settlers Church

This short drive along the R67 takes you through the lovely town of **Bathurst**, which is just loaded with settler memorabilia, historical buildings and **museums**. Most unusual is the **Toposcope**, which indicates the layout of the original settler farms. The **Pig and Whistle** was a stopping point for wagon trains in the early 19th century, and now offers very comfortable and significantly updated accommodation. It is also the oldest pub in South Africa, but if you're not spending the night and driving on ...

ON THE SIDE >> Biggest is best
The biggest pineapple in the world is in Bathurst. Standing 16.7m high, it's a beacon of all things fantastic and ananastic. Buy pineapple jams and preserves and a range of pineapple-themed gifts and whatnots. (In case you hadn't guessed, this is pineapple-farming country.)

Port Alfred is a great spot for a quick dip in the sea, a round of golf or more cultural input from the **Kowie History Museum** and the **1820 Settlers Church** and cemetery. For a fun break from driving and an interesting accommodation option, take a self-drive houseboat up the Kowie River.

Section ❸
Port Alfred to Grahamstown via Salem
Distance 56km
Driving Time 1.5hrs
Highlights Kariega Game Reserve, Salem

Head southeast on the R72 and then turn right on to the R343. After 14km you'll reach the **Kariega Game Reserve**, with its fabulous lodges and wonderful food. It's a great place to spend the night, to see some animals and to enjoy a river cruise. If you request it when you book, you can spend some time with the lodge manager, Alan Weyers, who is a renowned oral historian and recognised authority on the history of the area.

After about 18km you find the turn-off to the little town of **Salem**, which is reached after a short stretch of gravel road. This town is famous as the place where, during the Sixth Frontier War, the Quaker Richard Gush rode unarmed up to a huge impi of Xhosa warriors who were preparing to attack the village, and persuaded them to leave peacefully. The Methodist Church in the village still has the very uncomfortable pews Gush built in the 19th century. Those settlers were tough.

ON THE SIDE >> Peace – or something very much like it
Salem feels like an English country town, with cricket being played on the village green among the whitewashed houses. It's a sleepy little place that has, apparently, lived up to its name and continued in peace since the iconic incident described above. Well, mostly in peace. There is a fierce (but friendly) rivalry with the New Sidbury Club, which is all the more intense as the members of the respective clubs are almost all cousins, whose ancestors probably feuded over borrowed ox wagons that were returned with flat tyres (or something).

Toposcope

FRONTIER COUNTRY
Port Elizabeth to East London

Section 4
Grahamstown to Fort Beaufort
Distance 82km
Driving Time 1.5hrs
Highlights Bain memorial on Ecca Pass, Fort Brown, Martello tower, War of the Axe site

The R67, which was called the Queen's Road when it was made in 1842, was built by über-engineer **Andrew Geddes Bain**, whose **memorial** stands at the top of the **Ecca Pass**. It is said that the unusual rock formations of the Ecca sediments inspired his love of geomorphology and his subsequent publication of the first study of the geology of South Africa.

As you approach Fort Beaufort, you will see the police station on your right. It's worth stopping because the tower you can see at the heart of this building is the historical **Fort Brown** that was one of a chain of blockhouses built by the British along the frontier to defend the Cape Colony. Hang a right and spend a few days in the provincially-run Great Fish River Nature Reserve, where you will see lots of animals, including hippo in the eponymous river, and also get the chance to explore more historical sites and forts. In Fort Beaufort, visit the **Martello tower**, which is the northern-most of a chain of communications and defensive towers that were built in the 19th century to link Grahamstown and Fort Beaufort. It is unique in that it is the only Martello tower in the world built inland.

ON THE SIDE >> The War of the Axe
As you head into Fort Beaufort, ponder the beginning of the Seventh Frontier War, also known as the **War of the Axe**. An accused axe thief was being transported to Grahamstown to stand trial when his family attacked the soldiers escorting him. He was handcuffed to another prisoner, so the rescuers — some-what arbitrarily — cut off the poor guy's hand. He's buried here, just before the town — not the axe thief, the unfortunate shackle partner. C'est la vie, c'est la guerre. The axe thief got away, and the refusal of his community to hand him over to the British sparked the seventh of the frontier wars that came to be known as the War of the Axe.

'It is better to die for an idea that will live than to live for an idea that will die.'
Steve Biko

Martello tower

Section **5**
Fort Beaufort to East London
Distance 134km
Driving Time 2hrs
Highlights Fort Hare University, Steve Biko Garden of Remembrance

Steve Biko Museum

If it feels as if you've been travelling back in time over the past few days, this section is almost like a decompression stop on the way to the present. The history is here, but much of it is more recent, and it emphasises the fact that this area, which was designated a frontier by the British in the 19th century, continued in much the same vein over the next couple of hundred years.

The first place of interest is the town of Alice and **Fort Hare University**, which can number among its alumni such luminaries as Nelson Mandela, Walter Sisulu, Oliver Tambo, Seretse Khama, Govan Mbeki, Julius Nyerere, Robert Sobukwe and Desmond Tutu.

You can head off towards Hogsback to walk around some big old forests, gaze into gurgling streams and chill out after all the hectic history. Or you could carry on along the R63 to Dimbaza, which was one of those Bantustan-era tax-free industrial zones. Take a detour here by turning left to Keiskammahoek and look out for the weird circular depressions in the ground. This is the site of the 1818 Battle of Amalinda, where over 5,000 people were killed in what was arguably the biggest battle of the Eastern Cape — ever. And you've probably never heard of it. Now that's food for thought.

Another 20-odd kilometres further on, on the outskirts of King William's Town, is the **Steve Biko Garden of Remembrance**. There's not much there, but it sort of completes the circle, as Steve Biko was just one of a long line of people who died trying to create a viable society in this troubled part of the world. The house where he served out his banning order is also a monument, and the Steve Biko Centre is more than a museum — it's a living, breathing project that continues his work.

Stop at the Amathole Museum to see what's left of poor old Huberta, the adventurous hippo who was too trusting of people, and then do a detour through the provincial capital of Bhisho for another Bantustan flashback. When you hit East London, check out the statue of Biko in front of the city hall in Oxford Street and then go to the beach for a swim to clear your head.

Yes, we need to remember our history, but only so that we don't repeat it. Let's not dwell on it. It's a beautiful world. Dive into the waves.

FRONTIER COUNTRY Contact details

Amakhala Game Reserve
046 636 2750, 041 502 9400 or 086 767 9251
www.amakhala.co.za
Amathole Museum
043 642 4506
Fort Beaufort Historical Museum
046 343 2094 or 046 645 1555
Kariega Game Reserve
041 581 2606
www.kariega.co.za
Pig and Whistle
046 625 0673
www.pigandwhistle.co.za
Steve Biko Centre
043 605 6700
www.sbf.org.za

Regional info
www.ectp.co.za
www.nmbt.co.za
www.sunshinecoasttourism.co.za
www.travelgrahamstown.co.za
www.visiteasterncape.co.za

WILD COAST
East London to Port Edward

Over the years, I have done many short trips to the Wild Coast for various reasons, and every time I leave there having experienced something unique. It's like being sucked into an ever-changing kaleidoscope. The Wild Coast is a beautiful, mysterious location — an unspoiled (but not pristine) place that combines spectacular biodiversity and magnificent scenery with well-established communities and popular tourist destinations. I am not a cereal-for-breakfast kind of person but two of my most enchanting memories of this region involve, respectively, cornflakes and Coco Pops (neither of which I consume regularly). The first instance was when I rode down to a community camp site near Msikaba and ended up waiting a few hours for my hosts to arrive. Some local villagers saw me there alone and brought me cornflakes, fresh milk and Milo. The second was when I stayed at Morgan Bay Hotel on a hike. It's a family destination so it's not surprising that the breakfast buffet included Coco Pops and Strawberry Pops. Every hiker immediately had major childhood flashbacks. First Coco Pops I'd eaten in about 30 years. I do bits of this route regularly — by car, on foot, on horseback or by canoe — but one day, I promise myself, I will dedicate at least a month to exploring it in detail.

Total Distance ±1,100km
Driving Time 17.5hrs

....

Section ❶
East London to Kei River
Distance 98km
Driving Time 1.5hrs
Highlights:
Chintsa
Morgan Bay
Kei Ferry
SEE PAGE 94

....

Section ❷
Kei River to Dwesa
Distance ±320km
Driving Time 8hrs
Highlights:
Fabulous family-friendly hotels
Nonquase's Pool and Trevor's Trails
Wild Coast hikes
Crowned cranes
Most southerly mangroves
Dwesa serenity
SEE PAGE 95

....

Section ❸
Dwesa to Port Edward
Distance 660km
Driving Time 8hrs
Highlights:
Bulungula
Hole in the Wall
Awesome hikes
Nelson Mandela Museum
Horse trails
Waterfall Bluff
Mkambati Nature Reserve
SEE PAGE 96

WILD COAST
East London to Port Edward

Road tripper:
Jennifer Stern

In a nutshell:
An iconic coastal route linking up beautiful beaches, tranquil lagoons and picturesque villages.

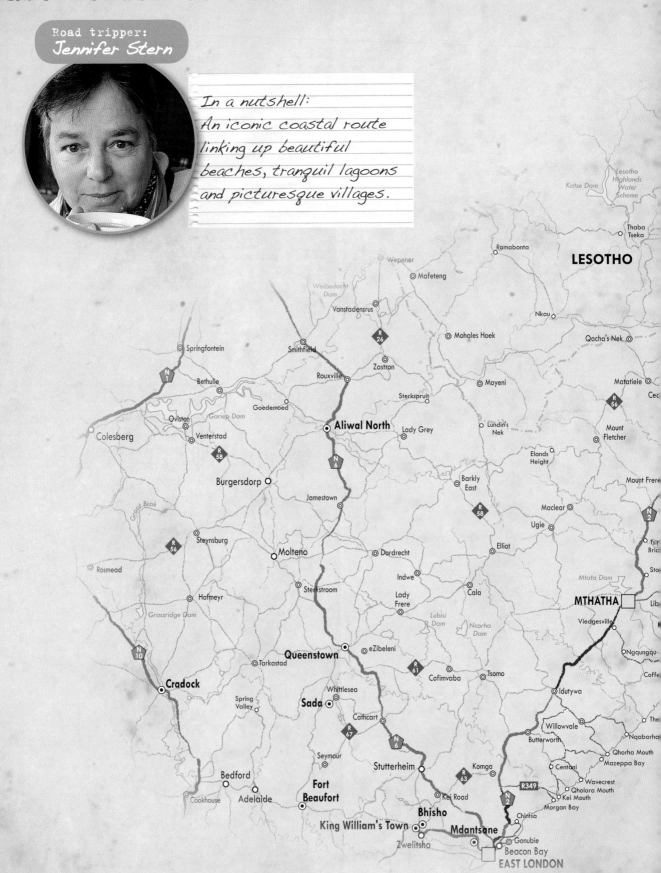

Logistics

While this is, theoretically, a linear route from point to point, it's impossible to do it as one direct route. The N2 goes through the whole of the Wild Coast but, to get down to the gorgeous little hotels, nature reserves and mini-resorts, you need to leave the national road and head off towards the coast.

Driving conditions

Most of the roads are tarred, all are potholed, and none are fenced. I repeat – the roads are not fenced. That means you will find dogs, chickens, children, cows, geese, donkeys and/or ponies contentedly ambling along the white line while, depending on species, they chew the cud, contemplate the mysteries of the universe, or simply move their legs while their heads remain empty. This is the main reason you really should not drive here at night. And, yes, there is talk of a new toll road along the coast but many people (myself included) believe that it is planned more for the convenience of the mining companies eyeing the titanium-rich dunes than it is to facilitate tourism or easier transport for the locals (most of whom don't own cars, anyway).

Pet-friendly rating ★ ★ ☆ ☆ ☆

1 = least suited   5 = most suited

Child-friendly rating ★ ★ ★ ★ ★

1 = least suited   5 = most suited

Low-slung vehicle-friendly rating ★ ★ ☆ ☆ ☆

1 = high clearance   5 = lowest slung

Don't miss

- Hole in the Wall
- Fabulous, fabulous hikes
- Beach horse rides
- Awesome waterfalls
- The ferry over the Kei
- Trevor's Trails
- Nelson Mandela Museum

Emergency service numbers

Emergency (from a landline) 10111
Emergency (from a cellphone) 112
AA roadside assistance 086 100 0234 or 083 843 22 (24 hours)

Best time

It's almost impossible to get a booking at any of the hotels in the December holidays because many families like to return to the Wild Coast year after year, and they book for the next year before they leave to drive home. Winters are not that cold and, like most places, spring and autumn offer the best weather. The sardine run is in winter, towards the end of June.

SUMMER			AUTUMN			WINTER			SPRING		
D	J	F	M	A	M	J	J	A	S	O	N

Background reading

The Sunburnt Queen by Hazel Crampton (Jacana 2006) tells the story of a young girl who was shipwrecked on this coast in the early 18th century and ended up living with the local people.
In Search of the Waratah, the Titanic of the South by David Willers (Highveld Press 2006) explores what may have happened to the *Waratah*, a passenger ship that disappeared without a trace off the Wild Coast in 1908.

WILD COAST
East London to Port Edward

Section ❶
East London to Kei River
Distance 98km
Driving Time 1.5hrs
Highlights Chintsa, Morgan Bay, Kei Ferry

East London is the gateway to the Wild Coast, but it is very much a quiet little seaside city. There are loads of hotels to choose from but I almost always stay at Meander Inn because of its connections with the slack-packing trails.

Leave East London on the N2 and, after about 11km, take the East Coast Resorts Road (R102). After about 15km the turn-off to **Chintsa West** is on the right, a bit further is Inkwenkwezi Game Reserve on the left, and then the turn-off to **Chintsa East**. I always stop at Buccaneers at Chintsa West because it is just such a laid-back place and it caters for everyone from families to backpackers. They also run great cultural and adventure tours.

Carry on with the R102 till it rejoins the N2. After about 10km on the N2, turn right towards Morgan Bay and Kei Mouth. **Morgan Bay** has got to be one of the prettiest coastal settlements around. Spectacular, grass-topped cliffs drop dramatically into the sea, offering fabulous hiking (on the top) and exciting rock climbing (on the cliffs). This is a family holiday destination of note. Another 8km further is Kei Mouth with some great surfing, and the **ferry across the Kei**, which costs R60 for a standard car. This was the border between the Ciskei and Transkei during the apartheid era, so it's quite a poignant ferry ride.

Ferry across the Kei

Section ❷
Kei River to Dwesa
Distance ±320km
Driving Time 8hrs
Highlights Fabulous family-friendly hotels, Nonquase's Pool and Trevor's Trails, Wild Coast hikes, crowned cranes, most southerly mangroves, Dwesa serenity

TIP

You have to plan ahead here. The coastal hotels are quite far apart, and driving from one to the other involves heading inland and travelling on a relatively good gravel road or returning to the N2. I suggest you do your homework and choose one or two destinations on this section.

After crossing the Kei, continue for about 16km on newly tarred roads to the mouth of the Qholora River and two of the real **iconic Wild Coast hotels**, Trennerys and Seagulls. Some families have been staying here every year for generations, and have even married on the strength of holiday romances spawned in those high school-era annual family holidays. Take a short hike up to **Nonquase's Pool** with **Trevor's Trails** and hear the sad story of the ill-conceived attempt of the Xhosa to end the Frontier Wars by supernatural means.

ON THE SIDE >> Wild Coast hikes
The Wild Coast has been a popular hiking destination for ages and there were loads of great hiking huts spread out all along the beach. But during the Bantustan era, fewer people hiked them, they started falling into disrepair and the vicious cycle continued until the hikes just sort of soaked into the sand. So, when people started walking along the coast again in the 1990s, they stayed in what were then rather scruffy coastal hotels that had only just managed to survive the bad years. The vicious cycle was reversed and the hikers contributed immensely to the revival of the hotels, and the Wild Coast in general. Wild Coast Holidays were the pioneers in designing and marketing hikes run in conjunction with the local communities. The many hikes available now range from short day-walks to long multi-day treks from hotel to hotel. The comfy accommodation, combined with the fact that most of the trails are guided, and porters can be arranged, makes these hikes a great option for not-so-tough hikers.

Another 70km on a good gravel road will take you through the typical rolling green hills and bright blue thatched huts of the Wild Coast to Wavecrest. Here you will find a community of endangered **crowned cranes** and the most southerly naturally occurring **mangroves** in Africa. From Wavecrest, you can continue 42km on the inland road to Mazeppa Bay, or head back to the N2 (64km). From the N2 you can drive down to Mazeppa Bay (72km) or carry on for 28km and turn off at Idutywa to drive the 70km to Kob Inn, which has a stunning position right on the beach. (You can drive from Mazeppa Bay to Kob Inn without going back to the N2, but only in a four-wheel-drive vehicle.) On the way to Kob Inn is the turn-off to **Dwesa Nature Reserve**. This is a little-known paradise with beautiful beaches, simple self-catering cottages and lots of peace and quiet.

Local woman and child at kraal

WILD COAST
East London to Port Edward

Section ❸
Dwesa to Port Edward
Distance 660km
Driving Time 8hrs
Highlights Bulungula, Hole in the Wall, awesome hikes, Nelson Mandela Museum, horse trails, Waterfall Bluff, Mkambati Nature Reserve

The big advantage of both Coffee Bay and Port St Johns is that they can be reached without travelling on dirt roads at all. From Dwesa, return to Idutywa on the N2 and continue east. After about 60km you will travel through the town of Qunu, with Nelson Mandela's house on the right-hand side of the road. A bit further on is the Qunu part of the Nelson Mandela Museum. Carry on for another 11km to the turn-off to Coffee Bay (about 20km before Mthatha.)

From the N2 it is about 80km to Coffee Bay. About 30km before Coffee Bay is the turn-off to **Bulungula**. It's a fantastic eco-friendly lodge that is largely owned by the local community. It's quite tricky getting there so, if you decide to go, get directions by phoning the lodge or visiting their website.

Coffee Bay is a great destination with lots of wonderful activities, a vibrant backpacking scene and some great family hotels. I particularly like Coffee Shack Backpackers for the vibe and activities, including surfing lessons. But when I need a bit of pampering, I opt for the very comfortable and family-friendly Ocean View Hotel that really does live up to its name. From Coffee Bay it's a rather adventurous drive of about 13km to **Hole in the Wall**, but it's also a **great hike**. A little further on is White Clay, which offers self-catering camping in a gorgeous spot with incredible views. Head back to the N2 and carry on another 25km to Mthatha. Don't miss the **Nelson Mandela Museum** in Nelson Mandela Boulevard (the N2). Keep a careful watch out for the turn-off to Port St Johns as it's right in the middle of town and is easily missed if you get distracted.

About 20km before Port St Johns is the turn-off to Umngazi River Bungalows, a very popular family holiday destination. Port St Johns is a bit of a party destination, definitely a beach destination, a fave backpackers haunt and a very popular location for international film-makers. Think *Blood Diamond*. There's

lots of accommodation to choose from but I like Cremorne, just on the other side of the river, because it has camping, self-catering and hotel accommodation. It was flooded out in early 2013 but they're busy mopping up.

From Port St Johns, cross the uMzimvubu River, travel about 40km and, just before Lusikisiki, turn off to Mbotyi, which is another 26km on, 19 of which are on gravel. Tidy green bushes line the road as you drive through the Magwa Tea Estate. There are so many great day-hikes and **horse rides** around Mbotyi, you could walk out every day for a week and not get bored. One of the big attractions (and only one of the many waterfalls in the area) is **Waterfall Bluff** — one of only a few waterfalls in the world that tumbles directly into the sea.

From Mbotyi return to Lusikisiki and then continue on the R61 towards Port Edward. Keep a careful eye out in Flagstaff as the R61 does a sneaky right turn (yes, I missed it). As you leave Flagstaff, turn right to Holy Cross Hospital and **Mkambati Nature Reserve**. Mkambati is about 65km from the R61 on a good gravel road. The reserve has quite basic self-catering accommodation and fabulous walks to waterfalls, lagoons, wetlands and forests, and is possibly the richest part of the Pondoland Centre of Endemism (PCE). The R61 roughly follows the route of the proposed Wild Coast toll road.

If you continue on the R61, you'll go through Bizana and then Port Edward where you cross the Mtamvuna River and leave the Eastern Cape for KwaZulu-Natal. This was the border of the apartheid-era Transkei, so there is a huge, glitzy casino and golf course (and not much else) on the Eastern Cape side and a small town on the KZN side. Weird.

ON THE SIDE >> Hole in the Wall
Of the many stories attached to this beautiful offshore sea arch, the weirdest and most oft-cited is the one that claims it was formed by a giant fish bashing a hole in a lagoon wall so that the sea people could abduct a pretty land-based maiden. It is also believed to be a gateway to the world of the ancestors — try swimming through there and you may well end up with your ancestors. It's known by the local people as *esiKhaleni*, which means 'the place of sound', and refers to the noise of waves slapping against the rock at high tide. Whatever the stories, whatever you call it, it's an amazing sight and well worth the drive or walk.

Hiking at Hole in the Wall

ON THE SIDE >> Pondoland Centre of Endemism

Stretching from Kei Mouth to Port Edward, the Pondoland Centre of Endemism is an area of about 19,000km² with well over 2,000 different plant species of which about a tenth are endemic, which means they grow naturally nowhere else in the world. What makes the PCE so interesting is that many of the endemics are restricted to a very small range. Some plants grow only on one river bank for a distance of about 15km upstream from the sea. For example, the Pondo Palm (*Jubaeopsis caffra*) is found only on the banks of the Msikaba and Mtentu rivers and — here's the weird bit — its closest relative is *Jubaea chilensis*, which is endemic to Chile. But this is just one of the fabulous plants, many of which probably haven't even been identified yet, that are at risk from the proposed construction of the Wild Coast toll road.

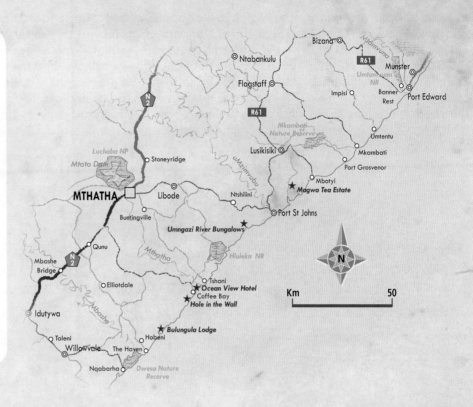

WILD COAST Contact details

Buccaneers Lodge & Backpackers
043 734 3012
www.cintsa.com
Bulungula Lodge
047 577 8900
www.bulungula.com
Coffee Shack Backpackers
047 575 2048
www.coffeeshack.co.za
Cremorne Estate
047 564 1110
Dwesa Nature Reserve
043 701 9600
www.ecpta.co.za
Inkwenkwezi Private Game Reserve
043 734 3234
www.inkwenkwezi.com
Kob Inn Beach Resort
047 499 0012
www.kobinn.co.za
Mazeppa Bay Hotel
047 498 0033
www.mazeppabay.co.za
Mbotyi River Lodge
082 674 1064
www.mbotyi.co.za
Meander Inn
043 726 2310
www.meanderinn.co.za
Mkambati
043 701 9600
www.ectourism.co.za
Morgan Bay Hotel
043 841 1062
www.morganbayhotel.co.za

Nelson Mandela Museum
www.nelsonmandelamuseum.org.za
Ocean View Hotel
047 575 2005/6
www.oceanview.co.za
Seagulls Beach Hotel
047 498 0044
www.seagullshotel.co.za
Trennerys Hotel
047 498 0004
www.trennerys.co.za
Trevor's Trails
073 575 7223
Umngazi River Bungalows
047 564 1115
www.umngazi.co.za
Wavecrest Beach Hotel & Spa
047 498 0022
www.wavecrest.co.za
White Clay
047 575 0008
Wild Coast Holidays
043 743 6181
www.wildcoastholidays.co.za
Wild Coast Meander and Amble
043 743 6181
www.wildcoastholiday.co.za

Regional info
www.coffeebay.co.za
www.visiteasterncape.co.za
www.wcha.co.za

MEANDERING THE MIDLANDS
Hilton to Karkloof

My grandfather worked for the Natal Parks Board and built Thendele Camp at Royal Natal National Park, so as a kid most of my holidays were spent in the Drakensberg. We used to travel from our home in Pietermaritzburg through the Midlands up to the Berg in my father's stunning TC sports car. Back then the roads were mostly dirt and in winter they even iced over. It was a beautiful journey but the classic convertible took a bit of a hammering. In my twenties I moved to Winterskloof and lived on a smallholding called Tanglewood. My room overlooked the paddocks onto the rolling hills of the Midlands and I developed a deep-seated love of the area. And I guess my love for convertibles also dates back to my early adventures driving through the Midlands — I now have a Z3 tucked away in my garage.

Total Distance 175km
Driving Time 2hrs 35mins

Section ❶
Hilton to Granny Mouse Country House & Spa, via Dargle
Distance 95km
Driving Time 1hr 45mins
Highlights:
Arts and crafts
Nelson Mandela's capture site
Beer and cheese
SEE PAGES 102–103

Section ❷
Granny Mouse Country House & Spa to Howick
Distance 44km
Driving Time 45mins
Highlights:
Arts and crafts
Howick Falls
SEE PAGES 103–104

Section ❸
Round trip from Howick to Karkloof
Distance 36km (18km each way)
Driving Time 30mins
Highlights:
Umgeni Valley Nature Reserve
Mountain-biking trails and picnic spots
Karkloof Canopy Tours
SEE PAGE 104

MEANDERING THE MIDLANDS
Hilton to Karkloof

Road tripper:
Shaen Adey

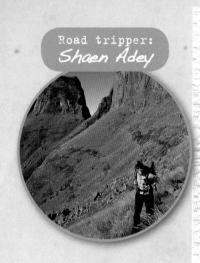

In a nutshell:
The Midlands start in Hilton, a village on a hill overlooking Pietermaritzburg, and stretch up to the toes of the Drakensberg. Venturing along the dusty back roads, you'll have a glorious bumble through the lush green hills and valleys of the KwaZulu-Natal Midlands, famous for horse studs, dairy farms, eclectic arts and crafts shops and wonderfully homely cafés, pubs and guesthouses.

Logistics

Both Hilton and Howick are a short hop off the N3. It takes just over an hour to get to Hilton from Durban and 4hrs 30mins to reach Howick from Johannesburg. Both are toll roads. The nearest international airport is King Shaka International just north of Durban. Stop at the information centre near Howick Falls or any of the places listed on the Midlands Meander and pick up a brochure for a few rand. It has a useful map of the various routes and heaps of information on what to see and do. Many of the places on the Midlands Meander are open from 09:00–16:30 but some keep different hours, so check out the brochure. Pack a camera – the scenery is stunning.

Driving conditions

Mostly tar with short sections of gravel, the Meander is twisty-turny, so take it slowly and enjoy. Before the N3 was built, the R103 was the main road between Durban and Johannesburg, which illustrates how things have changed with time.

Pet-friendly rating ★ ★ ★ ★

1 = least suited 5 = most suited

This applies if you skip Section 3, otherwise ★ as no dogs are allowed in the reserves.

Child-friendly rating ★ ★ ★ ★

1 = least suited 5 = most suited

There are a lot of stops en route that break the journey, making it fun for kids.

Low-slung vehicle-friendly rating ★ ★ ★ ★ ☆

1 = high clearance 5 = lowest slung

Sections of the road are dirt – they are well maintained but can be slippery when wet.

Don't miss

- Nelson Mandela's capture site
- Midlands Meander
- Howick Falls
- Umgeni Valley Nature Reserve
- Karkloof Canopy Tours

Emergency service numbers

Emergency (from a landline) 10111
Emergency (from a callphone) 112
AA roadside assistance 086 100 0234 or 083 843 22 (24 hours)

Best time

I love autumn, when the cosmos starts to bloom and the leaves start to change, but the Midlands are really nice any time of the year. In summer the rolling hills are a lush green, cows look fat and the afternoons are often rocked by thunder and lightning. Winter days are usually sunny but crisp and there's nothing nicer than a log fire.

SUMMER			AUTUMN			WINTER			SPRING		
D	J	F	M	A	M	J	J	A	S	O	N

Background reading

Spud by John van de Ruit, published by Penguin Books.
Also visit www.nightjartravel.com for more information.

MEANDERING THE MIDLANDS
Hilton to Karkloof

Section ❶
Hilton to Granny Mouse Country House & Spa, via Dargle
Distance 95km
Driving Time 1hr 45mins
Highlights Arts and crafts, Nelson Mandela's capture site, beer and cheese

Hilton is small and mostly residential so it doesn't take much time to explore but there are a few coffee shops and **arty places** worth visiting. The route I like most is to follow the Old Howick Road from the Old Main (a famous watering hole once known as Crossways Hotel) towards the Rotunda, which has a great farm stall, nursery, restaurant and other odds and ends. From there, turn left onto the N3 heading towards Harrismith. A few kilometres up the freeway, take the R103 turn-off to Midmar Dam. At the top of the off-ramp you get your first glimpse of the dam, which is especially pretty at sunset. Follow the road past the dam wall — which often overflows during summer — following the Umgeni River down towards Howick Falls. Just beyond the resort's gates you pass the Fern Hill Hotel, known for its good lunches.

Nelson Mandela's capture site

ON THE SIDE >> Midmar Mile
The Midmar Mile is recognised in the *Guinness Book of World Records* as the world's largest open-water event. The organisers are hoping to draw as many as 18,000 swimmers in February 2014 for their 40th anniversary celebrations.

Keep on the R103 heading towards Lions River, stopping to tickle your taste buds — and dent your pocket — at Florentines chocolates. A little further on you'll find **Nelson Mandela's capture site** and Truth Store. It's incredible to think this is where Mandela's freedom came to an abrupt end on 5 August 1962. Entrance to the museum is free but it takes time to really explore. The path to the Nelson Mandela sculpture is worth taking — a gentle reminder of his 'long walk to freedom'. Also based at the centre are the famous Impumelelo bead artists, the Truth Café and Truth Store.

Further up the road turn left towards Dargle/iMpendle. There are potters and craft places to visit along this stretch but what I like most are the patches of indigenous forest flanking the hills. St Andrew's Church is quaint and if the doors are open, have a peep at the stained-glass windows. When you reach the T-junction, turn right towards Nottingham Road. It's a winding dirt road and as it crawls uphill you get a great view of the Drakensberg. Look out for the beautiful Nguni cows farmed in the area and, if you see a cloud of dust coming, slow down. It's probably a local farmer — they know the dirt roads like the back of their hands and tend to fly along them.

The road passes a smaller road off to Fort Nottingham — if you like history, the fort's about 3km down the road. When you get there, ring the old brass bell; someone will emerge from nowhere and open up.

Back on the R103, aim for Balgowan and then on to Nottingham Road, a farming community. Heading left at the T-junction will take you to Rosetta, with a few interesting spots like the Ugly Duckling and Marrakesh Cheese Farm along the way. If you want to shorten your trip, turn right, heading under the bridge to another T-junction. Again you have choices and if your kids are asking 'Are we nearly there yet?', turn left and stop at the candle-dipping shop and stretch your legs with a wander around the beautiful little tin church opposite St Gowrie's Village. Also nearby is Sapore where you can get a delicious bite to eat and a jolly good latte. WildFly Travel is across the road; they'll help you choose your tackle or steer you to the best spots to cast a line, Excelsior being one of them. Notties Pub, back near the bridge, is legendary. Book room 10 if you're staying over and want to up your chances of seeing Charlotte the gentle ghost.

Otherwise, from the T-junction, turn right, and a hop and a skip down the road you'll find the Bierfassl, famous for its eisbein and, of course, local **beers.** Further down the road you'll find Rawdons Hotel, one of the older hotels in the area and home to The Nottingham Road Brewery. The names of their brews are the best: 'Pig-eyed Possum Pilsner', 'Tiddly Toad Lager' and, if you buy a case of 'Pickled Pig Porter', thirst aid as they call it, a portion of the profit lands in Project Rhino's piggy bank. They've donated a sweet fortune so far ... so drink more beer.

Down the road is Michaelhouse — the Hilton versus Michaelhouse game is one of the biggest and best schoolboy rugby derbies in the country.

After a spoil at Granny Mouse Country House & Spa, turn left as you head out of the gates. Not far down the road there's a turning to the right with a few interesting **arts and crafts** places to visit, like Hilford Pottery and Culamoya Chimes.

Return on the same road or take the link road back to the R103 then turn right. Spiral Blue, a colourful craft shop, seems to capture many a person's interest, but I'm a coffee fan so prefer to push on to Piggly Wiggly, which proudly claims to serve the best coffee in the area. It's generally a good place to eat, shop and play. Kids can play a round of putt-putt while you sit back and chill over your cuppa. Apart from the various galleries, there's Meander Fine Wines, which cracked the nod when I discovered that they sell my all-time favourite: Springfield 'Life from Stone'. Best of the Midlands sells high-quality food products, primarily from farms in the area, that are free of unnecessary additives, hormones and preservatives. Head back towards Spiral Blue and take the next dirt road right towards Caversham Mill.

The dirt road curves and curls, passing Ardmore Ceramic Art, a studio established by Fée Halsted who mentored Bonnie Ntshalintshali. As a polio sufferer, Bonnie was unable to work on the farm, so turned to art, and in 1990 she and Fée were jointly awarded the prestigious Standard Bank Young Artist Award. Though Bonnie sadly died, the studio has grown to include several of Ardmore's artists whose works are now recognised by Christie's (the acclaimed auction house) as 'modern-day collectibles'.

By now it is probably mid-afternoon and if you stop at Swissland Cheese the goats will be lining up for milking at 15:30 – but remember, they're all on maternity leave from the end of May to August. This is a good spot to buy **cheese** (duh), picnic hampers and a bag of nibbles to tempt the goats at Billy Goat avenue. There's a range of accommodation options in the area but for the ultimate spoil check into Granny Mouse Country House & Spa. One of the *grande dames* of the Midlands, it is child-friendly and has quaint thatched rondavels and very swish new suites, a great spa and a top-class restaurant.

ON THE SIDE >> Caversham Mill

Caversham Mill was built in the mid-1800s. The yellowwood and sneezewood that was carved into wheel buckets came from the local bush. A fire devastated the place in 1887 but it was soon rebuilt and continued to operate until 1935, when it was closed down by the Mealie Control Act. It then lay abandoned until David Walters, a local potter, bought and restored it to its former glory in 1978. He and fellow potter Ian Glenny then struck upon the idea of starting the Midlands Meander. In 1987 the Lions River flooded and destroyed the mill, so a heartbroken David sold up. It's changed hands a few times over the years but it's now been turned into a great restaurant overlooking the river, with a manor house and a few guest cottages.

Caversham Mill

MEANDERING THE MIDLANDS
Hilton to Karkloof

Continuing up the road and turning right at the intersection takes you past La Lampara, a gorgeous little Italian restaurant known for its delicious pizzas and the most amazing spaghetti gamberi.

Follow the dirt road up the hill and take the turning right towards Curry's Post; left would take you back to rejoin the R103. The winding dirt road will take you to the Balgowan-Curry's Post interchange, where you go straight over the N3 on the D369. The road continues to wind. At the T-junction turn right onto the Curry's Post road. A few of my favourite stops on this road are the Old Halliwell Country Inn, Ground Cover and Tumble Downs, the latter renowned for its food. You know you're about to enter Howick when you start getting great views towards Midmar Dam. The road takes you smack bang onto Howick's main road. Turning left will take you into the hub of the small town and, of course, to the **Howick Falls**.

ON THE SIDE >> Howick Falls

The Howick Falls are 95m high — and from the viewing platform they look really impressive — but they are significantly smaller than the uThukela (Tugela) Falls in the Drakensberg which, at 947m, are not only the highest falls in South Africa but the second highest in the world. Sadly, since 1851 there have been over 20 deaths recorded at Howick Falls, including young Charles Booker, a sixteen-year-old from Michaelhouse who took a bet of twenty pounds (in 1940) that he could dive into the pool at the bottom. The falls are known as *KwaNogqaza* to the Zulu people, which means 'Place of the Tall One'.

Howick Falls

Section ❸
Round trip from Howick to Karkloof Canopy Tours
Distance 36km (18km each way)
Driving Time 30mins
Highlights Umgeni Valley Nature Reserve, mountain-biking trails and picnic spots, Karkloof Canopy Tours

Leaving Howick, head out of town on the Karkloof road. After a short distance you'll pass the Yellowwood Café, a popular breakfast spot with mountain bikers. Kids also love the place for its animal farm playgound, and don't be surprised if you see a donkey leaning over the fence nibbling on a mountain bike while the biker's back is turned.

Not far up the road you'll find the **Umgeni Valley Nature Reserve**, a real gem of a place with stunning views down into the gorge (carved by the Umgeni River) and back to the Howick Falls. Apart from a fabulous game drive, the reserve offers fantastic **mountain biking** and hiking and there's a dedicated section of sport-climbing routes on its cliffs. It's also a good spot to do a bit of bird-watching, with over 270 bird species listed including the elusive nerina trogon and crowned eagle.

Back on the Karkloof road you'll pass the farmers' market, held every Saturday morning, and a little further on you come to the Karkloof Country Club. It's impossible to miss, with its neatly laid-out polo fields and white picket fence. If a game's on, it's worth stopping – not only to watch the horses in action but to see who's who in the horsey world. The club's a popular starting point for mountain bikers. The Karkloof area is very well known for its mountain-biking trails and hosts the annual Karkloof Classic race. Active Escapes, based in Howick, are fanatical about mountain biking and can guide you onto the best trails.

Opposite the club's entrance there's a small stone church, St Marks. It's only open on the first Sunday of the month but the grounds are beautiful and some of the graves date back to the 1800s.

Back on the Karkloof road you pass one of the larger dairy farms in the area. At milking time the herd will eyeball you as they follow the fence line up to the milking sheds. Shortly after you will come to a dirt road turning off to the right and leading to the Karkloof Falls. They aren't as spectacular as the Howick Falls but make a nice diversion and **picnic spot**. But if you really want a bit of fun, continue up the Karkloof road until you see a turning left to **Karkloof Canopy Tours**. Their eight slides zigzag through pristine forest scenery, passing a beautiful 20m waterfall en route. Return to Howick on the Karkloof road.

MEANDERING THE MIDLANDS
Contact details

Active Escapes
033 330 6131
www.active-escapes.co.za
Ardmore Ceramic Art
033 940 0034
www.ardmoreceramics.co.za
Bierfassl
033 266 6320
www.bierfassl.co.za
Caversham Mill
033 940 0145
www.cavershammill.co.za
Culamoya Chimes
033 234 4503
Excelsior
033 266 6908
www.excelsiorcottage.co.za
Granny Mouse Country House & Spa
033 234 4071
www.grannymouse.co.za
Ground Cover
033 330 6092
www.groundcover.co.za
Hilford Pottery
082 682 6294
Impumelelo Bead Shop
071 834 4349
www.thecapturesite.co.za
Karkloof Canopy Tours
033 330 3415
www.karkloofcanopytour.co.za
La Lampara
082 416 0195
lampara@mweb.co.za
Marrakesh Cheese Farm
084 352 8911
Meander Fine Wines
083 452 3350
www.pigglywiggly.co.za
Midlands Meander
033 330 8195
www.midlandsmeander.co.za

Nelson Mandela's capture site and Truth Store
083 227 2376
www.thecapturesite.co.za
Notties
033 266 6151
www.nottieshotel.co.za
Old Halliwell Country Inn
033 330 2602
www.oldhalliwell.co.za
Piggly Wiggly
076 803 1110
www.pigglywiggly.co.za
Rawdons Hotel
033 266 6044
www.rawdons.co.za
Sapore
033 266 6921
www.sapore.co.za
Spiral Blue
033 234 4799
www.spiralblue.co.za
Swissland Cheese
082 418 3440
www.swisslandcheese.net
The Nottingham Road Brewery
033 266 6728
www.nottsbrewery.co.za
The Ugly Duckling
033 267 7263
www.theuglyduckling.co.za
Tumble Downs
082 802 2837
www.tumbledowns.co.za
Umgeni Valley Nature Reserve
033 330 3903
www.wessa.org.za
WildFly Travel
033 266 6966
www.wildflytravel.com

Regional info
www.nightjartravel.com

GREAT TREK ROAD TRIP
Graaff-Reinet to Dundee and/or Makhado

Moving to South Africa some years ago, I was struck by the uniformity of place names. The ubiquitous Retief, Trichardt, Potgieter and Pretorius had stamped their names all over the map. It was only when the names started disappearing that I troubled to find out more about these so-called Voortrekkers and their epic journey 175 years ago. A friend and I decided to retrace their trip, albeit in a car rather than an ox wagon. We weren't the first to do so. In 1938 and 1988, ceremonial wagons were carried across the country, building cairns to mark the route. But those trips belonged to a different era, when Voortrekkers were rather more popular.

Total Distance 2,740km
Driving Time 33hrs 30mins

....

Section ❶
Graaff-Reinet to Bloemfontein
Distance 550km
Driving Time 6hrs
Highlights:
Pretorius statue in Graaff-Reinet
Moroka's Hoek and Victoria Nek near
  Thaba Nchu
First Raadsaal and Wagon Museum in
  Bloemfontein
SEE PAGE 110

....

Section ❷
Bloemfontein to Pietermaritzburg
Distance 660km
Driving Time 8hrs 30mins
Highlights:
Bell's Pass
Winburg Voortrekker Monument
Retief Rock at Kerkenberg
'Kaalvoet Vrou' statue
Sooilaer
Bloukrans Memorial
Saailaer
Van Rensburg koppie
Voortrekker Museum and Voortrekker
  buildings in Pietermaritzburg
SEE PAGES 111–113

....

Section ❸
Pietermaritzburg to Dundee (via Durban and
East Coast)
Distance 470km
Driving Time 6hrs 30mins
Highlights:
Congella battlefield
Durban Old Fort
uMgungundlovu and KwaMatiwane
Blood River Museum and battlefield
Ncome Museum
SEE PAGES 113–115

....

Section ❹
Bloemfontein to Potchefstroom
Distance 460km
Driving Time 6hrs
Highlights:
Bell's Pass
Winburg Voortrekker Monument
Sand River
Vegkop Battlefield and Museum
Potchefstroom
SEE PAGES 116–117

....

Section ❺
Potchefstroom to Makhado
Distance 600km
Driving Time 6hrs 30mins
Highlights:
Voortrekker Monument in Pretoria
Heroes' Acre in Pretoria
Moorddrift
Arend Dieperink Museum in Mokopane
Hugh Exton Photographic Museum in
  Polokwane
Schoemansdal Open-air Museum
SEE PAGES 117–118

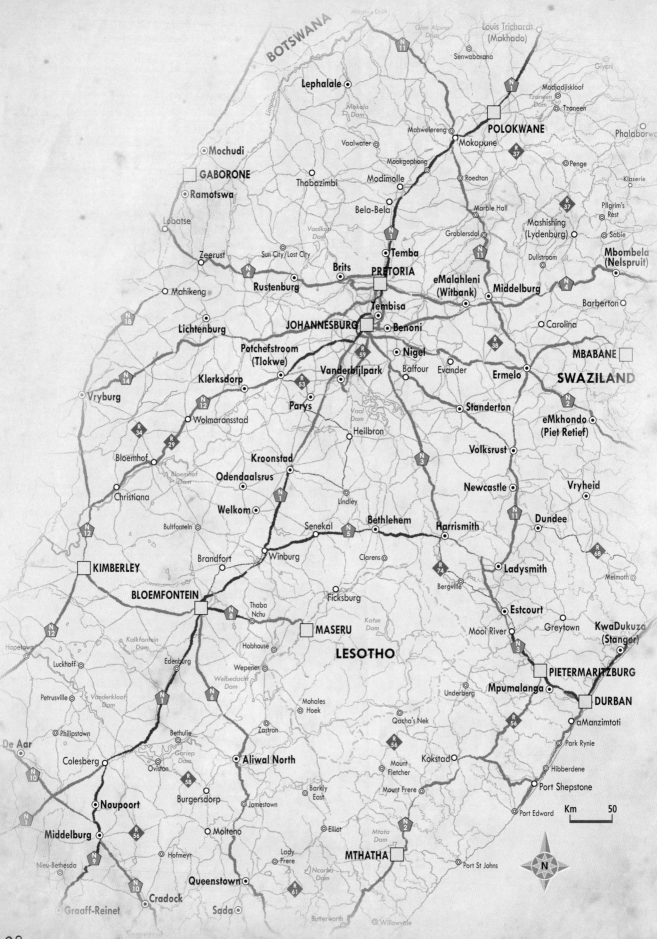

In a nutshell:
An adventure following the Voortrekkers' epic journeys, which can take you the length and breadth of South Africa.

Logistics
The nearest international airport to Graaff-Reinet is Cape Town, with Bloemfontein the closest domestic airport. This route overlaps with Not the N1 (see pages 8–21) to some extent and can link in to several routes through KwaZulu-Natal. Even following the Voortrekkers by car on tar roads is a vast undertaking, which will probably require the better part of a fortnight if you do all the possible detours and spend some time at the sites.

Driving conditions
Most of the journey is on good tar roads, though some in KwaZulu-Natal are in poor condition. The R74 over Oliviershoek Pass is particularly bad. A few sites (Retief Rock, the 'Kaalvoet Vrou' and Blood River) are accessed by dirt roads that can be tricky after heavy rains.

Pet-friendly rating ★ ☆ ☆ ☆ ☆
1 = least suited 5 = most suited
You're generally visiting memorials and graves.

Child-friendly rating ★ ☆ ☆ ☆ ☆
1 = least suited 5 = most suited
Aside from the Pretoria Voortrekker Monument and the museums at Vegkop and Blood River, most sites don't provide much information.

Low-slung vehicle-friendly rating ★ ★ ☆ ☆ ☆
1 = high clearance 5 = lowest slung

Don't miss
- The informative Voortrekker Monument near Pretoria
- The battlefields at Vegkop and Blood River
- Evocative sites in the Drakensberg and KwaZulu-Natal
- The sinister KwaMatiwane execution hill

Emergency service numbers
Emergency (from a landline) 10111
Emergency (from a cellphone) 112
AA roadside assistance 086 100 0234 or 083 843 22 (24 hours)

Best time
The drier winter months are a better time to visit the KwaZulu-Natal sites.

SUMMER			AUTUMN			WINTER			SPRING		
D	J	F	M	A	M	J	J	A	S	O	N

Background reading
The Voortrekkers by Johannes Meintjes, Corgi 1973.
The Great Trek by Oliver Ransford, Sphere Books, 1974.
The Historical Monuments of South Africa by J J Oberholster, Rembrandt Van Rijn Foundation for Culture, 1972.

ON THE SIDE >> The Great Trek
In early 1835, some 50 Dutch-speaking farmers, or Boers, led by Louis Trichardt crossed the Orange River, leaving behind the British-ruled Cape Colony in search of a new homeland. Larger parties soon followed, led by Hendrik Potgieter, Gert Maritz, Piet Retief, Piet Uys and Andries Pretorius. They left to escape the ravages of regular border wars with the Xhosa, plus meddlesome laws imposed by the British government, such as the abolition of slavery. Likening themselves to the Israelites quitting Egypt for the Promised Land, typically the only book they took with them was the Bible. In total, around 10,000 Boers left the Cape Colony, in what became known as 'the Great Trek'. Some went north across the Vaal River, others east over the Drakensberg Mountains into Natal. Neither was a trip for sissies. Of the six major trek leaders, four perished in 1838: Retief and Uys in battle, Maritz and Trichardt of disease. Only Potgieter and Pretorius survived long enough to see the British government finally recognise an independent Boer homeland in 1852.

GREAT TREK ROAD TRIP
Graaff-Reinet to Dundee and/or Makhado

Section 1
Graaff-Reinet to Bloemfontein
Distance 550km
Driving Time 6hrs
Highlights Pretorius statue in Graaff-Reinet, Moroka's Hoek and Victoria Nek near Thaba Nchu, First Raadsaal and Wagon Museum in Bloemfontein
Access to sites First Raadsaal and Wagon Museum: Monday to Friday 10:00–13:00, Saturday and Sunday 14:00–17:00. Free access to other sites.

In 1830, Graaff-Reinet was considered the last outpost of civilisation. Gazing down on it from the Valley of Desolation, it still looks that way — a small town huddled in a bowl, surrounded by vast empty space. The Voortrekkers set out from several locations, but **Graaff-Reinet** was the most common starting point. Hendrik Potgieter, Gert Maritz and Andries Pretorius all departed from here. There's a **bust of Pretorius** on the outskirts of town, gazing towards what was once the Promised Land but is now a township. That sort of encapsulates the Great Trek: wherever the Voortrekkers went, they found the best land already taken, precipitating numerous battles and scraps.

Armed with a map, GPS and *The Historical Monuments of South Africa* (1972 edition), we set off on our great trek north. By comparison, the Voortrekkers had only rudimentary maps to assist them, largely based on four expeditions sent out in 1834 to survey possible options. They also had no roads, whereas thankfully the N9 now cuts through the Sneeuberg and Bankberg mountains. On the Lootsberg Pass, a sign cautions for unexpected snow. The main hazard, however, is giant tortoises, waddling slowly across the road. I rescue four, who all repay my chivalry by urinating on me. The less said about the fifth, the better. To be fair, the Voortrekkers had to contend with slightly more menacing game, since all of South Africa was then Big Five country. On the plus side, hunting provided meat for their braais and ivory for trading.

At Colesberg we join the N1 and cross the Orange River. If Graaff-Reinet marked the last outpost of civilisation, the Orange River marked the edge of the known world. Now, it marks the start of the Free State: how times change. We leave the N1 for Thaba Nchu, where all trek parties headed

Valley of Desolation

to restock and regroup. It's taken us five hours from Graaff-Reinet, as opposed to the month it typically took the trekkers.

Then, as now, **Thaba Nchu** was home to the Barolong tribe, under Chief Moroka. A peaceable bunch, they allowed the trekkers to establish a camp at **Moroka's Hoek**, beneath the distinctive peak which the Barolong called 'black mountain' and the trekkers renamed Blesberg ('bald mountain'). A bronze plaque supposedly marks the site of the laager, but all we can find are a large empty field and deserted farm buildings. We have more luck on **Victoria Nek**, which the trek parties crossed once they'd re-hitched their wagons. On the right-hand side of the road, a stone cairn commemorates the route. The Barolong called this pass 'Rakgokgo', imitating the sound the wagon wheels made when jolting down the slope.

Beyond here, the trekkers divided. Some thought their Promised Land lay north, across the Vaal River; others believed it lay east in Natal, over the Drakensberg Mountains. We plan to follow both routes, but first visit nearby **Bloemfontein**, named after the abundance of flowers or cheetahs, depending on your ethnic tongue. The oldest surviving building is a modest structure on St George Street, with long whitewashed walls and a low, thatched roof. Built in 1849, the **First Raadsaal** has served as a school, church, poison store and assembly hall for the Orange River Republic, which the British recognised as an independent Boer state in 1854. It's now a **museum** exhibiting Voortrekker **wagons**, although making it in time for the limited opening hours requires some luck or planning. For a Saturday night, the country's judicial capital is in an appropriately measured, sober mood. On the plus side, it's a good place to catch up on sleep and replenish batteries for the trek ahead.

EERMAAL SAL DAAR WEL 'N WIEL OOR ONS WÊRELD
ROL WAT VIR U EN VIR MY ONKEERBAAR IS

ON THE SIDE >> Deviation to Boomplaats

At Trompsburg, you can leave the N1 and take the R704 to Boomplaats. A battle was fought here on 29 August 1848, between 500 Boers under Andries Pretorius and 1,500 British under Sir Harry Smith, who in his capacity as British Governor had annexed the land between the Orange and Vaal rivers, inciting the Boer settlers to revolt. Despite the poor odds, Pretorius managed to manoeuvre the British into a trap, but his men fired too early and superior numbers prevailed. There's a memorial to the battle dead on a farm outside Jagersfontein. Then again, it was a minor event in the Great Trek and will add some 50km to your journey.

The R74 over Oliviershoek Pass is in poor condition. The dirt roads leading to Retief Rock and 'Kaalvoet Vrou' are difficult after heavy rain. You can break the journey at Little Switzerland Resort near Bergville.

Section ❷
Bloemfontein to Pietermaritzburg
Distance 660km
Driving Time 8hrs 30mins
Highlights Bell's Pass, Winburg Voortrekker Monument, Retief Rock at Kerkenberg, 'Kaalvoet Vrou' statue, Sooilaer, Bloukrans Memorial, Saailaer, Van Rensburg koppie, Voortrekker Museum and Voortrekker buildings in Pietermaritzburg
Access to sites Voortrekker Museum, Pietermaritzburg: Monday to Friday 09:00–16:00, Saturday 09:00–13:00. Winburg Voortrekker Monument appears to be closed, though entry is possible. You might be asked to sign a register at Retief Rock. Free access to other sites.

Leaving Bloemfontein on the R30/R73, we head across flat plains punctured by koppies. Just south of Winburg, white stones on the flank of **Bell's Pass** indicate the Great Trek came this way. On crossing the Klein Vet River, the trekkers received a warm welcome from Chief Makwana and the Bataung tribe, who lived in mortal dread of their aggressive northerly neighbours, the Matabele. Offered land in return for allegiance, some trekkers decided to stay, building their first permanent town at **Winburg** in 1837. Voortrekker Street leads into what might be called the town centre. For all its intrepid history, it's now a sleepy place, where everyone seems to move at half pace. A couple of kilometres outside town, a **monument** commemorates the **Voortrekkers**. It's locked up, seemingly for good, and we have to scale a brick wall to get in. The tall concrete monument inside has a distinctly military edge.

Monument in Winburg

GREAT TREK ROAD TRIP
Graaff-Reinet to Dundee and/or Makhado

In April 1837, a large trek party from Grahamstown arrived at Winburg, led by Piet Retief, a distinguished figure, who believed their future lay in Natal. So, while Hendrik Potgieter's party stayed on the Highveld, Retief led the rest towards the Drakensberg Mountains. Leaving the N5 at Harrismith, we join the R74, skirting Sterkfontein Dam. The road is in such parlous condition, it feels as if we're travelling in a poorly sprung ox wagon.

Just before Oliviershoek Pass, a dirt road leads off to the left. While Retief went on to seek permission from Dingaan, King of the Zulus, to settle in Natal, the rest of the trekkers waited here, holding church services beneath a peak they called **Kerkenberg**. Like many Great Trek landmarks, it's identifiable by white stones on its flank, placed by commemorative trips. A footpath leads to an over-hanging **boulder**, bearing the legend 'P Retief Die 12 Nov 1837'. It was carved by Retief's daughter, Deborah, while he was away visiting the Zulus. A few days later, **Retief** sent word that Dingaan welcomed the settlers and they cheerfully descended into Natal. Graffiti's more acceptable when it's poignant.

Near here is Step's Pass, down which the trekkers lowered their wagons. It's not a bad place to get your cooler box out and take a break, looking out across the undulating green valleys, framed on your right by the Drakensberg peaks. After the flat, burnished Free State plains, perhaps it did look like the Promised Land. Then again, the trekkers weren't to know that when Retief went back with 100 men in February 1838 to seal the deal with Dingaan, they'd all be slain; that nearly 500 more trekkers would be killed by the Zulus later that month, in the so-called 'Great Murder'; and that, when the trekkers had finally defeated the Zulus and established their own homeland, the British would take it off them after just a few years. No, if they'd foreseen all that, they might not have bothered descending Step's Pass.

Also at Oliviershoek Pass, another dirt road leads to the '**Kaalvoet Vrou**', a bronze statue of a woman stomping bare-foot back towards the Highveld, with her *kappie* (bonnet) pulled up. It commemorates the defiant Voortrekker women who, when the British Commissioner announced the annexation of Natalia in August 1843, told him in no uncertain terms they were leaving for freedom back over the Drakensberg and north of the Vaal.

We descend into KwaZulu-Natal on the R74, which is safer than Step's Pass, if only just. Just outside Loskop, on the P600, a large stone cairn beside the Little Tugela commemorates **Sooilaer** laager, named after the defensive earth sod walls the trekkers built. They spent several bleak months after the Great Murder here, under Gert Maritz's leadership, and things got even bleaker when he died from illness in September 1838. Fortunately, two months later, Andries Pretorius arrived with a large party from Graaff-Reinet. And it was from Sooilaer that Pretorius set out on 27 November 1838 – with 470 men, 64 wagons and three cannons — on an expedition against the Zulus which culminated at the Battle of Blood River.

Around Estcourt, we visit several sites where trekkers were camping during the Great Murder. Having dispatched with Retief's party, Dingaan sent an impi of 10,000 warriors to 'eat up' the rest. The **Bloukrans Memorial** near Chievely is dedicated to the 482 trekkers killed in those few grisly days. At **Saailaer**,

'Kaalvoet Vrou'

Gert Maritz's party repulsed the attack, with their wagons tightly laagered in a horseshoe bend on the Bushman's River. A black obelisk and cairn mark this camp site. On a small **koppie** near Willow Grange, the **Van Rensburgs** also held out, saved by Marthinus Oosthuizen galloping through the impi to bring them ammunition. We reach it just as an afternoon storm breaks and, showing far less resilience than the Van Rensburgs, we promptly flee.

An hour later we reach **Pietermaritzburg**, the provincial capital of KwaZulu-Natal. It was formerly the capital of the Republic of Natalia, which the trekkers founded after their victory at Blood River. The town was named after the two pioneers who led them towards their Promised Land but didn't get to see it – Piet (Retief) and (Gert) Maritz. There are statues of both outside the **Voortrekker Museum**, with Retief perched atop a pile of stones collected from Kerkenberg.

Inside the museum is an original trek wagon. It's like seeing the Apollo 11 Command module – it's amazing that something so small and seemingly fragile could have survived such a journey. The museum's grounds contain the Church of the Vow, built in 1840 to honour a pledge the trekkers made before the Battle of Blood River. Pretorius's grand two-storey thatched home stands nearby; it was lovingly moved here in 1981 from his farm outside town. More authentically, some original **Voortrekker buildings** still grace Boom and Langalibalele streets, while at 225 Church Street is the former home of Piet Retief's widow. Sandwiched between shops, it's now a loan centre. On this trip you quickly learn that time is a great leveller.

Section ❸
Pietermaritzburg to Dundee (via Durban and East Coast)
Distance 470km
Driving Time 6hrs 30mins
Highlights Congella battlefield, Durban Old Fort, uMgungundlovu and KwaMatiwane, Blood River Museum and battlefield, Ncome Museum
Access to sites Durban Old Fort: 10:00–17:00. uMgungundlovu Multi-Media Centre: 09:00–16:00. Blood River Museum: 09:00–17:00. Ncome Museum: 08:00–16:30.

TIP

This is a long day, especially if you want to spend time at uMgungundlovu and Blood River. A historic, scenic place to stay near uMgungundlovu is Owen's Camp. The roads to Blood River battlefield and Ncome Museum can be difficult after heavy rain.

Given how many people run and kayak the 80km between Pietermaritzburg and Durban, you feel somewhat guilty cruising effortlessly down the N3. The British started a settlement in Durban in 1824 after King Shaka granted a large coastal strip to a young adventurer, Henry Flynn, in gratitude for nursing him after an injury. Originally called Port Natal, it was obsequiously renamed after the British Governor, Sir Benjamin d'Urban. The existence of this small British settlement was a key reason why Hendrik Potgieter stayed on the Highveld, and it proved a wise decision.

After the Voortrekkers established their own independent Republic of Natalia, the Great Trek seemed to be over. However, when the British heard that the trekkers had seized some slaves, they sent a force of 150 soldiers to intervene. Conversely, resolved not to become British subjects again, the trekkers assembled a commando. The two forces met on 23 May 1842 at Congella Bay, where the Boers thumped an inept British attack. Once a mangrove swamp, **Congella** is now a scruffy park across the highway from the port. A stone cairn marks where the first of many **battles**

GREAT TREK ROAD TRIP
Graaff-Reinet to Dundee and/or Makhado

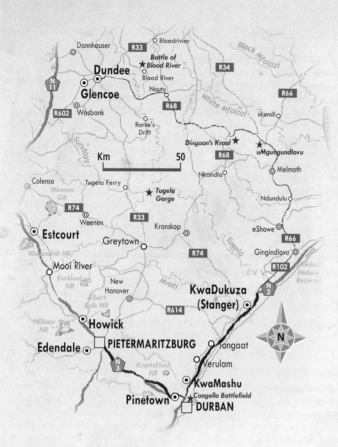

It's a long way from Durban city centre to Dingaan's kraal at **uMgungundlovu**, and the 250km distance is just the start of it. Having said that, the journey's far quicker now, courtesy of the N2 toll road which sweeps dismissively over the Tugela River and scythes up the coast, than when Retief paid two visits. At Gingindlovu we turn our backs on the ocean, taking the R66 to Ndundulu. After the musical Zulu names, Melmoth comes as a jolt. Some 30km beyond Melmoth on the R34 we reach uMgungundlovu, the 'place surrounded by elephants'.

There are no longer any elephants but there is a brand new multimedia centre with videos featuring traditional Zulu entertainment. By comparison, when Retief's party visited, Dingaan's palace was a collection of beehive huts with separate quarters for his large harem. For his day Dingaan was a cultured monarch, writing songs, designing costumes and choreographing dances for his harem to perform. But he'd also ascended the throne by assassinating his half-brother, Shaka, and bumping off most of his family. More pertinently, he viewed the trekkers as a threat and, notwithstanding initially promising to give them some land, decided to do away with them.

There's an observation tower outside the multimedia centre, offering panoramic views of the surrounding hills including **KwaMatiwane**, where Dingaan's enemies were executed and left out for the vultures. Having had to endure several days of traditional dancing, Retief's party were trussed up, dragged up the hill and murdered. The memorial to them looks uncomfortably like one of the spikes on which they were skewered. While the 70 Boers are listed by name (there are five Pretoriuses and four De Beers), the 30 loyal black retainers who died with them get one collective line. Retief gets his own grave lower down the hill. Though a long time has passed, it's still a sinister place where you can sense that bad things happened.

From uMgungundlovu we head northwest towards Dundee on the R68, kept alert by potholes and wandering cattle. Though KwaZulu-Natal boasts the best sites on this trip, it also has by far the worst roads. Having dispensed with Retief, Dingaan sent his warriors to exterminate the rest of the trekkers but, despite killing nearly 500, they failed in their task. Before the year ended this failure came back to haunt them.

On the R602 between Glencoe and Wasbank, a stone plinth marks where Andries Pretorius and his 470-strong commando passed in December 1838 on their punitive mission to crush Dingaan. It was here that Sarel Cilliers proposed making a vow that if they won the coming battle they'd build a church and honour the date each year. To the north rise the Mud Mountains, over which the trekkers then dragged their 64 wagons and three cannons.

between Boers and British took place. The plaque has been ripped off.

Huddled down by the foreshore, **Durban Old Fort** looks more like a toy castle than a proper sanctuary. After their shambles at Congella, the British soldiers retreated here, spending an uncomfortable month besieged by the Boers, subsisting on crows. They were rescued thanks to the endeavours of a British settler, Dick King, who rode to Grahamstown to raise help, covering the 960km in just 10 days. There's a statue of King on the foreshore, seated on his trusty mount, Somerset. The arrival of British warships bearing reinforcements marked the end of the spat and the Republic of Natalia was annexed by the British shortly thereafter.

Battle of Blood River Memorial

The battle was fought 40km north of present-day Dundee. On the battlefield stand 64 full-size replica bronze wagons drawn up in a laager. Naturally defended by a deep donga, a hippo pool and the Ncome River, this site was carefully chosen by Pretorius. On the evening of 15 December, the laager was surrounded by 10,000 Zulu warriors. Had they attacked then as planned, the trekkers' flintlock rifles wouldn't have functioned in the damp mist and the Zulus might have won. However, they mistook the camp lanterns for ghosts and withdrew, coming back the following morning. Rather bizarrely, there are two separate museums on opposite sides of the battle-field. The **Blood River Museum** tells the story from the Boer point of view, while the **Ncome Museum** offers the Zulu perspective. Neither make pleasant reading for Zulus. The **battle** started early, with insanely brave but hopeless Zulu charges at the Boers' elephant guns, which could down three men with one slug. The Zulus then thought about starving the trekkers out, but the requisite patience proved beyond them and some verbal taunts provoked another suicidal charge. When the Zulus finally retreated, they left behind 3,500 dead, many shot in the Ncome River, which the trekkers renamed Blood River and the Zulus vowed to never drink from again. In return, three Boers were wounded.

Defeat at Blood River marked the beginning of the end for Dingaan, who was murdered by his own advisers. Meanwhile, true to their promise, the trekkers built the Church of the Vow in Pietermaritzburg and declared 16 December a public holiday. Initially it was gloatingly called Dingaan's Day; in the 1960s it was renamed the Day of the Covenant; after an arcane theological row, it became the Day of the Vow; and now, rather more generously, it's known as Reconciliation Day. At this point, the Great Trek may well have ended but for the arrival of the British to annex Natalia. This prompted many trekkers to leave for the Highveld, which is where we're also now heading.

Ncome

GREAT TREK ROAD TRIP
Graaff-Reinet to Dundee and/or Makhado

Section ❹
Bloemfontein to Potchefstroom
Distance 460km
Driving Time 6hrs
Highlights Bell's Pass, Winburg Voortrekker Monument, Sand River, Vegkop Battlefield and Museum, Potchefstroom
Access to sites Vegkop Museum: 08:00–17:00. Free access to other sites.

If, like Hendrik Potgieter, you've decided to give KwaZulu-Natal a miss, then take the R30/R73 over **Bell's Pass** and visit the rather bombastic **monument** at **Winburg** (see Section 2). If you've already been there on Retief's trail however, stay on the N1 and speed past it. Some 30km past Winburg, just after crossing the **Sand River**, make a right-hand turn across the highway, hopefully dodging the fusillade of oncoming traffic. The dangerous manoeuvre is neatly symbolic of the journey the Voortrekkers also took to get to the Sand River Convention. Though we're getting rather ahead of ourselves, it was on this knoll, in January 1852, that the British signed an agreement recognising an independent Boer state north of the Vaal River. In many ways the establishment of Transvaal marked the end of the Great Trek. But it had been a torrid journey to get there.

Leaving the N1 at Kroonstad, we cut in-country to join the R725. If the trekkers' main adversary in Natal was the Zulu, up on the Highveld it was the Matabele, led by Chief Mzilikazi. When a party of trekkers crossed the Vaal River in August 1835, Mzilikazi sent his impi to wipe them out. Having massacred several groups camped near Parys, the 5,000-strong Matabele army descended upon Hendrik Potgieter's small party hunkered down in a defensive laager just south of modern-day Heilbron.

Driving along R725, I use my innate tactical brain to spot possible positions selected by Potgieter. The road continues past them and I'm rather taken aback when we reach what looks like a heavily vegetated slagheap with 'Vegkop' spelled out in white stones. At the southern end of the koppie, a **statue** of a stooped Voortrekker fends off a shower of assegai with his rifle while clutching a Bible. It was here that Potgieter positioned his laager and the omnipresent Sarel Cilliers led the Voortrekkers in prayer while the surrounding Matabele snacked on raw cattle. The **battle** was fast and furious, with the Matabele rushing the laager, and the 33 Boer men desperately shooting

them down, as the women and children reloaded their rifles. One hour later, when the gun smoke cleared, over 1,000 thrown assegais lay within the laager and nearly 500 Matabele lay dead outside it. Only two trekkers were killed, though the retreating Matabele drove off all the trekkers' livestock. The graves of the two trekkers are beside the quaint, tidy museum which houses imposing portraits of Potgieter and Cilliers. After his success at Vegkop, Potgieter raided Mzilikazi's kraal at Mosega, recapturing livestock and driving the Matabele over the Limpopo into modern-day Zimbabwe.

Vegkop

ON THE SIDE >> Mzilikazi's kraal at Mosega
Depending on your level of enthusiasm, you can follow Potgieter's remorseless 210km trail to Mzilikazi's kraal at Mosega. There aren't any monuments along the way, but the scenery is interesting. From Potchefstroom, take the R53/N14 to Groot Marico. This is the land described by Herman Charles Bosman, whose Oom Schalk Lourens tales evocatively capture trekboer life. In Groot Marico there's a Bosman Museum but don't set your expectations too high. Mosega is just south of Zeerust, where the R27 crosses the Klein Marico. Potgieter visited in January and November 1837, torching the Matabele homesteads and pursuing them over the Limpopo. Not surprisingly, nothing remains of Mzilikazi's kraal.

Leaving Heilbron and travelling northwest on the R723, we pass through Parys, where the Matabele massacred the Liebenberg family before their less successful foray at Vegkop. On the Vaal River, Parys has a laid-back, artistic charm, if not quite being Paris from which it takes its name. With the Matabele gone, many trekkers decided to settle around here, building a town some 50km northwest of Parys. Initially called Vryburg and then Mooiriviersdorp, it soon became known after the trekkers' authoritative leader, Hendrik Potgieter. Spaciously laid out, **Potchefstroom** was officially founded in 1838, with squares, gardens and, of course, a church. Until the church was completed, services were held outdoors on the town square. A cairn opposite the Magistrate's Court marks this spot. Potgieter himself lived 10km outside town at his inelegantly named Witstinkhoutboom farm.

TIP

Parys makes a pleasant overnight stop, with several riverside lodges, including the self-catering Otters' Haunt.

Section ⑤
Potchefstroom to Makhado
Distance 600km
Driving Time 6hrs 30mins
Highlights Voortrekker Monument in Pretoria, Heroes' Acre in Pretoria, Moorddrift, Arend Dieperink Museum in Mokopane, Hugh Exton Photographic Museum in Polokwane, Schoemansdal Open-air Museum
Access to sites Pretoria Voortrekker Monument: 08:00–17:00. Arend Dieperink Museum: Monday to Friday 08:00–16:00. Hugh Exton Photographic Museum: Monday to Friday 09:00–16:00, Saturday 11:00–13:00. Schoemansdal Open-air Museum: 08:00–16:00. Free access to other sites.

Though Potchefstroom is pleasant enough, it couldn't contain the restless Hendrik Potgieter, especially after trekkers returning from Natal started challenging his authority and the British announced that their laws extended to the 25°S parallel. So, in June 1845, he upped sticks and moved north, which is the way we head too.

Just south of **Pretoria** on the N14, a huge granite tower on a hilltop dominates the landscape. Built in the 1940s to commemorate the Great Trek, in supposedly Art-Deco style, the national **Voortrekker Monument** is powerful and imposing, if lacking in subtlety and grace. Inside, a 27-panel marble frieze depicts key events in the Great Trek and a cenotaph catches the noon sun on Reconciliation Day. Architectural quibbles aside, it's a fascinating, informative place.

Stopping in Pretoria, we visit **Heroes' Acre** in Church Street Cemetery. Any expectations that this may be South Africa's equivalent of Westminster Abbey are quickly dashed by the padlocked gate and the litter. Slipping in through a hole in the fence, we wander through rows of Boer War casualties, eventually finding Andries Pretorius's grave in the inner sanctum.

Inside the Voortrekker Monument

GREAT TREK ROAD TRIP
Graaff-Reinet to Dundee and/or Makhado

Pretorius died in July 1853, surviving long enough to see the Boers get their own independent state after the Sand River Convention, and then posthumously bestowed his name on the capital city. Next to him is a memorial to Hendrik Potgieter who was to have been re-interred here, but his family objected. In any case, the two great Voortrekkers never did get on after Potgieter refused to help Pretorius fight the British in Natal. Nearby lie the architects of apartheid, Hendrik Verwoerd and J G Strydom. The definition of a hero depends on your point of view.

Driving north on the N1 for nearly 200km we pull off at **Moorddrift**, or 'Murder Ford', so you can guess what happened here. A stone memorial is guarded by a pair of ancient camel-thorn trees. In 1854, Potgieter's brother, Hermanus, and his family were murdered here by Chief Mokopane's tribe. Allegedly, Potgieter was skinned alive while his children were beaten to death against the thorn trees. We were thinking of having a picnic here, but decide to push on instead.

Moorddrift

It's only 15km to the next town. Founded in 1852 and originally called Vredenburg (to commemorate the belated reconciliation between Hendrik Potgieter and Andries Pretorius just before they died), the town was quickly renamed Potgietersrus, in memory of Potgieter's son, Piet, who was killed on a retaliatory mission against Chief Mokopane. Besieged by the Boers, Mokopane and some 2,000 of his tribe starved to death in nearby caves. In 2003 the town's name was changed again, to **Mokopane**. The **Arend Dieperink Museum** tries to make sense of this grisly history.

Our next stop is 60km further along the N1 at **Polokwane** (previously Pietersburg). Confusingly, all the major towns up here have recently changed names. Then again, it's not a modern phenomenon: the Voortrekkers blithely renamed every geographical feature they came upon, regardless of what the incumbents called it. We visit the old Dutch Reformed Church housing the **Hugh Exton Photographic Museum** with its fascinating collection of 19th-century portraits.

Then we're back on the N1, crossing flat scrub plains and acacia-studded hills beneath a sea-blue sky and cottonwool clouds. Once you get into the rhythm of travelling, it's hard to stop: the vast open space seems to draw you on, especially if you've got the tax-mongering British behind you. The Tropic of Capricorn is marked by a graffiti-scarred monument at the side of the road. We're now at 23°26'S, which was beyond the rule of British law. There's a toll plaza near here, which wouldn't have impressed Potgieter.

Makhado (previously Louis Trichardt) is the northernmost limit of our journey. Trichardt's party reached here in May 1836 and Potgieter visited them a few months later, promising to return soon with the rest of the trekkers. However, fighting Matabele kept Potgieter otherwise engaged, and he only returned seven years later, by which time Trichardt had given up waiting and moved on.

Some 20km west of Makhado on the R523 is **Schoemansdal Open-air Museum**. Hendrik Potgieter finally settled here in 1848, after a brief, unhappy stay in Mpumalanga. The guards manning the gates look surprised to see us and the entrance book suggests they don't get bothered too often. At its peak, Schoemansdal boasted a church, a school and a population of 1,800. Now there's a dilapidated information centre, a collapsed observation tower and a few structures poking out from waist-deep grass. Potgieter died here in 1852, aged 59, of dropsy. Our search for his grave is curtailed by the guard's warning to watch out for snakes. Schoemansdal itself was abandoned in 1867 in the face of a Venda invasion. An untended grave in a derelict ghost town seems an ignominious end to such an incredible journey.

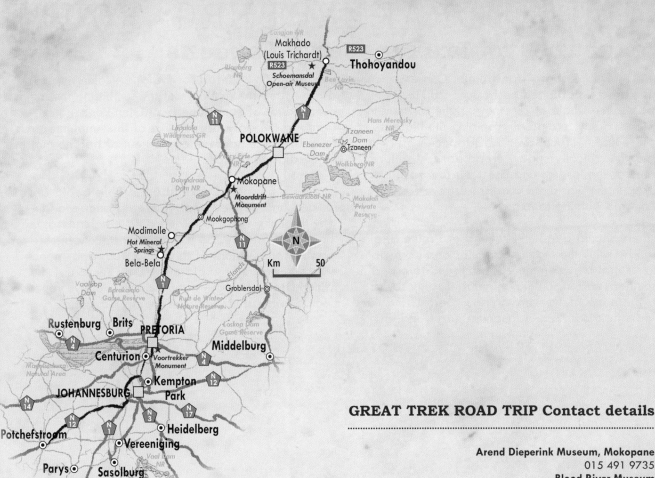

Arend Dieperink Museum, Mokopane
015 491 9735
Blood River Museum
034 632 1695
Durban Old Fort
031 304 4934
First Raadsaal and Wagon Museum, Bloemfontein
051 447 9609
Hugh Exton Photographic Museum, Polokwane
015 290 2186
Little Switzerland Resort near Bergville
036 438 2500
www.lsh.co.za
Ncome Museum
034 271 8121
Otters' Haunt
056 818 1814
www.otters.co.za
Owen's Camp
078 817 9949
parthur@iafrica.com
Vegkop Museum
058 853 0781
Voortrekker Monument, Pretoria
012 326 6770
www.voortrekkermon.org.za
Voortrekker Museum, Pietermaritzburg
033 394 6834

Regional info
www.graaffreinet.co.za

ON THE SIDE >> Extension to Mpumalanga and Kruger National Park

In between quitting Potchefstroom and moving to Schoemans-dal, Potgieter established a new settlement at Andries-Ohrigstad (named after one of his Christian names and a friendly Dutchman). It's a sensational drive to get here, on the R36 over the Abel Erasmus Pass. The settlement itself is a disappointment, with just some ruined fort walls, a superfluous concrete needle and a red brick hall bearing Potgieter's name. It was malaria that put an end to Potgieter's dream, and you'll find the graves of some of the victims in a cemetery on the Burgersfort Road. Whereas Potgieter then went off to Schoemansdal, other survivors moved 40km south to Lydenburg ('the town of suffering'), so named to remind them of their losses. Some original Voortrekker buildings remain here, including a simple school (built in 1851) and an ornate church (built in 1853). The town was recently renamed Mashishing.

Having left the Soutspansberg in August 1837, Louis Trichardt led his party towards the supposed safety of the Portuguese colony at Lourenço Marques (present-day Maputo). It was an epic journey over the eastern Drakensberg and through the Kruger National Park. Just inside Numbi Gate, a memorial marks the end of the Great Trek for Willem Pretorius, an ill-fated member of Trichardt's party. Another 100km into the park, just beyond Tshokwane, a red brick cairn notes that Louis Trichardt's party passed this way. They finally reached Lourenço Marques in April 1838, where most of them, including Trichardt, promptly died of malaria.

MALUTI DRAKENSBERG ROUTE
Ficksburg to Drakensberg Gardens

The Maluti Drakensberg Transfrontier Conservation (MDTC) area, established on 11 June 2001, encompasses the whole of Lesotho and the surrounding mountains. Home to dinosaur remains, the highest falls in southern Africa, over 2,500 species of flowers, the critically endangered bearded vulture and one of the largest and finest outdoor rock art galleries in the world, it's a treasure-trove for adventurers wanting to explore.

But where should a Maluti Drakensberg route begin and end? I think the most spectacular and accessible section is that between the eastern Free State and the southern end of the uKhahlamba/Drakensberg Park. These mountains were my soul food during the six years that I worked in Johannesburg – at least

once a month I'd head for the hills. Waking up at dawn to see the first rays of the sun hitting the multi-hued bands of sandstone from Glen Reenen Rest Camp or the dark basalt cliffs of the Amphitheatre from Thendele had me leaping out of bed no matter how exhausted I was.

It is in the northern Drakensberg, where peaks are jagged and defined, that you really understand why the Zulus refer to the Berg as uKhahlamba, the 'Barrier of Spears'. So if time is short, concentrate on the first four sections of this route. You really need weeks to properly explore even this section of the Maluti Drakensberg – but whichever valleys you decide to head up, you can't really go wrong.

Total Distance 847km
Driving Time 16hrs 35mins

Section ❶
Ficksburg to Witsieshoek Mountain Resort
Distance 161km
Driving Time 2hrs 30mins
Highlights:
Die Blikplek
Golden Gate Highlands National Park
The chain ladders
SEE PAGES 124–125

Section ❷
Witsieshoek Mountain Resort to Royal Natal
National Park
Distance 118km
Driving Time 2hrs
Highlights:
The view of the Amphitheatre
A stay at Thendele camp
The uThukela Gorge trail
SEE PAGES 125–126

Section ❸
Royal Natal National Park to Cathedral Peak
Distance 98km
Driving Time 2hrs
Highlights:
Any one of the many hikes
A stay at the charming Cathedral Peak Hotel
Didima Rock Art Centre
SEE PAGE 126

Section ❹
Cathedral Peak to Giant's Castle (including
detour to Champagne Valley)
Distance 155km
Driving Time 3hrs 20mins
Highlights:
A canopy tour
A performance of the Drakensberg
  Boys' Choir
A drink or meal at one of Izimbali
  Restaurant's outside tables
SEE PAGE 127

Section ❺
Giant's Castle to Garden Castle
Distance 315km
Driving Time 6hrs 45mins
Highlights:
A stay at Cleopatra Mountain Farmhouse
Game Pass Shelter
A trip up Sani Pass
SEE PAGES 128–129

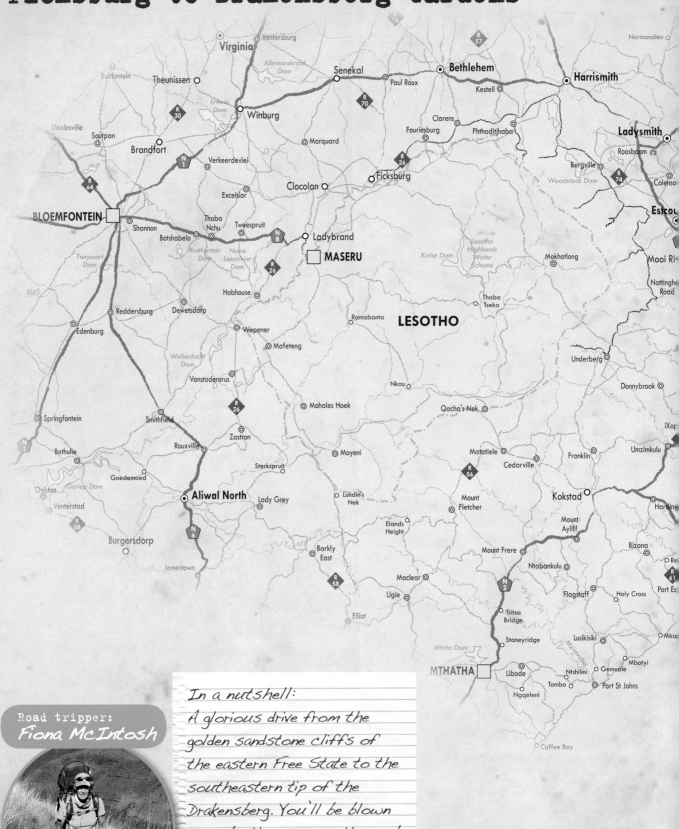

Road tripper:
Fiona McIntosh

In a nutshell:
A glorious drive from the golden sandstone cliffs of the eastern Free State to the southeastern tip of the Drakensberg. You'll be blown away by the scenery, the rock art, the bird life and the wild- flowers of southern Africa's highest mountain range.

Logistics

Ficksburg is an easy drive from Bloemfontein airport on the N5. It's about 4hrs from Joburg via the N3 and N5 (see Not the N1, pages 8–21). From Garden Castle, head back to the N3 and on to Durban (or back north), extending your route by linking in to the Midlands Meander (see pages 98–105) if you wish.

Driving conditions

Much of this route is on unfenced dirt or poor quality tar roads, so take it slowly and carefully. At the time of writing the R74 from Harrismith to the Oliviershoek Pass was in an appalling state, with numerous deep potholes and a one-way system causing extended delays, so check the status quo with local accommodation venues or tourism offices before setting out. If it's still bad, the easiest and quickest alternative is to head down the N3 to the R616 off-ramp then join the R74 to the south of Royal Natal National Park.

Pet-friendly rating ★ ☆ ☆ ☆ ☆

1 = least suited 5 = most suited
Pets are not allowed in the reserves.

Child-friendly rating ★ ★ ★ ★ ★

1 = least suited 5 = most suited
Distances are short, the scenery is bewitching and the resorts are child-friendly.

Low-slung vehicle-friendly rating ★ ★ ★ ☆ ☆

1 = high clearance 5 = lowest slung

Don't miss

- Golden Gate Highlands National Park
- The Amphitheatre
- Didima Rock Art Centre
- The Drakensberg Boys' Choir
- Sani Pass

Emergency service numbers

Emergency (from a landline) 10111
Emergency (from a cellphone) 112
AA roadside assistance 086 100 0234 or 083 843 22 (24 hours)
Mountain Rescue – KwaZulu-Natal: 080 000 5133 (EMRS), 082 990 5876 (Gavin Raubenheimer, convenor);
Free State (also Gauteng & Mpumalanga): 074 125 1385

Best time

May, when the cosmos flowers, and November are my favourite months. There is less chance of rain and temperatures are moderate. There's a very good chance of seeing snow on the Berg from June to September.

SUMMER			AUTUMN			WINTER			SPRING		
D	J	F	M	A	M	J	J	A	S	O	N

Background reading

Barrier of Spears: Drama of the Drakensberg by R O Pearce is a wonderful account of the mountain range and the intrepid men who tried to scale its peaks.
www.nightjartravel.com

Don't forget

Your passport, in case you fancy a trip up Sani Pass.

Hiking safely

- These are big mountains, so plan your trip carefully and stay within your capabilities. If you are inexperienced, take a guide.
- Always sign the mountain register before setting out and on your return.
- If you are venturing onto the plateau, check the weather forecast. Go prepared for everything from snow to thunderstorms and lightning. Watch the weather carefully.
- Carry a fully charged cellphone with the Mountain Rescue numbers loaded in.
- Snake sightings are rare, but keep your eyes open. If you encounter a snake, keep still and allow it to move on.

Ficksburg to Drakensberg Gardens

Section ❶
Ficksburg to Witsieshoek Mountain Resort
Distance 161km
Driving Time 2hrs 30mins
Highlights Die Blikplek, Golden Gate Highlands National Park, the chain ladders

The magnificent sandstone peaks of the Malutis are what draw me to the eastern Free State, so it seemed fitting that Ficksburg, surrounded by towering sandstone cliffs that have long been hewn for building, should be the start of this route. The Union Buildings in Pretoria are built from sandstone quarried in the surrounding area, and the old mill at Gumtree, just outside Ficksburg, is the tallest sandstone structure in the country. Sandstone from this part of the world is still much in demand, so you might like to swing by Koos van der Merwe's sandstone cutting works before leaving town.

Like Clarens, Ficksburg is full of somewhat eccentric artists who have escaped the rat race. Sandra Netherlands is one, and a visit to **Die Blikplek** ('the tin place'), where she'll demonstrate how old steel ceilings, enamel and other scrap metal is recycled into works of art, is a good way to get your bearings. Selling OPJ (other people's junk, as a fellow visitor coined the funky objects of desire) has developed into a successful business that is complemented by Blikskottel, a great coffee house/restaurant. Sandra is a fundi on the area and she'll fill you in on the annual Cherry and Steam Train festivals, organise tailor-made tours or point you in the direction of handmade chocolates, riverboat cruises, goose down feathers and cheese tastings. Her guesthouse, the Green Acorn, has a wonderfully eclectic selection of rooms.

The quaint town of Clarens, the hub of the eastern Free State, is a great spot to spend a day or two (see Not the N1, pages 8–21). A number of artists call Clarens home, and the town is justifiably proud of its Art Route. Most of the interest is on Main Street and the central square, so you can take it all in on an easy stroll, stopping to stock up with goodies for the road at 278 on Main's deli.

But to really appreciate the area you need to get out and hike. The dramatic Mushroom Rock, balanced high on a sandstone ridge on the St Fort farm, 5km out of town on the R711 (the Fouriesburg road), is a two-hour return walk that affords spectacular views. Alternatively, head east on the R712 to the trails of the **Golden Gate Highlands National Park**.

Golden Gate Highlands National Park

The drive through this unfenced national park is a delight. Pictures of the imposing buttresses grace every marketing brochure for the region and a good place to capture the *National Geographic* winning shot is from the Glen Reenen Rest Camp, where many of the short trails begin. The geological history of the area is writ in the sandstone rock bands — the hard orange/brown of the surface rocks overlying yellow, pink and white softer layers. Once through the Gates you can take a number of scenic detours or continue down the pass, stopping off at viewpoints and admiring herds of white-faced blesbok and other plains game.

TIP

Golden Gate Highlands NP offers a range of accommodation options — from basic camping to the spoils of the Golden Gate Hotel, which has stupendous views of the photogenic Brandwag Buttress — as well as day and overnight hiking, horse riding, canoeing and abseiling.

The Basotho Cultural Village is well worth a visit. The 'living museum' is a colourful insight into Basotho culture, and the rondavels are very comfortable should you wish to overnight.

ON THE SIDE >> Game in the park
The highlands are home to a variety of game, including black wildebeest, eland, blesbok, oribi, springbok and Burchell's zebra. Some 177 species of birds are listed, including the rare bald ibis, which breeds on the sandstone cliffs, and 2012 saw the opening of a vulture hide which allows visitors to enjoy sightings of the endangered bearded vulture (lammergeier) and Cape vulture.

Sheep and Pumpkins For SALE

The sprawling settlement of Phuthaditjhaba comes as something of a shock after the tranquil rolling grasslands. Turn right here to Witsieshoek Mountain Resort, the gateway to the northern corner of the Drakensberg. The recently renovated mountain retreat enjoys a truly spectacular setting with the whole amphitheatre spread out behind it, so you can chill there (and believe me it's so high that even in summer you will chill), but if you're up for a moderately strenuous hike, make your way to the Sentinel car park, then lace up your boots, sign the mountain register and head out on the obvious path that takes you round to the **chain ladders**.

TIP

The condition of the road from Witsieshoek to the Sentinel car park (well, actually, until 1km from the car park where you're suddenly presented with a good brick road) varies from bad to appalling. While (provided you are very careful) you CAN usually negotiate it in a sedan, unless you have a high-clearance vehicle I'd advise arranging a transfer from the resort.

Scaling the double set of ladders is fairly intimidating, but it's the easiest way (other than driving up Sani Pass in a 4x4) for non-mountaineers to reach the top of the Berg plateau. If the weather is kind, this is one of the most magical hikes in the world. At the top, take the short hike to the top of the uThukela (Tugela) Falls, the world's second-highest waterfall. The view across the high cliffs of the Amphitheatre to Devil's Tooth, one of the Berg's iconic peaks, is incredible, but take care, it's a looooooong way down!

Section 2
Witsieshoek Mountain Resort to Royal Natal National Park
Distance 118km
Driving Time 2hrs
Highlights The view of the Amphitheatre, a stay at Thendele camp, the uThukela Gorge trail

From Witsieshoek, head back through Phuthaditjhaba and turn right onto the R712 in the direction of Harrismith, then south onto the R74. At the time of writing this road was under repair, so do your homework before setting out. The road is unfenced so requires caution even at the best of times.

The road takes you past the vast expanse of Sterkfontein Dam. On your right, about halfway along, there's a vulture restaurant, which makes a good spot to stretch your legs.

It's a steep descent down Oliviershoek Pass into KwaZulu-Natal (see the Great Trek route, pages 106–119) from where the magnificent panorama of the Drakensberg mountains unfolds.

The road to Royal Natal National Park is on the right, a few kilometres from the base of the pass. The main attraction of this spectacular reserve is the **view of the famous Amphitheatre**, a 500m-high crescent-shaped rock face with the great promontories of the Eastern Buttress and Sentinel as bookends.

ON THE SIDE >> uKhahlamba/Drakensberg Park World Heritage Site
The uKhahlamba/Drakensberg Park, inscribed into the World Heritage List in 2000, is an area of exceptional natural beauty, and its diverse habitats protect a number of rare endemic and threatened species of plants and birds. The high concentration of rock paintings in its caves and rock overhangs make the park one of the largest and most spectacular natural galleries in the world.

Tackling the chain ladders

Thendele, at the end of the road, is one of the more expensive of Ezimvelo KZN Wildlife's camps, but trust me, it's worth every cent for the views. You can see the Amphitheatre from every chalet, so you could sit all day just soaking up the magnificence of the mountain scenery that is played out all around you. But to do that would be to miss out on some of the country's most stupendous hikes. Easy walks include the gentle walk to Fairy Glen, but if you only do one hike, make it the **uThukela Gorge walk** – this hike rewards you with views of one of the iconic sandstone structures in the Berg, the Policeman's Helmet, and a photogenic vista of the uThukela River with the Amphitheatre as the backdrop.

TIP

If you're in need of an adrenalin shot, or fancy exploring the area on a quad or mountain bike, stop off at All Out Adventures for a heart-stopping swing or foefie slide.

If Thendele is full (which it often is), or you prefer to camp, there's the option of the lovely Mahai camp site or nearby Rugged Glen, from where you can ride out into the mountains on horseback, enjoying the views and sightings of buck. Trout fishing, picnicking and swimming in the clear mountain streams are other popular pastimes.

TIP

Don't miss a visit to the stunning **Didima Rock Art Centre**.

Didima Rock Art Centre

Section ❸
Royal Natal National Park to Cathedral Peak
Distance 98km
Driving Time 2hrs
Highlights Any one of the many hikes, a stay at the charming Cathedral Peak Hotel, Didima Rock Art Centre

A rough dirt road follows the west side of the Woodstock Dam and leads to the Cathedral Peak road at the Hoffenthal Mission, but it is kinder to your car to return to the R74 – which has sufficient potholes and cattle to make it exciting enough.

Take a right just past Bergville then, after 18km, go right again onto the R394. Alternatively (if you have missed out Royal Natal, or didn't feel like braving the bad section of the R74), take the N3 to the Ladysmith turn-off and follow the R616 west to Bergville.

The 30km-long winding gravel road to Cathedral Peak takes you up and down dales and across several rivers, the scenery all the while getting better and better. But keep your eyes peeled for cows, chickens, children and the odd drunk wandering into your path! Like most of the roads on this route, it's not one to drive after dusk.

Cathedral Peak is my favourite destination in the Maluti Drakensberg – actually one of my favourite places in the world. In the cradle of majestic mountains, it's a wonderful base for **hikers**, mountain bikers, anglers, birders, lovers of rock art or, indeed, anyone who enjoys gazing up at dramatic peaks and taking in the fresh mountain air. The accommodation options are the camp site in the trees, the cleverly designed, up-market chalets of Didima Resort, and the charming, and even more up-market, **Cathedral Peak Hotel**. This family-owned hotel, which opened in 1939, has upped the ante over the last decade and now has a modern spa, nine-hole golf course, tennis, and all the necessary trappings of an up-market resort, but it has not lost its soul and, among other attractions, offers free guided hikes.

If you're fit and have a head for heights, sign up for the 9hr return trip to the top of Cathedral Peak. The hike involves some fairly exposed rock scrambling but the views are mind-blowing. The guided walk to see the rock art at Eland Cave is also strenuous but thoroughly recommended, while the riverside trails and those to the photogenic Mushroom Rock and Rainbow Gorge are less exhausting.

On your way out of Champagne Valley, stock up with goodies and know-how at Thokozisa (on your right at the crossroads, about 11km from Champagne Sports Resort, where you turn onto the Loskop road to head south). The fab little lifestyle centre is home to the Central Drakensberg Info Centre and has a deli where you can buy some local trout and wine for dinner (good wine shops are very scarce on the route, so don't pass up the chance!) as well as a variety of arty and practical clothing stores. Or you could simply wander around checking out the sculptures that lie buried among the garden plants.

Section ❹
Cathedral Peak to Giant's Castle
(including detour to Champagne Valley)
Distance 155km
Driving Time 3hrs 20mins
Highlights A canopy tour, a performance of the Drakensberg Boys' Choir, a drink or meal at one of Izimbali Restaurant's outside tables

I'd suggest at least two nights at Cathedral Peak before you bid the valley farewell and head south along the R600 into Champagne Valley in the Central Drakensberg. There's plenty to do in the area. The nearby **canopy tours** are a big hit, and on your way in you'll also pass the turn-off to Four Rivers Rafting & Adventures, a one-stop shop for a range of adrenalin-pumping and fun activities. If possible, time your visit for a Wednesday afternoon and stop off at the auditorium of the **Drakensberg Boys' Choir School** to enjoy a performance by the world-famous choir. Their large repertoire ranges from classical music to contemporary pop – and there's a good chance that you'll be treated to an entertaining gumboot dance.

Again hiking, mountain biking, horse riding and fishing are the top pursuits, with the three-hour Blue Grotto trail from the Drakensberg Sun one of the best if time is short. The trail leads through an indigenous forest to a magnificent grotto with waterfall and pool. The grave of Dick Barry, a little further on, is something of a pilgrimage for mountaineers. Barry was one of the pioneers of Berg climbing until his untimely end in 1938, when, at the tender age of 22, he fell off Monk's Cowl, the ominous fang that you can see from his grave.

There's a camp site and two family-friendly and popular resorts, the Drakensberg Sun and Champagne Castle Resort, should you wish to stay over, otherwise enjoy a snack at the Tea Garden before retracing your route out of the valley and on to Giant's Castle.

Garden Castle is one of my favourite Ezimvelo KZN Wildlife camps, with a grand setting, very pleasant chalets and the surprisingly good **Izimbali Restaurant**. One of the major attractions is the Vulture Hide, at which you can get up close and personal with a wide variety of birds including bearded vultures and Verreaux's eagles. The hide is open year round but advance booking is required. The waterfalls that tumble off the back of Giant's Castle freeze in winter, a particular treat for fit mountaineers who gamely carry ice axes, crampons and camping gear up the long, steep Grey's Pass for a few days of ice climbing.

Thokozisa

If you have time en route to Giant's Castle, detour into the Little uThukela Valley to Injisuthi. This lovely hutted camp is a great base from which to explore the trails of the Little Berg, and is the trailhead for assaults on Mafadi (3,446m), the highest peak in South Africa. The rock art at Battle Cave can be visited on a short guided tour and there is excellent trout water if fishing is your game.

Harrismith
Rosendal
Clarens
Van Reenen
R712
Golden Gate Highlands NP
Sterkfontein Dam NR
Oliviershoek Pass
Ladysmith
N11
R70
Fouriesburg
Phuthaditjhaba
R711
Marquard
Witsieshoek Mountain Resort
R74
R616
Roosboom
R26
Joel's Drift
Thendele
Bergville
Colenso
Ficksburg
Butha-Buthe
Royal Natal NP (World Heritage Site)
Woodstock Dam
Spioenkop Dam NR
Weenen GR
R708
Hlotse
Zunckels
Clocolan
Peka
Cathedral Peak
R600
Loskop
Estcourt
Rainbow Gorge
Drakensberg Sun
Ladybrand
Teyateyaneng
Champagne Castle
Ntabamhlope
N
Giant's Castle
Mooi River
MASERU
Lesotho Highlands Water Scheme
A1
Mokhotlong
uKhahlamba Drakensberg Park (World Heritage Site)
Rosetta
Nottingham Road
N3
Katse Dam
LESOTHO
Waggndrift NR
Kamberg
Lidgetton
Midmar NR
A3
A3
Thaba Tseka
Mantsonyane
Vergelegen
iMpendle
Ramabanta
A5
Garden Castle
Cobham NR
Himeville
Himeville NR
R617
Km   50
Underberg
Bulwer
Nkau
DRAKENSBERG
Sehlabathebe National Park
R612
Donnybrook

MALUTI DRAKENSBERG ROUTE
Ficksburg to Drakensberg Gardens

Section ⑤
Giant's Castle to Garden Castle
Distance 315km
Driving Time 6hrs 45mins
Highlights A stay at Cleopatra Mountain Farmhouse, Game Pass Shelter, a trip up Sani Pass

Following the foothills of the mountains south from here takes you on a rough gravel road past the Bill Barnes Crane and Oribi Nature Reserve, which actively conserves South Africa's three species of crane – the critically endangered wattled crane, the threatened South African grey crowned crane and the blue crane – as well as various other bird species and the endangered oribi. You can't just drop in, but guided tours can be booked in advance.

After a few more kilometres a road on the right leads up steeply to Highmoor Dam, a very popular trout-fishing area (note that advance booking is required). The high moorland, with its dams and streams, reminds me of my native Scotland.

TIP
Gourmets, and romantics, should book a stay at **Cleopatra Mountain Farmhouse**, on the Highmoor road. Richard Poynton's passion for food is legendary – every meal is a work of art.

The neighbouring Kamberg Nature Reserve offers plenty of picturesque rambles – both in the foothills of the Berg and along the Mooi River – as well as great fishing, but the main drawcard here is **Game Pass Shelter**. One of the first sites to be seen by Europeans, it's of particular significance as it enabled archaeologists to understand the meaning of San rock art, so is sometimes referred to as the 'Rosetta Stone'. Community guides lead tours to the shelter at 09:00, 11:00 and 12:30.

Lotheni and Vergelegen nature reserves are pretty and worth the detour if you have time, otherwise keep going south towards Himeville.

TIP
Twitchers will love Lotheni, which has a bird list of 172 species. Anglers have 16km of the well-stocked Lotheni River in which to cast their flies.

If time is short, Himeville is a good spot to end this trip. But, before you do (if you have remembered your passport), park your car and take a tour up the **Sani Pass**. Do NOT be tempted to try this spectacular mountain road in your sedan. The road is for 4x4s only and is in really bad condition near the top. (A friend of mine tried in his BMW, and yes, he – I stress 'he' – did get horribly stuck and had to be rescued. Most embarrassing!)

A highlight of any trip up to the 'Roof of Africa' is a drink in Sani Mountain Lodge (formerly Sani Top Chalet), the highest pub in Africa. The food and accommodation at the lodge is also good, but an overnight stay is expensive, so unless you're planning to climb Thabana Ntlenyana, southern Africa's highest peak at 3,482m, you're probably better off saving your pennies.

Cleopatra Mountain Farmhouse in autumn

MALUTI DRAKENSBERG ROUTE Contact details

But an even better finale to the trip is to continue to Underberg and then turn west along the R617 for 5km, then right towards the Drakensberg Gardens Golf & Spa Resort. In the shadow of the distinctive Rhino Peak, Garden Castle Nature Reserve is very different in character from the more northerly sections of the Berg, with dramatic sandstone buttresses and wind- and water-sculpted landforms. At 3,051m, Rhino Peak is a demanding day-hike, but the mountain acts like a beacon to peak baggers wanting a challenge, and the views from the top are ample reward for the effort. Otherwise enjoy the more relaxed trails, which lead to rock-art sites and through the wildflowers of the veld. Keep your eyes open for game — this is one of the few places where you are still likely to see eland in the Drakensberg.

A drink at the Drakensberg Gardens is a good way to celebrate a fine road trip before heading on to Durban or home.

All Out Adventures
036 438 6242
www.alloutadventures.co.za
Bill Barnes Crane and Oribi Nature Reserve
www.kzncrane.co.za
naturereserve@kzncrane.co.za
Cathedral Peak Hotel
036 488 1888
www.cathedralpeak.co.za
Champagne Sports Resort
036 468 8000
www.champagnesportsresort.com
Cleopatra Mountain Farmhouse
033 267 7243
www.cleomountain.com
Didima Resort/Cathedral Peak camp site
033 845 1000
www.kznwildlife.com
Drakensberg Boys' Choir
036 468 1012
www.dbchoir.co.za
Drakensberg Canopy Tour
083 661 5691
www.drakensbergcanopytour.co.za
Drakensberg Gardens
031 813 5288
www.drakensberggardensresort.co.za
Drakensberg Sun
086 144 7744 or 011 461 9744
www.tsogosunhotels.com/resorts/drakensberg-sun/pages/overview.aspx
Ezimvelo KwaZulu-Natal Nature Conservation
033 845 1000
www.kznwildlife.com
Ficksburg Tourist Information Office
051 933 2130
Four Rivers Rafting & Adventures
036 468 1693 or 083 785 1693
www.fourriversadventures.co.za
Giant's Castle Vulture Restaurant
036 353 3718
Golden Gate Highlands NP and Basotho Cultural Village
012 428 9111
www.sanparks.org
Golden Gate Hotel
058 255 1000
Green Acorn
051 933 2746
www.greenacorn.co.za
Kamberg Rock Art Centre
033 267 7255
www.kznwildlife.com
St Fort
058 256 1345
www.stfort.co.za
Witsieshoek Mountain Resort
058 713 6361/2 or 073 228 7391
www.witsieshoek.co.za

Regional info
www.cdic.co.za
www.goficksburg.co.za
www.kznwildlife.com
http://southernbergescape.co.za

Sani Pass

ANGLO-ZULU WAR BATTLEFIELD ROUTE

Dundee to Durban

Battlefields fascinate me, with their charged atmosphere and ghosts. This three-day trip includes the world-famous Isandlwana and Rorke's Drift, plus several more sites from the 1879 Anglo-Zulu War. Some are easy to find, others less so, requiring some patience and a sense of adventure. Indeed, you should probably treat this trip as a live history lesson crossed with a treasure hunt. It's also an excuse to see some spectacular countryside you probably wouldn't otherwise visit.

Total Distance 570km
Driving Time 10hrs

Section ❶
Dundee to Fugitives' Drift
Distance 80km
Driving Time 2hrs
Highlights:
Isandlwana and Rorke's Drift battlefields
Fugitives' Drift
SEE PAGES 134–135

Section ❷
Fugitives' Drift to uLundi
Distance 190km
Driving Time 3hrs
Highlights:
Prince Imperial Memorial
uLundi
Useful GPS Coordinates:
Prince Imperial Memorial – 28°07'57"S,
30°47'57"E
SEE PAGES 136–137

Section ❸
uLundi to Durban
Distance 300km
Driving Time 5hrs
Highlight:
The spectacular drive to Cetshwayo's grave
Useful GPS Coordinates:
King Cetshwayo's grave – 28°45'17"S,
31°04'29"E
Fort eShowe – 28°53'04"S, 31°29'48"E
eShowe Military Cemetery – 28°53'41"S,
31°29'47"E
Ultimatum Tree – 29°12'52"S, 31°25'33"E
SEE PAGES 138–139

ANGLO-ZULU WAR BATTLEFIELD ROUTE
Dundee to Durban

Road tripper:
Matthew Holt

In a nutshell:
Journey deep into
KwaZulu-Natal, visiting
heroically charged
battlefields from the
1879 Anglo-Zulu War.

Logistics

Isandlwana and Rorke's Drift museums are open from 08:00 to 16:00 (from 09:00 at weekends). There is free access at the other sites. While it's fun searching for remote sites on your own, it's also worthwhile doing a guided tour of a major battlefield. For information, see www.battlefieldsregionguides.co.za or www.fugitivesdrift.com

Driving conditions

Most of the route is on tar or good gravel roads, but watch out for potholes and cows.

Pet-friendly rating ★ ☆ ☆ ☆ ☆

1 = least suited 5 = most suited
You're visiting memorials and war graves.

Child-friendly rating ★ ★ ☆ ☆ ☆

1 = least suited 5 = most suited
Guided battlefield tours are compelling history lessons for older children. Fugitives' Drift Lodge has dedicated tours for under 12s.

Low-slung vehicle-friendly rating ★ ★ ★ ☆ ☆

1 = high clearance 5 = lowest slung

Don't miss

- Isandlwana and Rorke's Drift battlefields
- Driving through the heart of rural Zululand

Emergency service numbers

Emergency (from a landline) 10111
Emergency (from a cellphone) 112
AA roadside assistance 086 100 0234 or 083 843 22 (24 hours)

Best time

May to September are best. The British invaded in January, during the rainy season.

SUMMER			AUTUMN			WINTER			SPRING		
D	J	F	M	A	M	J	J	A	S	O	N

Background reading

The National Army Museum Book of the Zulu War by Ian Knight, Pan Books 2004.
Battles of KwaZulu-Natal by Ken Gillings, Art Publishers.

ANGLO-ZULU WAR BATTLEFIELD ROUTE

Dundee to Durban

Section ❶
Dundee to Fugitives' Drift
Distance 80km
Driving Time 2hrs
Highlights Isandlwana and Rorke's Drift battlefields, Fugitives' Drift

The starting point for our tour is Dundee — a mecca for history buffs, with scores of battlefields nearby. Our first stop, **Isandlwana**, is 60km away. This is where the Zulus defeated the mighty British Empire in the first major battle. It's an atmospheric place, with a sinister dark rock jutting abruptly out of the plain and white cairns marking where British soldiers fell. Joining a guided battlefield tour, we see where Chief Mkhosana spurred on the faltering Zulu attack, paying for his courage with a bullet through the head; where Colonel Durnford's line was overrun, triggering the British re-treat; and the small cave where the last British soldier fought on alone, till late in the afternoon.

ON THE SIDE >> Battle of Isandlwana
Having crossed the Buffalo River into Zululand, Chelmsford's army camped at Isandlwana. Early on 22 January 1879, Chelmsford took most of the column to engage the Zulu army, which was reportedly nearby. While decoys led Chelmsford on a wild-goose chase, 25,000 Zulus encircled the British camp, where 1,900 men remained. Initially, the British firing lines held, but the Zulus' stupendous bravery eventually overwhelmed them. Retreat quickly turned to rout. The British lost 1,357 men, including 52 officers, in one of their worst ever de-feats. The battle was a great Zulu victory, but it also sealed their doom, with the humiliated Chelmsford now intent on destroying Cetshwayo's kingdom.

The few British survivors escaped via the Fugitives' Trail, swimming the Buffalo River en route. You can retrace their rugged 7km route. Alternatively, you can drive round to **Rorke's Drift** on the 15km gravel road. There's a small museum here, set amid the aloes. This is where the 1964 movie *Zulu* was set, with Michael Caine and Stanley Baker repelling a Zulu impi against the odds. The cast also included Chief Mangosuthu Buthelezi, playing his great-grandfather, King Cetshwayo.

ON THE SIDE >> Defence of Rorke's Drift
When the main British Army crossed into Zululand, 140 men stayed on at Rorke's Drift, a trading post on the Natal bank of the Buffalo River. On 22 January, survivors from Isandlwana rode past with alarming news of the massacre. Worse still, shortly after that, 4,000 Zulus arrived and attacked. The plucky British garrison repelled them throughout the night, fighting from behind hastily constructed barricades of biscuit boxes and mealie bags. At dawn, the Zulus retired, leaving 600 dead. The British lost only 17 and awarded 11 Victoria Crosses, seven to one regiment, a record for a single engagement.

Our final stop is 10km along the D31, at **Fugitives' Drift**, visiting the graves of Lieutenants Coghill and Melvill. They died trying to save their regimental Colour at the end of a torrid day. Our day ends much better, with evening drinks around the fire at Fugitives' Drift Lodge.

TIP

Do not trust your GPS for directions to Fugitives' Drift — the coordinates are wrong! Coordinates for Fugitives' Drift Lodge: 28°23'23"S, 30°36'21"E

Isandlwana

Rorke's Drift

A leading authority on the war and spellbinding raconteur, David Rattray, and his wife, Nicky, established Fugitives' Drift Lodge on the site where Lieutenants Melvill and Coghill died. David was tragically murdered in 2007, and his son, Andrew, now leads the battlefield tours. The lodge is not your budget option, but it's a very special place, brimming with memorabilia. You'll feel immersed in history the moment you walk in. Whether you stay here or not, their battlefield tours are highly recommended.

ON THE SIDE >> Saving the Colour

British soldiers fled from Isandlwana back to Natal along the so-called Fugitives' Trail. White cairns mark where they were cut down by pursuing Zulus. Among the fugitives was Lieutenant Teignmouth Melvill, who had orders to save the regimental Colour (a Union Jack flag mounted on a wooden pole). Swept off his horse in the Buffalo River, he ended up clinging to a rock. Lieutenant Nevill Coghill, who'd already reached the Natal bank, rode back and helped him across. Stopping for a breather on the steep bank, they probably thought they'd made it. Instead, they were spotted and killed by some Zulus who lived in Natal. At least their efforts weren't totally in vain. The flag was later found wedged in some boulders and they were posthumously awarded Britain's highest military honour, the Victoria Cross.

ON THE SIDE >> The Ultimatum

The new British High Commissioner, Sir Bartle Frere, arrived in Cape Town with instructions to mould South Africa into a confederation. Viewing the independent Zulu kingdom as a security threat, he used a minor border incident as an excuse to demand that King Cetshwayo dismantle his army within 30 days. This ultimatum was presented to Cetshwayo's representatives on 11 December 1878 at the so-called Ultimatum Tree. One month later, when Cetshwayo failed to comply, British troops under Lord Chelmsford invaded Zululand.

ANGLO-ZULU WAR BATTLEFIELD ROUTE

Dundee to Durban

Section ❷
Fugitives' Drift to uLundi
Distance 190km
Driving Time 3hrs
Highlights Prince Imperial Memorial, uLundi

TIP

Coordinates for Prince Imperial Memorial: 28°07'57"S, 30°47'57"E

Leaving Fugitives' Drift Lodge, we drive through a light morning mist, almost straight into a herd of giraffes ambling across the road. Like Chelmsford's army, we're headed for uLundi, though travelling a bit faster than the 4km per day they managed. At Nqutu, we leave the R68 to visit the war's most exotic casualty, the French **Prince Imperial**. A narrow dirt track leads towards a kraal and glade of trees. Children besiege us until a large matronly lady bustles over and shoos them away, while producing a visitors' book from the folds of her voluminous dress. Although only 70km from Fugitives' Drift Lodge, it feels much further. The **memorial** is beneath trees planted by the Prince's mourning mother. This is a poignant spot, well off the beaten track and a long way from the glitzy ball-rooms of Europe.

ON THE SIDE >> Death of the Prince Imperial
After Napoleon III was deposed and exiled to England, his only child, Louis Napoleon, was at a loose end. Having attended British military school, he persuaded Queen Victoria to let him join the Zulu campaign. Despite being officially an observer, the hot-headed 23-year-old still managed to almost get himself killed several times. On 1 June he led a small mounted party to scout an area considered safe. Stopping at a deserted kraal for coffee, the seven-man party was surprised by 40 Zulus who crept up in the tall grass, killing two British soldiers. The rest mounted and bolted, except for the prince, who fell off his horse when the saddle snapped. He put up a spirited fight, but was overpowered and ritually disembowelled. A year later, his mother visited the site of his death and met one of the warriors who'd killed him.

Rejoining the R68, at Melmoth we turn north to uLundi. It's an exhilarating drive, sweeping over passes with views across forests and cane fields. Just outside uLundi, there's a sign to Fort Nolela, where the British camped before the battle. We follow a dirt track past a British soldier's grave up to a small stone enclosure, overgrown by grass. This might be Chelmsford's stone redoubt or a shepherd's kraal. Either way, it will do.

uLundi battlefield is beside the P700, opposite the airport. An avenue of aloes leads to an elegant domed memorial. This was where the British soldiers formed their hollow square, which the Zulus heroically charged, with horrendous casualties. Amidst the acacia trees and aloes are the graves of the 13 British dead, plus a memorial to 1,500 anonymous Zulus. The traffic drones indifferently past.

ON THE SIDE >> Battle of uLundi
After the Isandlwana debacle, Lord Chelmsford retreated to Pietermaritzburg to plan his next step more carefully. The second invasion commenced in late May 1879, with Chelmsford again commanding the central column, which left Dundee heading for Cetshwayo's royal kraal near uLundi. Scouting the route, building forts and burning Zulu homesteads, they moved cautiously, taking a month to cover 120km. Cetshwayo sent emissaries suing for peace, but Chelmsford wasn't interested. In late June, Chelmsford reached the White uMfolozi, where he built a stone redoubt, called Fort Nolela. Cetshwayo's military kraal lay across the river at Ondini, where his army was gathered. On 4 July, the British army crossed the river and shuffled across the plain in a huge square formation. Having surreptitiously surrounded them, the Zulus attacked, but were scythed down by the hailstorm of lead. Within an hour the battle was over, leaving 1,500 Zulus dead. After torching Ondini, the British marched back to Natal.

Prince Imperial Monument

Just along the road at Ondini Historical Reserve is a reconstruction of King Cetshwayo's royal kraal, before it was torched by the victorious British. And nearby is Ondini battlefield, where King Cetshwayo was defeated again, four years later, this time by fellow Zulus. That night at Umuzi Bush Camp, we're treated to a braai and traditional Zulu dancing. Considering the trouble we rooineks caused here, it could have been much worse.

PADKOS

Being British I don't even know how to spell 'padkos', never mind make it, and once I'm in the car I tend not to stop till I get to my destination. However, if someone wants to feed me while I'm driving, I'd go for a ham and cheese roll with the added luxury of Woolworths' Italian basil.

ANGLO-ZULU WAR BATTLEFIELD ROUTE

Dundee to Durban

Section ③
uLundi to Durban
Distance 300km
Driving Time 5hrs
Highlights The spectacular drive to Cetshwayo's grave

Cetshwayo's Grave

You could go home from uLundi the way you came, as Chelmsford's army did. But then you'd miss out on a **spectacular drive** and the thrill of a treasure hunt through deepest KwaZulu-Natal. Looking for **King Cetshwayo's grave**, we take the Nkandla road, which sweeps and dips over hills and through the indigenous forest. Some 40km beyond Nkandla, we turn right on the Kranskop road and, 7km later, right again by a panel beater. (If you reach President Zuma's refurbished kraal, you've gone too far.) Then we follow a sensational line along the spine of the hills for 14km. Cetshwayo's grave is in a shady grove on the left. It's a peaceful spot, which he probably deserved after all his troubles.

Elated by success, we move on to eShowe. Just out of town, a stone cairn marks Fort eShowe, where Colonel Pearson's men spent two months under siege, while dysentery picked them off. Surrounded by telegraph poles and power lines, it's not an evocative site. The British cemetery is back towards the R66, down a dirt track on the left. Overgrown and littered, it hardly brings to mind 'a corner of a foreign field that is forever England'.

ON THE SIDE >> Fort eShowe and Gingindlovu

While Lord Chelmsford led the main British army across the Buffalo River, Colonel Charles Pearson took a column up the coast, with orders to attack uLundi from the east. After crossing the Tugela (uThukela) at Fort Pearson, they built Fort Tenedos on the opposite bank. At Nyezane, on 22 January, they were attacked by a Zulu impi. For a while the outcome hung in the balance, but eventually firepower prevailed, with the Zulus losing 350 men and the British 11. On reaching eShowe and learning of the Isandlwana disaster, Pearson's men built an earthwork fort. Besieged by Zulus, they played cricket and concerts to keep up their spirits, but disease set in. They were only rescued in April, when Lord Chelmsford arrived with a relief column, having defeated the Zulus en route. The battle at Gingindlovu on 2 April was a turning point. With 1,200 Zulus killed versus only 12 British, it proved to Chelmsford that defensive square formations were the key.

Taking the R66 towards the coast, we're seeking Nyezane battlefield, where Pearson's column saw off a Zulu impi. Ten kilometres beyond eShowe, a sign promisingly directs us to turn right – into cane fields. We spend 30 minutes driving in circles before giving up. It's all part of the treasure hunt and maybe you'll have more luck. Another 10km along the R66 is Gingindlovu battlefield, right beside the road. With traffic humming past and sugar cane swaying in the breeze, it's difficult to imagine death and glory here.

On reaching the ocean, we head down the coast towards the uThukela River, the traditional border between Natal and Zululand. After a frustrating and fruitless search for Fort Tenedos, we aim for Fort Pearson and the Ultimatum Tree on the Natal bank. They're within the Harold Johnson Nature Reserve, off the R102. We get there at dusk, just as the reserve is closing. Parking outside the gate, we sprint along the trail, past some British graves and up to the site of Fort Pearson, on a bluff overlooking the river. The N2 toll road cleaves unsympathetically through this historic landscape. A steep footpath drops down to the river bank, where the British presented their ultimatum to Cetshwayo's delegates, under a fig tree. The historic tree was destroyed by fire in 2004 and a stone now marks the spot. It seems a fitting place to end our

ON THE SIDE >> Cetshwayo's downfall

After the Battle of uLundi, Cetshwayo was imprisoned in Cape Town Castle. The British then split Zululand into 13 territories, which proved a perfect recipe for conflict, as the competing chiefs squabbled. Meanwhile, Cetshwayo travelled to London to meet Queen Victoria, who agreed to restore him as monarch, albeit with reduced powers. It was too late, however, and Cetshwayo's attempt to reassert authority triggered a bloody civil war. In July 1883, his newly restored palace at Ondini was destroyed again. Escaping with a wounded leg, Cetshwayo took refuge in Natal. He died in February 1884, a broken man.

TIP

Coordinates for King Cetshwayo's grave:
28°45'17"S, 31°04'29"E
Fort eShowe: 28°53'04"S, 31°29'48"E
eShowe Military Cemetery: 28°53'41"S, 31°29'47"E
Ultimatum Tree: 29°12'52"S, 31°25'33"E

tour: where the war effectively started and the death warrant of the independent Zulu nation was signed. Besides, it's just 80km down the N2 to the bright lights of Durban.

Depending on your itinerary and enthusiasm, you can retrace the campaign by Colonel Evelyn Wood's column, which was sent to control the area around Vryheid and fought two major battles in March 1879. On Hlobane Mountain, 20km out of Vryheid, the British were almost caught in a trap, escaping with the loss of 80 men. A rough dirt road leads up to the saddle, where you can see the infamous Devil's Pass, down which the British escaped. Visiting the summit requires a 4x4, plus permission from the mining company that owns the land.

Hlobane's casualties included Petrus Uys, a Boer settler who rode with the British. The Zulus were a nemesis for his family, having also dispatched his father and elder brother. There's a memorial to Uys in Utrecht, opposite the Dutch Reformed Church.

The day after Hlobane, the Zulus attacked Wood's camp at Kambula. Some 10km north of Vryheid, there's a dirt road off the R33 on the left. After winding unpromisingly through forestry plantations, the vista suddenly opens up to rolling hills. A stone-walled enclosure contains memorials to the 29 British dead. The Zulus lost over 2,000.

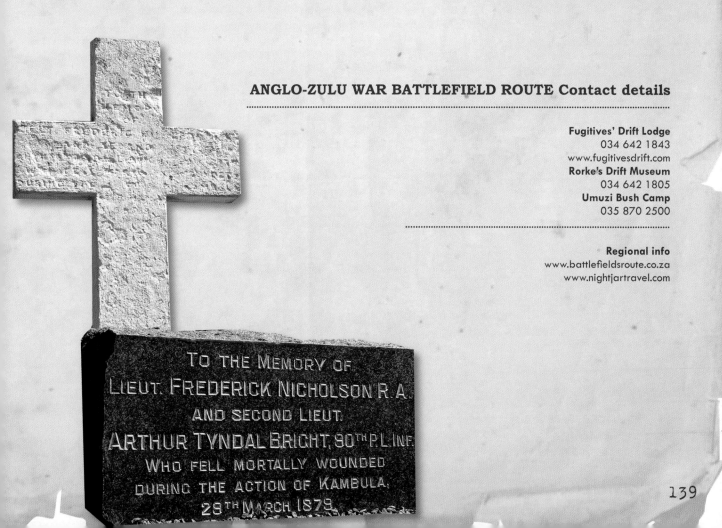

ANGLO-ZULU WAR BATTLEFIELD ROUTE Contact details

Fugitives' Drift Lodge
034 642 1843
www.fugitivesdrift.com
Rorke's Drift Museum
034 642 1805
Umuzi Bush Camp
035 870 2500

Regional info
www.battlefieldsroute.co.za
www.nightjartravel.com

THE ULTIMATE SAFARI
St Lucia, through Swaziland to Kruger National Park

Since South Africa has 19 national parks and at least 10 major private game reserves running alongside Kruger National Park, and several more in KwaZulu-Natal, plus Swaziland's six game parks, the complete ultimate safari could take quite a long time! The challenge was to find a self-drive route that would take in the greatest diversity of landscapes and animals in some of the most renowned game reserves, while also encountering diverse cultures, languages and a visit to our neighbouring landlocked country of Swaziland.

It's debatable who gets the accolade of being named an 'expert', but perhaps having visited over 200 safari lodges in southern and East Africa and having a number of coffee-table safari books to her name – as

well as a blog cheekily called www.safaritart.com – qualifies Carrie Hampton to write this chapter.

In this Ultimate Safari road trip, you'll find out where to see crocodile, hippo, rhino and elephant on the same day, where you can watch warthog while catching a tigerfish, and the best place to walk within sight of rhino, while you still can.

It's amazing that this journey can go from one game reserve to another with no boring bits in between for 10 whole days (and longer if you choose). There isn't a day when you are not surrounded by Africa's glorious diversity of animals, plants and splendid scenery in areas where the people have a deep connection with nature. Enjoy the ride!

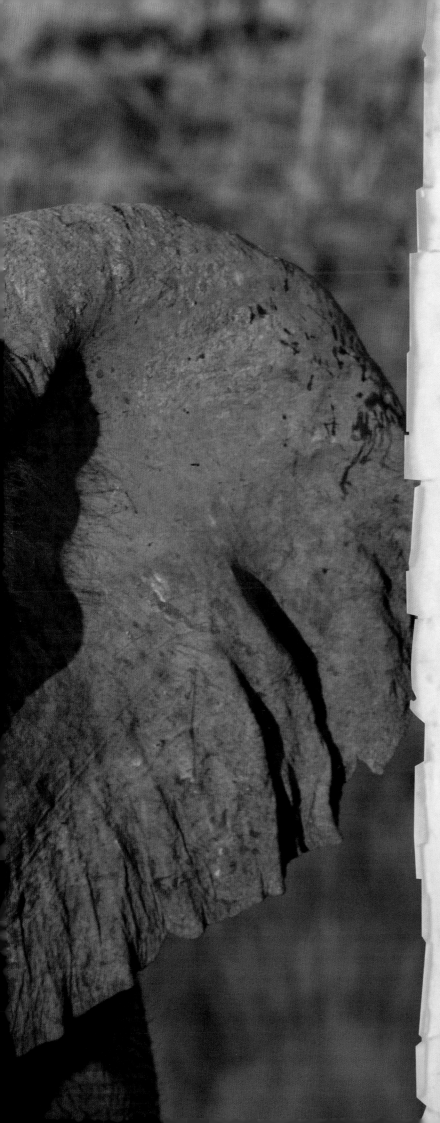

Total Distance about 850km (plus detours and loops)
Driving Time about 10 days

Section ❶
KwaZulu-Natal Safari to Swaziland border
Distance about 350km
Driving Time about 3–4 days
Highlights:
Hippos on St Lucia Estuary
Turtle watching on northern KZN beaches
   (Nov–March only)
Rhino and elephant in Hluhluwe-iMfolozi Park
Ilala Weavers
Tiger fishing on Lake Jozini
SEE PAGES 144–146

Section ❷
Swaziland
Distance about 200km (plus detour of 270km)
Driving Time 3 days (add 2 days for the detour)
Highlights:
Swazi culture and monarchy
Walking with rhino
Swazi crafts
Traditional ceremonies
SEE PAGES 146–149

Section ❸
Kruger National Park
Distance 290km if exiting through Orpen Gate, or less if exiting at Numbi Gate
Driving Time minimum 3 days, maximum up to you
Highlights:
Big Five
Bush camps
Wild dog (if you're lucky)
Ground hornbill
SEE PAGES 150–152

THE ULTIMATE SAFARI
St Lucia, through Swaziland to Kruger National Park

In a nutshell:
A linear route through the top game reserves in KwaZulu-Natal, Swaziland and into Kruger National Park to witness Africa's wildlife in all its variety and glory.

Background reading

Jock of the Bushveld by Percy Fitzpatrick — book and films.

The Elephant Whisperer by Lawrence Anthony with Graham Spence.

IRhino by Angus Begg — this new ibook is an interactive, definitive guide to everything rhino.

Sasol Birds of Southern Africa is a meticulously illustrated trusted field guide.

Scatalog: Quick ID Guide to Southern African Animal Droppings by Kevin Murray. This book should give kids something different to talk about.

A Field Guide to the Tracks and Signs of Southern, Central and East African Wildlife. Navigate quickly and find out who's been there before you with this updated and improved version of the ever-popular guidebook by Chris and Mathilde Stuart.

Shaping Kruger by Mitch Reardon is a fascinating insight into decades of groundbreaking research into animals and their environment, and how Kruger National Park manages its wildlife.

Roberts Bird Guide Kruger National Park and Kruger's *Bird Checklist*: you can rely on Roberts for superb bird books and this one is specifically for Kruger, or just get the checklist.

www.safaritart.com — a review of everything safari by our road tripper Carrie Hampton.

Don't forget

Your passport, binoculars and bird and animal field guides.

TIP

Malaria does occur along this route, so consult your doctor before you start. There's also a Kruger Malaria Hotline: 082 234 1800.

Logistics

The Ultimate Safari is a linear road trip travelling south to north (or vice versa). It starts on the Indian Ocean coast at St Lucia in KwaZulu-Natal (fly into Durban and hire a car) and goes north through the Kingdom of Swaziland, then it's a short drive before entering Kruger National Park. Upon exiting Kruger it's about 5+ hours' drive to Johannesburg, or you have a choice between two airports near Kruger: Eastgate Airport (Hoedspruit) or Kruger-Mpumalanga International. Alternatively, just keep heading north and explore the rest of Kruger, or join the Tumbling Waters road trip (see pages 154–161), taking in the Panorama Route's waterfalls and gorges. The R95 on the route from Durban is a toll road.

Driving conditions

You'll be travelling on several dirt roads, the majority of which are in good condition. You'll have no trouble finding petrol as long as you don't let the tank get too low. Good grocery shops are less frequent, so stock up when you can.

Pet-friendly rating ☆☆☆☆☆

1 = least suited 5 = most suited

Child-friendly rating ★★★★☆

1 = least suited 5 = most suited
Not suitable for toddlers.

Low-slung vehicle-friendly rating ★★★★☆

1 = high clearance 5 = lowest slung

Don't miss

- Rhino and elephant in Hluhluwe-iMfolozi Park
- Tiger fishing on Lake Jozini
- Walking with rhino
- Big Five Safari
- Great birding

Emergency service numbers

Emergency (from a landline) 10111
Emergency (from a cellphone) 112
AA roadside assistance 086 100 0234 or 083 843 22 (24 hours)
Swaziland Emergency 999
Manzini Clinic Private Hospital, Swaziland +268 505 7430
Nearest hospital to Kruger Park: Nelspruit Mediclinic
013 759 0500
Car repairs in Kruger Park: Skukuza Rest Camp
013 735 5879/4247

Best time

Winter (Jun–Sep) is usually considered best for game viewing as it's dry, the bush is sparse and animals come to water holes. Spring (Oct–Dec) is baby season, with some beautiful sights like gangly newborn impala. In April and May the land is still green from summer rains and the climate is perfect. January to March is hot and wet, making it rather humid, with mosquitos and malaria a consideration.

SUMMER			AUTUMN			WINTER			SPRING		
D	J	F	M	A	M	J	J	A	S	O	N

THE ULTIMATE SAFARI
St Lucia, through Swaziland to Kruger National Park

Section ❶
KwaZulu-Natal Safari to Swaziland border
Distance about 350km
Driving Time 3–4 days
Highlights Hippos on St Lucia Estuary, turtle watching on northern KZN beaches (Nov–March only), rhino and elephant in Hluhluwe-iMfolozi Park, Ilala Weavers, tiger fishing on Lake Jozini

Our mission is to see the creatures of Africa in their natural environment and St Lucia, along the Elephant Coast of Zululand in KwaZulu-Natal, is the perfect launching pad for our Ultimate Safari adventure.

Coral trees, hibiscus and other subtropical plants crowd the gardens of St Lucia, but what the lush suburban streets don't reveal is that this cute village is literally cornered into a triangle between the Indian Ocean, the river estuary and the iSimangaliso Wetland Park. There's only one way in and out of **St Lucia** – over a bridge spanning the estuary. **Hippos** wandering through town at night and leopard spoor indicate the close proximity of these wilderness areas. They combine to create a World Heritage Site that is the third largest protected area in South Africa, including the largest estuarine lake in the world.

Information centres and tour operators lining St Lucia's main street are all geared towards helping you choose from a mind-boggling array of activities: day or night game drives, kayaking, horse riding, estuary boat rides, sea or shore fishing and boat-based whale- and dolphin-watching. This coast is also the best place to see loggerhead and leatherback **turtles** laying eggs on the beach and later the babies emerging (November to March). Ponder the options while staying overnight at the well-run Umlilo Lodge or over a snack at Fisherman Restaurant and Sport Pub, where the decorative flotsam and jetsam remind you that the ocean is very close. Take one of their fishing excursions and they'll cook your catch for supper.

Travelling past the Crocodile Centre (stop here to see some of the largest crocs in the country) and into the iSimangaliso Wetland Park, it's 32km on a tar road to Cape Vidal's beach and Coastal Forest Reserve. Look out for samango monkeys at Cape Vidal and start your birding tick-list with some localised rarities like green twinspots, southern-banded snake eagles and rosy-throated longclaws.

Turtle tour

About halfway to Cape Vidal is Mission Rocks lookout, from where you can see all five eco-systems: lakes, estuaries, grasslands, subtropical forests and ocean. Cape Vidal's drawcard is surf fishing and deep-sea fishing, or the more gentle activity of whale- and dolphin-watching. The sandy beach is endless and the snorkelling is reasonable at low tide, but scuba diving isn't allowed. On the other side of the highest vegetated sand dunes in Africa is a forest that shelters animals like elephant, leopard and antelope, but it's a night drive with one of the concession tour operators that's most rewarding for the possibility of seeing nocturnal animals like chameleon, bushbaby, porcupine and aardvark. You can stay overnight at Cape Vidal in a camp site or basic log cabins in the forest, where you'll probably hear some of the creatures of the night. There's only one way in and out of this park, but the reversal is no hardship when you can tick off a few more of the 500 birds found here on the 30min drive through swampy grasslands back to the gate.

Before our safari heads inland, take to the water of the St Lucia Estuary in a kayak with St Lucia Kayak Safaris or a St Lucia Safaris double-decker cruising boat. Kayaking takes you very close to nature but not too close to hippo, of which there are about 800 in the estuary – and there are even more crocs. The boat, on the other hand, gets within metres of both for amazing photo opportunities and provides an overdose of hippos to last you the rest of the trip. You'll be able to tick off birds such as fish eagles, woolly-necked stork, various kingfishers and herons, including the statuesque Goliath heron.

ON THE SIDE >> Bird spotting
If you're a keen birder, there's no reason why you shouldn't clock up 150 different bird species on this Ultimate Safari road trip. Get the kids involved, with rewards for spotting certain birds, as sometimes in the heat of the day our feathered friends are the only creatures to be seen.

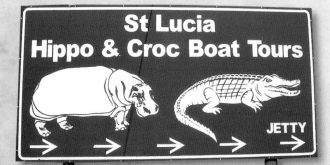
St Lucia Hippo & Croc Boat Tours
JETTY

With rhino poaching decimating the population, we're very privileged on our Ultimate Safari to visit several reserves where rhino thrive. **Hluhluwe-iMfolozi Park**, in the heart of Zululand, is one of them.

Established in 1895, Hluhluwe-iMfolozi Park is where Zulu kings such as Dingiswayo and Shaka would have hunted the Big Five, which still abound here. It's about 60km from St Lucia on the tarred R618 to the Nyalazi Gate, and the route around the park is up to you — south into the original iMfolozi portion or north into the Hluhluwe section, both of which will provide good big-game sightings of **rhino, elephant** and buffalo. The beautifully presented Ezemvelo KZN Wildlife map book (*Maps of the Zululand and Maputaland Reserves*) available at the entry gate shouldn't be considered 100% accurate. You may find yourself on roads that don't exist on the map and coping with steep, sometimes rutted dirt roads for which a basic hire car wasn't exactly designed.

Stop off at the Centenary Centre, just a few kilometres from Nyalazi Gate, where captured animals may be viewed in their bomas ready for auction — this is done to help spread the gene pool and populate other reserves. Since the start of 'Operation Rhino' here in the 1960s, over 10,000 rhino have been translocated worldwide. The Hluhluwe-iMfolozi game-capture team set the benchmark for game capture and have perfected the art. They now move 5,000–6,000 animals per year, including antelope, black and white rhino, zebra, hippo and giraffe. The history and techniques of game capture are illustrated through videos and displays at the Centenary Centre.

Elephants in Hluhluwe-iMfolozi Park

With 96,000ha of park and an immense diversity of nature, keep your animal and bird field guides handy. Guided walks are also available, most rewarding in early morning and late afternoon. There's a variety of accommodation inside Hluhluwe-iMfolozi, such as the rustic Hilltop Muntulu Bush Lodge overlooking the Hluhluwe River. A good option outside the park is Umkhumbi Lodge, owned by local 'Crocodile Dundee' character Anton Roberts, who'll dash off to rescue a black mamba from a neighbour's home in the middle of a story about grappling with a lion. Ask him nicely and he'll show you his snake collection, which includes Gaboon adders, forest cobras and a large, friendly boa constrictor called Fluffy!

Umkhumbi Lodge is very close to **Ilala Weavers**, where Zulu craftwork melds traditional and contemporary design in well-priced Zulu baskets, beadwork and a variety of arts and crafts. You aren't going to find many better places to buy ethnic artworks than here.

Cruising the smooth, tarred N2 heading north to our next safari destination — **Lake Jozini** near Pongola — you can't help but notice the endless trucks heading in both directions, loaded with logs, sugar cane and supplies. This is a good reason to divert left along a good dirt road to Bayete Zulu Reserve and their elephant interaction at 11:00 daily. Learn how Rambo and Rachel were rescued and get up close and personal with them and baby Jabulani. About 3.5km into the reserve is a beautiful lodge that must be booked out for sole use, with a minimum of six guests and a maximum of 24. Bring your own food and the chef prepares it.

THE ULTIMATE SAFARI
St Lucia, through Swaziland to Kruger National Park

If you have ample funds, consider sidetracking to some of the superb private game reserves in KwaZulu-Natal: the five-star Thanda Private Game Reserve, &Beyond Phinda, and Zululand Rhino Reserve. Or, a little further on, there's KZN Wildlife's Mkhuze Game Reserve, where you can drop a nought off the private reserve tariffs and delight in the 450-plus bird species found here.

The name of our next destination gets confusing: Phongolo, Pongolapoort, Jozini or all of the above! The Pongola River is dammed at Jozini, forming an enormous body of water 27km long and 5km wide known as Lake Jozini. The KZN Wildlife Phongolo Nature Reserve borders the lake along its western boundary. It's the only place in South Africa where you can catch **tigerfish** and you can do that on an excursion from private lodges, or by chartering a boat from Tiger Hunters Tours and Safaris. You'll probably get an involuntary game experience at the same time, with the likes of rhino and elephant visiting the water's edge and antelope and warthog permanent shoreline grazers.

Camping is cheap as chips at Phongolo Nature Reserve, where facilities extend to ablution blocks, electric plug points, braai sites and a boat slipway. A leap up in price, but still reasonable, gets you excellent dinner, bed and breakfast at Shayamoya Tiger Fishing and Game Lodge (see below about their Shayamanzi Houseboat). The pinnacle of accommodation in the area is the five-star White Elephant Lodge.

ON THE SIDE >> Shayamanzi Houseboat on Lake Jozini
If floating on Lake Jozini, catching fish, watching game and wallowing in a Jacuzzi with cold beer in hand sounds good, then drive the eastern rim of the lake to Jozini town, pull into Jozini Tiger Lodge and Spa, and step aboard a Shayamanzi Houseboat for a few nights. These are fully catered and licenced, and have spacious cabins and cheerful staff who know all the best fishing spots.

Section ❷
Swaziland
Distance about 200km (plus detour of 270km)
Driving Time 3 days (add 2 days for the detour)
Highlights Swazi culture and monarchy, walking with rhino, Swazi crafts, traditional ceremonies

The wonderful thing about Swaziland is that in just three hours of driving you can witness four different geo-regions: the Drakensberg Highveld on the western border with South Africa, the Lebombo Mountains on the eastern border with Mozambique, the middleveld cultural heart, and the eastern savannah lowveld, which is where we are headed on safari.

Swaziland is laid-back – slow even, but who's in a rush? It's a tiny country (180km north to south and 130km east to west) and the roads are good. We enter Swaziland through the Golela/Lavumisa Gate – no visas are required for South Africans and most overseas visitors. Suddenly there are no cars! The tar road north is almost empty and this becomes an attractive feature of driving in Swaziland. Not quite so appealing are the frequent road bumps, which prohibit any kind of constant speed and result in longer-than-expected journeys.

The first logical bathroom and lunch stop, 30 minutes from the border, is Nisela Safaris. This is your first introduction to traditional thatched Swazi beehive huts (should you wish to stay overnight), with doorways fit for hobbits! Their restaurant, overlooking a crocodile pond with fish jostling for your breadcrumbs, serves the kind of man-size portions of food you're going to get used to in Swaziland.

ON THE SIDE >> Currency and communication
The South African rand is accepted throughout Swaziland and you can usually ask for change in rand instead of emalangeni. In many areas 3G is available, and MTN cellphone coverage is widespread but requires international roaming.

Tiger fishing on Lake Jozini

ON THE SIDE >> Swaziland hazards

The smooth tarred roads and lack of traffic can lull you into gaining a reasonable speed, but be warned: pedestrians, goats and cattle may appear on the roads at any time and speed bumps occur unexpectedly, particularly near settlements and bus stops, and they usually come in sevens. Poor maps, lack of signage and people giving wrong directions just add to the adventure.

Rhino bushwalk

Sugar cane plantations line the roadsides near Big Bend, indicating the soil's fertility, which also provides sweetveld grazing for the wild animals we are about to see. It's only 50km from Nisela to the first of Swaziland's Big Game Parks on our route: Mkhaya Game Reserve. Unexpectedly, the timetable runs like clockwork and you must be at the gate at either 10:00 or 16:00 for your transfer into the park, or face being left behind. You'll leave your car at a secure homestead a few kilometres inside the gates, then jump on an old Land Rover for a game drive en route to the lodge. This is rhino country (white and black), and you are definitely going to see them here.

There's been a huge turnaround in rhino numbers since the Rhino Wars from 1988–92, when Swaziland lost 80% of its white rhinos to poachers. King Mswati III, Swaziland's much revered **monarch**, who may have faults but is generally adored, is a great conservationist. He takes it personally if Swazi rhino are poached and I sensed the message that 'you poach our rhino, you die!'

There's probably nowhere better in Africa than Mkhaya to do a **rhino bushwalk**. If you're lucky enough to get Bongani as a guide, you'll be in the hands of one of the best. Rhinos are seen on 95% of guided walks here, and that includes the shy and easily agitated black rhino. Walking into rhino is a thrill that may not be available to future generations, so count your blessings that Swaziland is so good at protecting them. You will be treated to excellent bird sightings at Mkhaya too, with a twitcher's dream of nesting narina trogon in the middle of camp by the giant sausage tree.

Another feature that makes Mkhaya very different are the low-thatched bedrooms with no walls. Well, there's a little wall to push the mosquito-netted bed up against, but that's it. You sleep with the gentle breeze wafting through the room and share your bathroom with anything that cares to join you. It's kept very clean, so you aren't subjected to many bugs unless you leave the lanterns burning — did I forget to say there's no electricity?

Close encounters

147

THE ULTIMATE SAFARI
St Lucia, through Swaziland to Kruger National Park

Hlane Royal National Park is 80km further north on the MR16, but it takes over an hour as you have to slow down for potholes and speed bumps. Hlane, the largest of Swaziland's game parks at 30,000ha, is dominated by hardwoods like knob-thorn and is home to lion, elephant and white rhino. There is some separation of species for security (anti-poaching) and safety (walking or mountain biking) reasons. You can self-drive in the rhino/elephant portion, but only guided game drives are allowed where the lions reside. Hlane is one of the best locations to have your sleep interrupted by roaring lions. It can go on all night, but this magnificent sound is worth losing sleep over. Accommodation ranges from camping to basic rondavels, self-catering cottages and family houses.

Platefuls of *nyama* (meat) are served at Hlane's restaurant, with equivalent-sized helpings of vegetables and salad. Just a few metres from where you dine, little bats hang from the reception entrance rafters. Look in the other direction to see hippos in the dam. But you've seen so many at St Lucia – in and out of the water – that you might not bother. Birders may note that Hlane has the largest population of white-backed vultures in the country.

The MR3 road bisects Hlane and it's just 15 minutes' drive to the adjoining Mlawula Nature Reserve and Mbuluzi Game Reserve on the eastern side of the road. You're now in the foothills of the Lebombo Mountains and signs to the Mozambique border start to appear. These reserves boast game not harmful to walkers and mountain bikers. Mbuluzi offers a remote camp site in the northern sector for absolute solitude, or a charming riverside tented camp in the southern sector, with three luxury en-suite tents and a stone-and-thatch lounge, kitchen, fireplace and braai area. You book out the whole camp, and it comes with your own private swimming pool. It's great for a bunch of friends travelling together. A few other cottages are available on the reserve, all along the river bank, and the rest are privately owned by shareholders. Don't be tempted to swim in the river – there are crocs (albeit small ones) – and apply insect repellent when hiking as it helps prevent pepper ticks from biting. Go for a walk and test your tracking skills: follow the spoor of giraffes – of which there are many here – and you may bump right into one. Giraffes are never alone, so look around and you're sure to find more.

ON THE SIDE >> Swazi ceremonies

Umhlanga (Reed) Dance in August/September celebrates purity through the nation's virgins, who cut reeds to repair the home of the Queen Mother (Ndlubukasi – she elephant). The King (Ngwenyama – the lion) usually reveals his next wife here (the choice and negotiations have already been completed). King Mswati III still has a long way to go before reaching his father's tally of 69 official wives and hundreds of children.

Incwala is the most sacred Swazi ritual, held on an astronomically auspicious date in December or January. It unites the country in seeking blessings from ancestors for the harvest, in sanctifying the kingship and giving hope for a fruitful harvest. Key players perform in a spectacular pageant on the fourth day of celebrations, and the king and his regiments dance in full war dress.

Birders should keep a lookout for rare sightings of African finfoot, seen preening on rocks in the river right in front of the tented camp.

We haven't seen all there is to see on safari in Swaziland, but it's time to decide whether to continue north or west and exit Swaziland at the Mananga or Matsamo/Jeppes Reef Border Gates and head up to Kruger. I suggest a detour (see opposite) to the western side of Swaziland to visit Phophonyane and the Mlilwane Wildlife Sanctuary, and shop for **crafts** in the Malkerns Valley.

ON THE SIDE >> Dos and don'ts at Swazi ceremonies

Women should wear skirts or sarongs, and men should not wear hats (except traditional headgear). Shoes are not worn in the dance arena; you can take pictures but not of the Inhlambelo (the king's sanctuary), and you can sing and dance.

Swazi baskets

ON THE SIDE >> Swaziland's adventure activities

Swaziland is all-encompassing in the adventures it offers: whitewater rafting, the Malolotja Canopy Tour, Chubeka Trails overnight horse rides, caving, hiking and authentic cultural village visits. The best operator is Swazi Trails (for contact details, see page 153).

Detour: Malkerns, Mlilwane and Phophonyane

Head for Manzini and suffer a short dose of traffic as the main road goes right through the city. It soon turns into a free-flowing highway, from which you turn off towards Ezulwini Valley/Mlilwane. Pick up the free newspaper *What's Happening* and use the Ezulwini Valley map as your guide. Make sure you've got money as you'll want to spend it at Swazi Candles, roadside craft markets and at House on Fire, which has the most exquisite weaving and craft shops like Gone Rural. There's also a very popular restaurant and a wildly artistic concert venue where the annual Bush Fire Festival of big-name bands is held (it takes place in May/June).

You are now in close proximity to Mlilwane Wildlife Sanctuary, where Ted Reilly started Swaziland's first wildlife conservation reserve in the 1950s. His efforts have been supported by King Mswati III and by his father before him, leading to the formation of Swaziland's Big Game Parks.

Mlilwane is the weekend retreat of expats and locals who come with mountain bikes and jogging shoes to exercise among non-threatening wildlife like zebras, who hardly move off the sandy road. The hippos famed for being in the dam at Hippo Haunt Restaurant may still be camped out in the neighbour's pond (she says they are ruining her lawn!).

There's camping, as well as basic huts, a beehive village and self-catering cottages, but the pinnacle of accommodation at Mlilwane is Reilly's Rock Hilltop Lodge. It's the original Reilly colonial homestead, with an enormous century-old jacaranda tree at the entrance, glowing purple with exotic blossom come spring (October). Walk through the Gilbert Reynolds Memorial Gardens, with their outstanding collection of aloes, and find a lookout rock to survey Mlilwane's grassland domain. At the lodge you'll get close sightings of klipspringers, whose favourite spot is on top of the stone bird table in the middle of the lawn. Stick around for the nightly bushbaby banana feast and, if one clambers onto your knee, sneak a feel of the softest fur ever.

Game drive

The MR1 road north to Pigg's Peak – a town now sporting a KFC and a few South African chains – is dramatically scenic as it rises and falls, offering views across to the Malalotja peaks of the northeastern highlands. Make sure to take the loop to the Maguga Dam wall and viewpoint to appreciate the magnitude of this feat of engineering. You'll find Lightleys House-boats (formerly of Knysna) on Maguga Dam, and an overnight lake trip would make a refreshing change in transport. This loop returns to the MR1 just before Pigg's Peak. Thereafter, look out for signs to Phophonyane Falls and Lodge, and brave the steep, bumpy downwards track (with which most ordinary cars can cope). This family-owned piece of paradise is a place to chill out by the swimming pool or in the refreshing forest pool filled by a chute from the waterfall. Birding's good (narina trogon, gorgeous bush shrike and crowned eagles), and so is the food and hospitality. Stay in their cavernous beehive huts for something different, or in a safari tent by the river.

From here, head north out of Swaziland – next stop, Kruger National Park.

Masked weavers in aloes

THE ULTIMATE SAFARI
St Lucia, through Swaziland to Kruger National Park

Section ❸
Kruger National Park
Distance minimum 290km if exiting through Orpen Gate, less if exiting at Numbi Gate
Driving Time minimum 3 days, maximum up to you
Highlights Big Five, bush camps, wild dog (if you're lucky), ground hornbill

What better place to start in Kruger National Park than at the beginning? By this I mean the southern-most section proclaimed by President Paul Kruger in 1898. He pronounced that the area between the Crocodile and Sabie rivers would become the Sabie Game Reserve. The region is renowned for the highest rainfall in Kruger, resulting in unique plant diversity and a mixture of bushveld, grass plains, rolling hills and rocky koppies. The sweet grass attracts a variety of grazers and the carnivores that feast on them: lion, leopard, cheetah, hyena and elusive packs of wild dog. This makes it one of the best places in Kruger to see big game.

It's less than 50km on the R570 from Swaziland's Matsamo/Jeppe's Reef border post to the Malelane Gate of Kruger National Park. Once across the broad Umgwenya River, you've arrived in what is considered one of the finest and indeed largest game reserves in Africa. **Note:** the speed limit in Kruger is 50km/h on tarred roads, 40km/h on gravel roads.

The nearest public rest camp is Berg-en-Dal, with a vista to the east of the softly undulating Malelane Mountains. This camp, like most SANParks accommodation in Kruger, offers camp sites, bungalows, cottages, and a family guesthouse. They are all self-catering, but there's a cafeteria and a restaurant, a grocery shop, a petrol station, a laundromat, an internet café and a postbox for sending the 'Wish you were here!' postcard. While cooling off in the swimming pool, pat yourself on the back for booking ahead for a guided night drive, a bush walk or the three-night Bushmans or Wolhuter wilderness walking trails in camps far from the crowds (departing Wednesdays and Sundays only). If you don't pre-book these activities, you may be out of luck (especially during school holidays).

Our suggested route heads east from Malelane, skirting the enormous Tlhalabye outcrop (630m), and across the Matjulu River onto the Crocodile River road. Quite quickly you get off the beaten track and after about 5km on this good sand road you'll see a 'No Entry' sign. If you take it, you'll end up on one of the private concessions within Kruger – in this case at the five-star Lukimbi Safari Lodge. They have 15,000ha all to themselves. Rather take an alternative side road to one of the river viewpoints to be rewarded with the sight of hippos, which are plentiful in this river. All the **Big Five** are regularly seen around here.

The riverine thickets open up at the Biyamiti Bridge, which you cross to get to Biyamiti **Bush Camp** (where you've booked your accommodation in advance – right?). It's one of the most beautiful camps in Kruger, hidden by delagoa thorn thickets and tucked between huge fig and jackalberry trees alongside the Biyamiti River. It's a secluded camp, with a mini-shop and little else. It's just you, a few cottages and a vast amount of flora and fauna to entertain you day and night.

Our loop of the southern portion of Kruger continues northeast towards Lower Sabie Rest Camp. There are choices between tarred, secondary or sand roads, all leading to Lower Sabie through open grasslands dominated by knob-thorn and marula trees. Large herds of zebra and wildebeest are often found together here (zebras graze the longer, tougher grass, while wildebeest prefer the sweeter new growth). This is also lion and cheetah territory, so keep your eyes open.

White rhino

Lower Sabie is a large, popular camp with many facilities and accommodation options, including camping and caravan sites, river-view safari tents and wheelchair-friendly units. Its location by the perennial Sabie River is beautiful and there's shade from giant sycamore figs, marula and mighty Natal mahogany trees. Roads lead out of Lower Sabie in every direction except east, because it's only about 8km across the rugged Lebombo Mountains to the Kruger/Mozambique boundary.

ON THE SIDE >> The top five creatures to spot around Lower Sabie
- Cheetah
- Leopard
- White rhino (hopefully!)
- Goliath heron
- Giant kingfisher

An alternative route from our entry point into Kruger would be to head north. After about 20km, you'll reach the Afsaal picnic area — an untamed wilderness where transport riders and hunters used to camp. The location was strategically chosen because a slice of sweetveld protrudes into the sourveld grassland, attracting grazing animals as well as lion, cheetah, sometimes leopard and, if you're really lucky, **wild dog**.

Do a head count of how many different mammals you've seen so far: Kruger has about 148, including 5 primates, 27 carnivores, 22 antelopes and 42 bats. And get out the birding list and add a few of Kruger's 517 different bird species, keeping a particular eye open for raptors.

ON THE SIDE >> Kruger's Big Six birds
See if you can clock up Kruger's Big Six birds:
- Saddle-billed stork
- Kori bustard
- Martial eagle
- Lappet-faced vulture
- Pel's fishing owl
- **Ground hornbill**

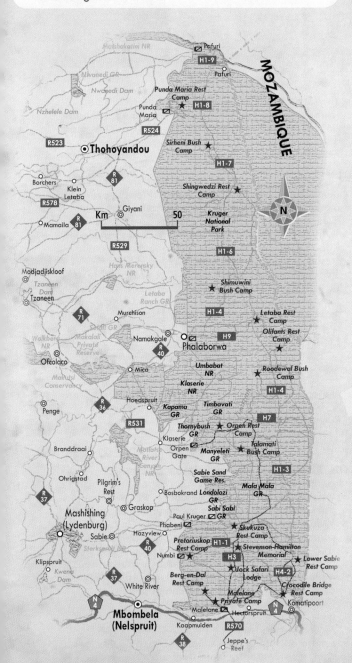

A majestic lion

THE ULTIMATE SAFARI
St Lucia, through Swaziland to Kruger National Park

A drive in a dedicated game-viewing vehicle is likely to reveal more than if you're in a city car – it's higher, of course, and the rangers radio each other with sightings. If it's in your price range (R4,000+ per person per night fully inclusive), you might consider a night or two at Jock Safari Lodge. This luxury lodge is on the first private concession inside Kruger, established in 2002, with 6,000ha of exclusive traversing rights off the main H3 road just north of Afsaal. The lodge is entirely themed around Jock of the Bushveld, the little Staffie made famous in Percy Fitzpatrick's book and subsequent films, epitomising the pioneering spirit of the 1880s. The old wagon route from Delagoa Bay (now Maputo, Mozambique) to the interior passed this way, and Jock's character features frequently in restaurants, shops and monuments in many parts of southern Mpumalanga.

Continue north but take the S113 onto the S23 dirt road to link up with the S114 secondary road and follow signs uphill to the giant granite boulders of the Stevenson-Hamilton Memorial. Stand in contemplation, admiring the astounding view over the entire southern portion of Kruger. Stevenson-Hamilton was *Skukuza* – the 'new broom' (a Tsonga Shangaan name given to him) – who swept Kruger clean of poachers and outlaws. Stevenson-Hamilton's greatest legacy is the diversity of wildlife in Kruger National Park. It's at this majestic site that his and his wife's ashes were strewn.

You've dedicated a certain amount of time for your ultimate safari, so do you follow in Jock's footsteps and head west towards the sunset and the exotic trees and flowers of Pretoriuskop Rest Camp then exit at Numbi Gate, or do you continue north through Kruger National Park?

Whether heading north from Lower Sabie or from the Stevenson-Hamilton Memorial, you'll want to avoid staying overnight at the largest rest camp in Kruger – Skukuza – which is akin to a small town (although it's a good place to stop for food, fuel or a round on the nine-hole golf course). Satara might be the next logical rest camp because of its plentiful game and good facilities but, if you like things more intimate, make a booking at Talamati Bushveld Rest Camp. Bring your own food as there's only a mini-shop here. It's in a large open valley but underground water keeps vegetation lush along the dry river bed. Grasslands attract herds of grazers (look out for sable antelope) and so you know predators won't be far away.

Impala fighting

The Ultimate Safari road trip could be an infinite journey around South Africa, but our route is almost at an end. We will exit at the Orpen Gate, but the finale of an ultimate safari (funds allowing) would be two nights at a lodge in one of the private game reserves bordering Kruger: Sabie Sand, Manyaleti, Lion Sands, Timbavati, Kapama, Thornybush, Klaserie... the pinnacle-of-luxury lodges are priced for the overseas market, but boy, you won't ever forget a stay at the likes of Singita, Royal Malewane or Camp Jabulani. There are more affordable options – some lodges in Kapama, or Elephant Plains in Sabi Sand, nThambo Tree Camp and Africa on Foot Camp in Klaserie. This doesn't even scratch the surface of available private lodges, but they're all listed on the MapStudio Mpumalanga, Kruger and Panorama Route fold-out map and the Mpumalanga Kruger National Park road atlas book.

Congratulations, you've completed the South Africa and Swaziland Ultimate Safari. But there are so many more reserves in South Africa that we haven't managed to get to. So start planning your next safari now: Waterberg, Limpopo, Eastern Cape, Garden Route, Kalahari and beyond...

ON THE SIDE >> Activities in Kruger

To get the most out of Kruger, take a look at the activities on offer by SANParks and pre-book:

- Backpacking trails over four days and three nights
- Wilderness trails, spending three nights in a wilderness camp and walking through unspoilt wilderness each day
- 4x4 adventure trails on a self-drive route from Satara or Pretoriuskop, negotiating dongas and river beds
- Malopeni Eco-Trail – a guided motorised adventure accessing remote roads near Phalaborwa Gate
- Guided walks and game drives
- Bush braai
- Mountain-bike trails

See more on: http://celtis.sanparks.org/parks/kruger/tourism/activities/default.php#olifants

THE ULTIMATE SAFARI Contact details

Advantage Tours
035 590 1259
www.advantagetours.co.za
Big Game Parks (accommodation in Mkhaya, Hlane, Mlilwane and Reilly's Rock)
+268 2528 3943/4
www.biggameparks.org
Fisherman Restaurant and Sports Pub
035 590 1257
Kayak Safaris
035 590 1233
www.kayaksafaris.co.za
Kruger National Park
012 428 9111
www.sanparks.org
KZN Parks (iSimangaliso Wetland Park, Crocodile Centre, Cape Vidal, Hluhluwe-iMfolozi, Mkhuze and Phongolo Nature Reserve)
033 845 1000
www.kznwildlife.com
Lightleys Houseboats
+268 2444 1744
www.hawane.co.sz/pages/houseboat.html
Mbuluzi Game Reserve
+268 2383 8861
www.mbuluzigamereserve.co.sz
Mlawula Nature Reserve
+268 2416 1516
www.sntc.org.sz
Phinda Private Game Reserve
011 809 4314
www.phinda.com
Phophonyane Falls and Lodge
+268 2431 3429
www.phophonyane.co.sz
Shayamanzi Houseboat
034 413 2299
www.shayamanzi.co.za
Shayamoya
034 435 1110
www.shayamoya.co.za
Swazi Trails
+268 2416 2180
www.swazitrails.co.sz
Thanda Private Game Reserve
087 806 1210
www.thanda.com
Tiger Hunters Tours and Safaris
072 976 6002
http://jozinitigerfishing.wozaonline.co.za
Umkhumbi Lodge
076 1641134
www.umkhumbilodge.co.za
Umlilo Lodge
035 590 1717
www.umlilolodge.co.za
Zululand Rhino Reserve
035 595 8550
www.zululandrhinoreserve.co.za

Regional info
Kruger Park: www.sanparks.org
KwaZulu-Natal Tourism: www.zulu.org.za
Swaziland Tourism Authority: www.thekingdomofswaziland.com

PADKOS

Roadside padkos options in KZN and Swaziland are few and far between and when you find someone selling something, it's not usually not for instant eating. Clumps of honeycomb fearlessly liberated from eucalyptus plantations make the steering wheel sticky, as do small sweet pineapples, and giant forest mushrooms could be dodgy. So you'd better take your own padkos on the Ultimate Safari, but think twice about warthog or kudu biltong, as watching the wild animal while eating it just isn't right!

A sleeping lion cub

TUMBLING WATERS
Long Tom Pass to Sabie, Pilgrim's Rest, Motlatse River Canyon and Graskop

The rivers and waterfalls that tumble down the Drakensberg Mountains of Mpumalanga into the lowveld, and the gorges they cut into the landscape, make a fitting theme for this highly scenic road trip, which is just as good on a motorbike as in a car. If you drive the Panorama Route with the goal of swimming in the most waterfall pools possible, you'll have the opportunity to plunge into four or five of them.

With a density of only around 50 people per square kilometre, Mpumalanga is renowned for its dramatic passes leading to gently undulating roads. These link small towns like Sabie and Graskop, and the National Monument town of Pilgrim's Rest — a living museum dedicated to the gold-rush era of the 1870s.

We start our Tumbling Waters tour on the top of Long Tom Pass. Why? Because it sets us at a high point over the Sabie Valley with only one direction possible — down — like the waterfalls we are in search of!

Total Distance about 230km
Driving Time 3 days

Section ❶
Long Tom Pass to Sabie
Distance 35km plus visiting local waterfalls in Sabie
Driving Time 30mins plus local trips
Highlights:
Swimming in Bridal Veil Falls
Water activities like rafting and tubing
SEE PAGES 158–159

Section ❷
Sabie to Pilgrim's Rest
Distance 36km
Driving Time 30mins
Highlights:
Living in a time warp
Panning for gold
SEE PAGE 159

Section ❸
Pilgrim's Rest to Motlatse River Canyon, ending in Graskop
Distance about 160km
Driving Time all day
Highlights:
Three Rondavels viewpoint
Bourke's Luck Potholes
Swimming in Lisbon Falls
SEE PAGES 160–161

TUMBLING WATERS
Long Tom Pass to Sabie, Pilgrim's Rest, Motlatse River Canyon and Graskop

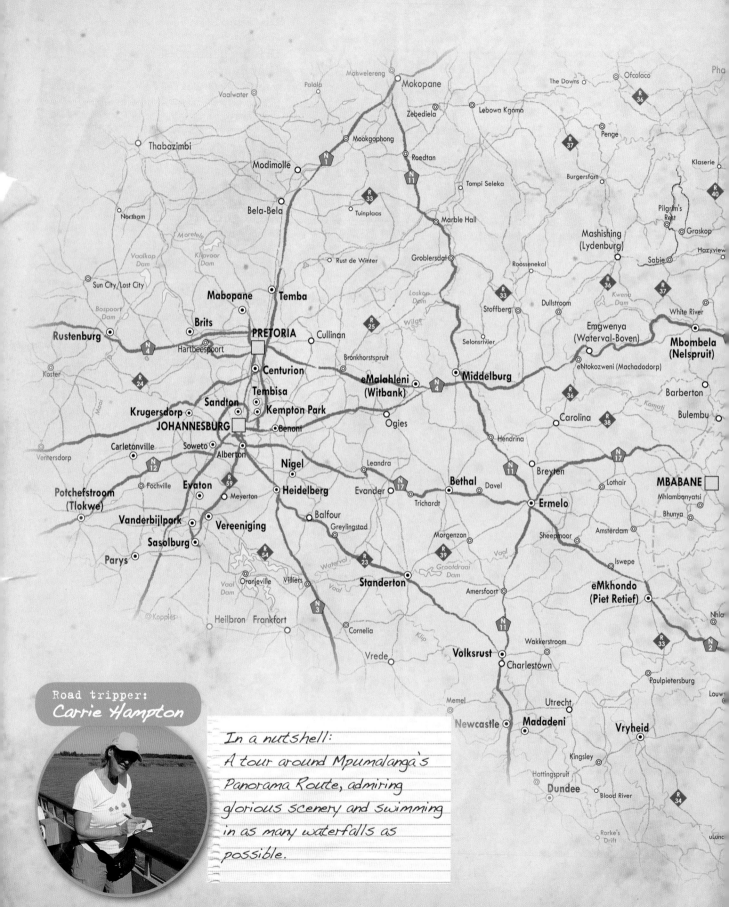

Road tripper:
Carrie Hampton

In a nutshell:
A tour around Mpumalanga's
Panorama Route, admiring
glorious scenery and swimming
in as many waterfalls as
possible.

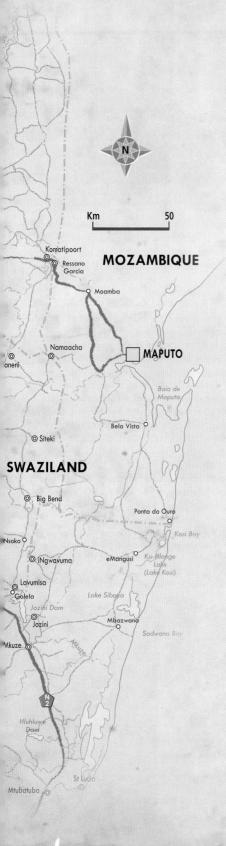

MOZAMBIQUE

Km [50]

Komatipoort
Ressano Garcia
Moamba

Namaacha

☐ MAPUTO

aneni

Baia de Maputo

Bela Vista

Siteki

SWAZILAND

Big Bend

Ponta do Ouro

Kosi Bay

Nsoko

iNgwavuma
eMangusi
Ku-Hlange Lake (Lake Kosi)

Lavumisa
Golela
Jozini Dam
Jozini
Mbazwana
Lake Sibaya
Sodwana Bay

Mkuze

N2

Hluhluwe Dam

St Lucia
Mtubatuba

Logistics
This journey may well originate in Johannesburg or Pretoria en route to Kruger, but is also a logical extension of the Ultimate Safari road trip (see pages 140–153), which can start in Kruger and go through Swaziland and into KwaZulu-Natal, or the other way around. The beautiful town of Sabie acts as our first base from where we can explore numerous waterfalls. This is followed by a scenic, winding road to the old gold-rush town of Pilgrim's Rest, then north on a scenic dirt road to Vaalhoek, following the Motlatse River to the strangely weathered Bourke's Luck Potholes. Then it's onwards to the Motlatse River Canyon's Three Rondavels viewpoint, then a quick backtrack along the edge of the canyon, diverting to waterfalls and viewpoints with evocative names like Wonder View, God's Window and The Pinnacle. Graskop is the final stop on this tour. The closest International airport is Kruger-Mpumalanga International Airport.

Driving conditions
Roads are good, including the only dirt road on this journey (from Pilgrim's Rest to Bourke's Luck Potholes). Small towns are dotted along this route, so there should be no problem sourcing fuel and supplies, but don't get stuck at the far end of Motlatse River Canyon with an empty tank. Some waterfalls are closed to the public in the height of summer, when heavy rains turn them into thundering torrents. There are no toll roads on the route.

Pet-friendly rating ★ ☆ ☆ ☆ ☆
1 = least suited 5 = most suited

Child-friendly rating ★ ★ ★ ★ ★
1 = least suited 5 = most suited

Low-slung vehicle-friendly rating ★ ★ ★ ★ ☆
1 = high clearance 5 = lowest slung

Don't miss
- Waterfall swims
- Eating trout, venison and pancakes

Emergency service numbers
Emergency (from a landline) 10111
Emergency (from a cellphone) 112
AA roadside assistance 086 100 0234 or 083 843 22 (24 hours)
Nelspruit Mediclinic 013 759 0500
Sabie Provincial Hospital 013 764 1222

Best time
The best months to travel are March to September, spanning late summer through winter to early spring. And if you combine this trip with the Ultimate Safari road trip (see pages 140–153) in the cool, dry months from May to August, you'll be there during the best game-viewing time. It can get cold, with snow on the mountains in midwinter, and nights on average 3°C in Sabie. In the rainy summer season (October to April) it gets hot and humid (26°C to 32°C during the day) and the higher you are, the wetter it is; Graskop has an average of 2,500mm of rain in summer, while Sabie gets 1,200mm. It falls mostly as soft, penetrating rain over several days, or late-afternoon thunderstorms, peaking in January and February. These conditions often create mist in the low-lying valleys – good for atmospheric photography.

SUMMER			AUTUMN			WINTER			SPRING		
D	J	F	M	A	M	J	J	A	S	O	N

Background reading
T V Bulpin's *Discovering Southern Africa*
Percy Fitzpatrick's *Jock of the Bushveld* (book and films)

TUMBLING WATERS
Long Tom Pass to Sabie, Pilgrim's Rest, Motlatse River Canyon and Graskop

Section ❶
Long Tom Pass to Sabie
Distance 35km plus visiting local waterfalls in Sabie
Driving Time 30mins plus local trips
Highlights Swimming in Bridal Veil Falls, water activities like rafting and tubing

We begin our tour at the highest point on Long Tom Pass (2,150m above sea level), some 35km before Sabie. At the strange rock formations of Devil's Knuckles viewpoint, you're in luck if the blanket of mist commonly over Sabie town doesn't obscure the magnificent vista of the entire Sabie Valley. Take a long look and admire the vast expanse of lowveld before you, while imagining the amount of water that tumbles down the escarpment in waterfalls and rivers. They have a dramatic effect on the landscape, as we are about to see.

Before the 30-minute drive down into Sabie, take a look at the Long Tom Cannon replica, which gives the pass its name. Long Toms were long-barrelled Boer War cannons nicknamed by the British against whom they were used. The monument marks the spot where, in September 1900, these two cannons were used for the last time.

It's a 21km winding descent on smooth tarmac road into Sabie, closely following the original treacherous track blazed by the wagons of late 19th-century pioneers. How the wooden wagon wheels negotiated the rocky montane grasslands and unexpected cliffs and gorges is hard to envisage.

Right near the highest point on the pass is Hops Hollow Country House and Brew Pub, with a selection of home-brewed English, German and Belgian-style ales. They'll welcome you for a tasting on every day but Sunday. But if you happen to be travelling at breakfast time, stop a little further on at Misty Mountain Chalets — it's a natural heritage site with one of South Africa's last remnants of undisturbed northeastern sourveld and is a rare breeding site for endangered blue swallows. There's no guarantee you'll see them, but you'll get a good breakfast.

At the foot of Long Tom Pass, a turn-off leads for 10km through pine and eucalyptus plantations to the little town of Sabie.

Stay a night in pretty subtropical Sabie and use it as your base for seeing the sights, swimming in three refreshing waterfalls, eating good food and buying curios. It's well set up for all these, with the Wild Fig Tree Restaurant the best in town for speciality trout and venison dishes. Petena Pancakes are tasty, and the Smokey Train Diner, in train carriages, serves traditional South African *kos* like potjies, oxtail stew and steaks.

Lone Creek Falls

Travel writer and historian T V Bulpin, who died in 1999 while updating his informative tome, *Discovering Southern Africa*, tells us that Sabie grew as a result of gold found on a local farm during a picnic in 1895. The men lined up bottles for target practice and the bullets hitting the rock exposed a reef of gold. And so the town of Sabie was born. A timber industry then burgeoned after local resources had been exhausted, and today, the area is covered with one of the largest man-made pine and gum-tree forests in the southern hemisphere. This could imply monotonous scenery, but that's not the case. The northern Drakensberg Mountains rise dramatically behind Sabie, rivers course into the valley and the nearby great chasm of Motlatse Canyon ensures enough spectacular vistas for any road tripper. Roads lined with plantations become an antidote to the melodrama of such marvels of nature.

Which waterfall pool shall we dive into first? Horseshoe Falls, Bridal Veil and Lone Creek Falls are all off the Old Lydenburg road heading west, so let's have a **swim** in them all. If you must choose only one, **Bridal Veil** lives up to its name, with an outstandingly pretty, diaphanous cascade dropping 70m. Have some change with you as Horseshoe and Lone Creek charge a small entrance fee. Don't be stingy — it's worth it because at both you can walk through indigenous forest, have a picnic or braai and enjoy the falls. Horseshoe Falls has

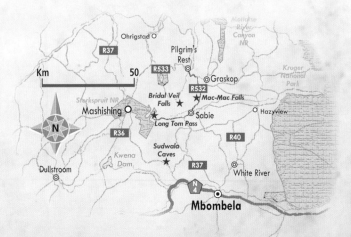

the added attraction of a trout farm, where you can catch a fish and braai it right there and then. They have rustic wooden chalets and camp sites, too. But for me, the biggest draw is swimming at the base of the waterfalls and braving the cascade of tumbling water. It's something that makes you feel truly alive!

Sabie has a whole choice of accommodation, many owner-run and recommended by Trip Advisor reviewers, like Wayfarers Guest House, Villa Ticino Guest House and Hillwatering Country House. There are also a couple of family resorts — the best seems to be Jock Sabie Lodge's self-catering log cabins. You'll see many references to the little Staffie, Jock of the Bushveld, as this was the pioneering territory of his owner.

ON THE SIDE >> Adventure sports
There are several other ways to have adventures, and Sabie Backpackers and Xtreme Adventures offer to get you 'wet, high and physical'. This means whitewater **tubing, rafting** and canyoning/kloofing (which is a nature and adventure mix). Or an even bigger adrenalin rush: headfirst on an anvil raft as you scoot down rapids kicking with your fins. For the 'high' they mean the Sabie Gorge Big Swing, or abseiling or repelling down a rock face into the Sabie Falls. Sissies can do a dry rock abseil. 'Physical' involves crawling into the belly of the earth and exploring a natural cave system. Who'd have thought that the owner of this adventure business is Sarel Loots, competitor in 2012 South African MasterChef? Funny, there's no mention on the website of getting fed!

...d workers at the General Dealer store, Pilgrim's Rest

ON THE SIDE >> Gold Panning Championship
Gold fever isn't over in Pilgrim's Rest, and 2012 saw the World Championship Gold Panning Competition held here. This attracts dedicated gold panners, who use anything from the traditional frying-pan style to the Batea cone-hat pan favoured by Eastern Europeans, or the latest, and some say fastest, the dead flat disc. You have to be fast to find all the nuggets secreted into your sand by the Chief Justice of Gold Panners. The bonus is that you get to keep the gold, but the minus is that the medals you win aren't gold! The next national championships are in Pilgrim's Rest during the September/October school holidays.

Section ❷
Sabie to Pilgrim's Rest
Distance 36km
Driving Time 30mins
Highlights Living in a time warp, panning for gold

There's one road heading out of Sabie in each direction, and we're going north on the R532 towards Graskop. Shortly after leaving Sabie you'll see signs to Mac-Mac Falls — named after Scotsmen who came seeking their fortune in alluvial gold. Mac-Mac Falls may be renowned for cascading 100m into a narrow ravine, but they aren't as accessible as Sabie's waterfalls. You look down on Mac-Mac from a caged viewing platform after countless steps down — kids may grumble. The craft market that has grown around the entrance is great, with bargains in wood and stone. Pause again at Mac-Mac pools, 10km along the R532, for children to paddle and swim; the first pool is right by the car park/picnic area, with a couple more just five minutes' walk upstream.

Now that you've had your morning dip, you can head west along the beautiful, winding R533 up to Pilgrim's Rest. There couldn't have been a more romantic setting to have a gold rush than here. It's a national heritage site and a living museum oozing with authentic Victorian nostalgia. The gold rush started in 1873 when Alec 'Wheelbarrow' Patterson panned for gold in a little stream. Word soon got out that he'd struck it lucky and hundreds of prospectors arrived. Within a year there were over 20 stores, numerous canteens and several houses of ill repute.

Start at Pilgrim's Rest Information Centre, situated in what is locally known as 'Uptown' (open daily 09:00–16:00), to help you get your bearings and pick up maps and information about museums, restaurants, craft and curio shops, diggings and accommodation. You'll need a few hours to discover all the interesting places. The best way to experience Pilgrim's Rest is to stay overnight in the Royal Hotel. It was painstakingly restored to its former glory and the late 19th-century buildings house 50 richly decorated bedrooms, complete with antique brass beds, washstands, and ball-and-claw baths. It's like **living in a time warp**!

Alternatively, Crystal Springs Mountain Lodge, 8km from the village and positioned overlooking a ravine on Robbers Pass, will serve you well with amenities like a spa and gym, swimming pools, restaurant and bar, tennis, mini-golf, a fireplace and free firewood for cold winter nights, and the list goes on... Note that this area was not called Robbers Pass for nothing: there's a monument to the last mail coach robbery in South Africa that occurred here on 7 June 1912.

While in Pilgrim's Rest, why not do what they did best here — **pan for gold**? It's not that hard and you might get hooked, just as the old prospectors did, when you spot some glinting gold dust and tiny nuggets in the mud. You aren't allowed to keep your small fortune, though!

TUMBLING WATERS
Long Tom Pass to Sabie, Pilgrim's Rest, Motlatse River Canyon and Graskop

Section ❸
Pilgrim's Rest to Motlatse River Canyon, ending in Graskop
Distance about 160km
Driving Time all day
Highlights Three Rondavels viewpoint, Bourke's Luck Potholes, swimming in Lisbon Falls

Having slowed the pace in Pilgrim's Rest, there's no need to speed things up, so we're going to take the well-maintained 27km dirt road to Bourke's Luck Potholes, as a reminder that this is a road trip for the sake of it and not for reaching our destination as fast as possible. The road generally follows a contour line with a ridge of mountains to your left, while you cross five loops and bends of the Motlatse River. Very occasionally, it'll be closed when bridges are under water. Ask Johnny at The Vine Restaurant (in downtown Pilgrim's Rest, serving South African fare like potjie, tripe and bobotie) and he'll fill you in on local knowledge.

Keep right and drive the last scenic 8km to the R532 main tar road. What you won't now realise is that the Motlatse Canyon is right beside you and the earth dramatically drops ±800m to the river bed. You can't see this from the road, so you have to stop at viewpoints for vistas that truly take your breath away.

One such is a little way north on the R532 and is perhaps the most spectacular, marking the northern end of the 26km long canyon: the **Three Rondavels** or Three Sisters. Three huge rock spirals of quartzite and shale rise out of the far canyon wall. With rounded domes iced in green vegetation and their sides stained with orange lichens, they impart a golden hue to the scene. Beyond and below you'll catch a glimpse of the Blydepoort Dam.

Backtrack south to **Bourke's Luck Potholes**, where the Blyde River ('river of joy', now the Motlatse River) and Treur River ('river of sorrow') meet. Their whirling waters have, over millennia, created surreal cylindrical rock sculptures and a series of dark-water pools. It's a remarkable geological phenomenon and the many bridges allow you to see this bizarre spectacle from every angle. It draws plenty of visitors and every time a car or tour bus enters, the informal dance troops burst into song and dance and you have to wonder: 'Shouldn't those kids be at school?'

Bourke's Luck Potholes

We're only 35km from Graskop and it's a good, smooth tar road to get there, but it's not going to be a speedy return on the southwards loop of this Tumbling Waters tour. There are still more waterfalls to swim in and views to admire.

ON THE SIDE >> Recommended hiking trails on the Tumbling Waters tour
- The fantastically scenic Fanie Botha Hiking Trail from Graskop to Sabie is two to five nights, over 50km if you make it the whole way.
- The Belvedere Day Walk from Bourke's Luck Potholes is a beautiful 8km down into the canyon and up to the old Belvedere Hydro Power Station.
- The Loerie Trail, running past Bridal Veil Falls in Sabie, covers about 10km.
- The Secretary Bird route of 3km from Mac-Mac pools is suitable for the whole family.
- The Forest Falls Nature Walk is a circular 4.5km route through the forest; get a permit from the Sabie or Graskop tourist information office.
- Kruger's Gold Hike takes you down into Graskop Gorge and up the other side over 1–2hrs.

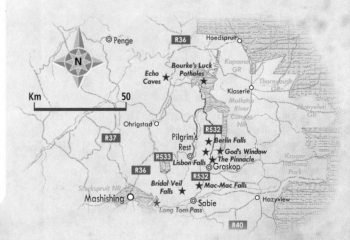

You may overdose on scenery, so select your scenic stops from the self-explanatory: Wonder View, God's Window and The Pinnacle on the R534 loop. If you think you might miss out, do them all — they're all glorious. But what about a waterfall swim? Berlin Falls and Lisbon Falls are off the main Graskop R532 road but, unlike at Sabie, we're up on the escarpment and seeing the waterfalls from above, not below. View Berlin Falls from a special observation platform and watch it plunge 80m. Nearby **Lisbon Falls** is a fantastic double whammy 90m-high waterfall, which cascades in two channels over a semicircular convex rock face. Tread carefully and follow the rainbow to find treasure at the bottom of the path and have your final waterfall swim of this tour. Not many people bother to descend, so you'll probably be alone down here.

Life's good, the car window's down and Christopher Cross is singing 'Ride Like the Wind' on the CD. You are cruising the last 7km of smooth rolling road towards Graskop where our Tumbling Waters tour ends. You've witnessed some of the most spectacular scenery on earth right here in southern Mpumalanga and have embraced the spirit of adventure with waterfalls cascading over you. What more could you ask from a three-day road trip?

Berlin Falls

TUMBLING WATERS Contact details

Autumn Breath B&B
013 767 1866
www.autumnbreath.co.za
Crystal Springs Mountain Lodge
013 768 5000
www.crystalsprings.co.za
Dar Amane Guest Lodge
013 767 1983
www.daramane.co.za
Graskop Information
013 767 1886
www.graskop.co.za
Hillwatering Country House
013 764 1421
http://hillwatering.co.za
Hops Hollow
013 235 0910
www.hopshollow.com
Jock Sabie Lodge
013 764 2178
www.jock.co.za
Misty Mountain Chalets
013 764 3377
www.mistymountain.co.za
Pilgrim's Rest
013 768 1060
www.pilgrims-rest.co.za
Sabie Backpackers and Xtreme Adventures
013 764 2118
http://sabiextreme.co.za
Sabie Tourist Information
013 764 3599
www.sabie.co.za
The Royal Hotel, Pilgrim's Rest
013 768 1044
www.royal-hotel.co.za
Villa Ticino Guest House
013 764 2598
www.villaticino.co.za
Wayfarers Guest House
013 764 1500
www.wayfarers.co.za
Zur Alten Mine
073 236 9289
www.zuraltenmine.co.za

Regional info
www.lowveldtourism.com
www.mpumalangahappenings.co.za
www.pilgrimsrest.org.za
www.sabie.co.za

ON THE SIDE >> Don't miss in Graskop

- Harrie's Pancakes (try the one with smoked trout mousse and horseradish cream)
- Buy local macadamia nuts from street sellers
- Delagoa Craft Shop (colourful authentic African artefacts and contemporary tribal arts and crafts)
- Graskop Silk Weavery (throws, bedspreads, scarves and more, hand-woven from a local silk farm)
- The 68m freefall cable gorge swing or the 131m foefie slide across the gorge 80m above the ground
- Accommodation: Zur Alten Mine log cabins, Dar Amane Guest Lodge and Autumn Breath B&B

LAND OF LEGEND
Circular route around Makhado via Elim and Thohoyandou

I am a long-time lover and resident of Limpopo, and one of my favourite escapes is into the delicious heights of the Soutpansberg in the Vhembe district. The area has all the right ingredients for a good road trip: beautiful mountain scenery, ancient culture and traditions, and a sense of magic. I first started visiting the area when I began working — a wide-eyed young travel writer driving around the place in a shabby little Golf that I forced to go places even 4x4 drivers feared. In the years since then I have visited the area many times, reporting on it for radio, writing about it for various magazines and newspapers, and finding a thousand nights of joy and comfort in the many special hideaways in these mountains. *Ku dya hiku engeta*, as they say in Xitsonga (Shangaan) — once you have tasted, you will want to return...

The Land of Legend route takes you around the Soutpansberg, South Africa's northernmost mountain range. It rises in the arid west near the little bushveld town of Alldays and heads east for some 120km in a series of dramatic peaks and gorges towards rainy, subtropical Thohoyandou. The route takes you into the ancient heart of the Vhembe district, with its baobabs and blue-green hills, bright green tea plantations, sacred lakes and waterfalls. The region is steeped in the rich cultural traditions of the Venda and Tsonga (Shangaan) people. A beautiful but relatively unexplored route, it has a great sense of escape with a distinctly African twist.

Total Distance 348km
Driving Time 15hrs

....

Section ❶
Makhado to Wylie's Poort via Vivo
Distance 144km
Driving Time 5hrs
Highlights:
Madi a Thavha
Leshiba Wilderness
Blouberg
Baobab trees along the R523
SEE PAGES 166–167

....

Section ❷
Wylie's Poort to Thohoyandou
Distance 101km
Driving Time 5hrs
Highlights:
Tshipise
Rural villages
Nwanedi Nature Reserve
SEE PAGE 167

....

Section ❸
Thohoyandou to Makhado
Distance 103km
Driving Time 5hrs
Highlights:
Thathe Vondo forest and Lake Fundudzi
Wylie's Poort Pass and Hendrik Verwoerd
Tunnels
Mashovhela Lodge
Shiluvari Lakeside Lodge and Albasini Dam
Zoutpansberg Skirmish Route
SEE PAGES 168–169

LAND OF LEGEND
Circular route around Makhado via Elim and Thohoyandou

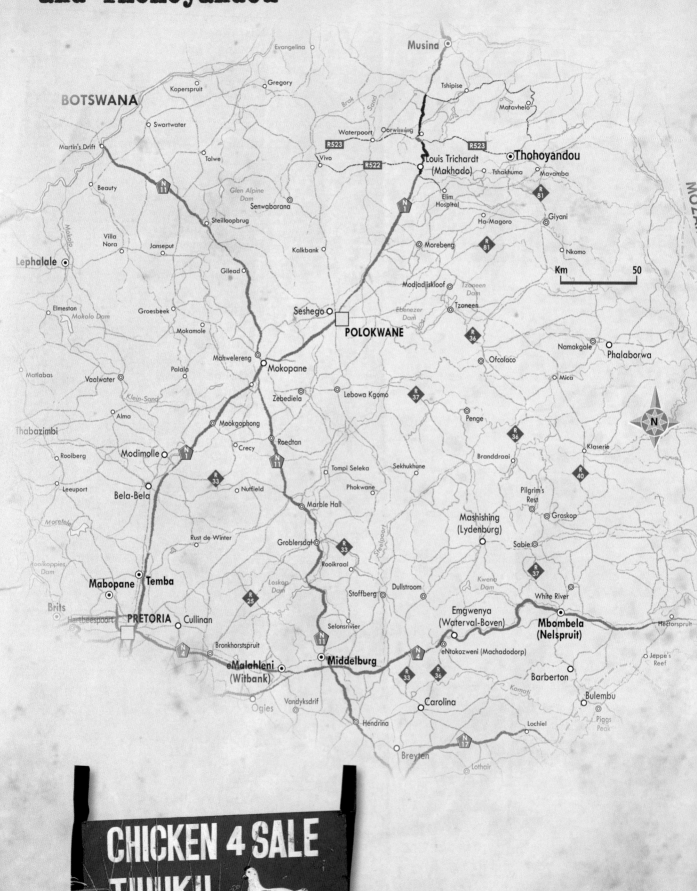

CHICKEN 4 SALE
TIHUKU
KHUHU ➤

Road tripper:
Bridget Hilton-Barber

In a nutshell:

A figure-of-eight trip from Makhado (Louis Trichardt) that takes you west along the base of the Soutpansberg, then east along the top, then eventually down a spectacular pass back to Makhado. The route features amazing mountain scenery, artistic and sacred spots, astonishing baobab specimens, laid-back rural villages and great feats of road building.

Background reading
For a fascinating account of the dying days of the South African War in the Soutpansberg area, read *The Legend of Breaker Morant is Dead and Buried: A South African version of the Bushveldt Carbineers in the Zoutpansberg May 1901–April 1902* by Charles Leach, published in 2012 by Leach Press.
Another fabulous read on the area is *Lost Trails of the Lowveld* by T V Bulpin, the classic book written in the 1950s offering stories about the people, the legends, the area and more.

Don't forget
Tree field guides, hats, walking shoes and picnic gear.

Logistics
The closest commercial airport is Polokwane International in Limpopo's capital, Polokwane, which is 98.5km away from Makhado. Private chartered flights are possible to airfields near Makhado or Musina, 65km away.

Driving conditions
The road from Makhado to Vivo is a single-lane mountain track. Watch out for trucks, taxis and potholes. The road from Vivo to Wylie's Poort is in better condition. On the N1, be careful of slow-moving big vehicles. On the R508 to Tshipise, look out for potholes, pedestrians, cows and children, and the same applies as you approach Thohoyandou. Focus your mind and go slowly. The final stretch down the N1 back to Makhado is steep, with lots of slow-moving trucks.

The daily distances are just over 100km per section, each requiring a minimum of four hours to take in all the scenery and attractions.

The area is generally safe but you should take the usual precautions.

There is a toll road on the N1 between Polokwane and Makhado – the Baobab Plaza.

Pet-friendly rating ★ ☆ ☆ ☆ ☆
1 = least suited 5 = most suited
The route takes you in and out of conservation areas, which generally don't allow pets.

Child-friendly rating ★ ★ ★ ☆ ☆
1 = least suited 5 = most suited
The route is better suited to older children. There are relatively few stop-overs along the way, so it's best to carry everything you need with you in the car. The most child-friendly part is Tshipise Forever Resort, which has tailor-made activities for children, as well as having child-minders available.

Low-slung vehicle-friendly rating ★ ★ ★ ☆ ☆
1 = high clearance 5 = lowest slung

Don't miss
- Soutpansberg Mountains and baobab trees
- Lake Fundudzi and Phiphidi Falls
- Wylie's Poort and tunnels
- Leshiba Wilderness
- Madi a Thavha
- Mashovhela
- Shiluvari Lodge and Albasini Dam
- Blouberg Mountains
- Nwanedi Nature Reserve
- Artists' Route

Emergency service numbers
Emergency (from a landline) 10111
Emergency (from a cellphone) 112
AA roadside assistance 086 100 0234 or 083 843 22 (24 hours)
Regional Towing – Louis Trichardt Tow-in Services 015 516 4479

Best time
Late summer is the best time to visit the Vhembe area, when the rains have filled the dams, the mountains are green and the weather is cooler.

SUMMER			AUTUMN			WINTER			SPRING		
D	J	F	M	A	M	J	J	A	S	O	N

LAND OF LEGEND
Circular route around Makhado via Elim and Thohoyandou

Section ❶
Makhado to Wylie's Poort via Vivo
Distance 144km
Driving Time 5hrs
Highlights Madi a Thavha, Leshiba Wilderness, Blouberg, baobab trees along the R523

The Land of Legend route has great scenic appeal — think lichen-clad cliffs, yellow mountain rumps, blue-green subtropical hills. And never mind the hundreds of charming baobab trees. The route also has diversity — you will go from open bushveld to mountain tops, from highways to single-lane roads.

The Soutpansberg range reveals its full drama almost as soon as you head out of Makhado town on the R522 towards Vivo. Instant views means an instant road trip buzz. The single-lane road winds beneath the foothills of *tha vhani ya muno*, the 'mountain of salt', which takes its name from the many saltpans here. The mountains are part of the Soutpansberg Conservancy, which is a 9,000ha mix of provincial, municipal and private parks and wilderness areas especially designed to protect the special habitat of these mountains.

Open road to Vivo

ON THE SIDE >> Did you know?
The Soutpansberg, or *tha vhani ya muno* (mountain of salt), is South Africa's northernmost mountain range. It gets its name from the many saltpans that have been here for centuries.

The Soutpansberg and the Limpopo River Valley host over 540 bird species, making this is a rewarding birding route. It includes northern parts of the Kruger, Mapungubwe National Park and the Soutpansberg range. The Blouberg also has a large population of vultures.

About 10km along the R522, on the right, is **Madi a Thavha**, a charming and friendly guesthouse and gallery that is the best place for information on the local Artists' Route. Enjoy a light breakfast or lunch and browse around the gallery called The Dancing Fish. Madi a Thavha has pleasant accommodation and offers breakfasts, light lunches and dinners on request.

The quirky but interesting Schoemansdal Museum is further along the R522, some 14km from Makhado. It has memorabilia and exhibits from the days when the Voortrekkers trekked to these parts with their ox wagons and Bibles. There are also exhibits from the early indigenous San and Khoi inhabitants of this area.

The R522 travels below the mountains, with amazing views and a variety of spots to visit and stay overnight. One of the nicest is the Venda Village at **Leshiba Wilderness**. Designed by acclaimed artist Noria Mabasa, this magical lodge is set in a wild garden and has a courtyard filled with pots and sculptures of mythological creatures — lions, maidens, giant feet, moulded benches. Leshiba's reserve has indigenous forests and open mountain plains with game. This is hiking, strolling, botanising country. Go on a game drive, or take a guided hike to see the San rock art hidden in the caves here.

Other fabulous options are Medike Mountain Reserve and Buzzard Mountain. You will drive past the little village of Buysdorp, which was started by Coenraad de Buys, a fugitive Voortrekker who began the region's first so-called coloured community.

The distinct **Blouberg** mountain rises up as you travel westwards to Vivo. This inselberg, or granite koppie, is the centrepiece of a 9,000ha reserve. There are no hiking trails, but self-drive game drives are possible. Stop for supplies in Vivo — the remainder of the 70km+ journey to Wylie's Poort has no garages and few spots to stop.

TIP
Visit the vultures at the Blouberg Nature Reserve. The reserve is famed for its 600-strong breeding population of endangered Cape vultures. The vulture restaurant here is visited by the Cape vulture, as well as lappet-faced, hooded, white-headed, white-backed and the rare Rüppell's vultures. The reserve has a great combination of mountains and plains, with impressive baobabs, yellowwood and mashatu trees, and a small sycamore fig forest and wetland.

From Vivo turn right onto the R521 and then after 6km turn right again on to the **R523**, which leads you towards Wylie's Poort past amazing **roadside baobabs** and ancient bushveld scenery. You can visit the saltpans here, or stop along the roadside and have a picnic under a baobab and take photographs. Vhembe district is famed for its thousands of baobab trees, the source of much folklore and a tourism icon of Limpopo province. *Adansonia digitata*, as the baobab is scientifically named, has one of the longest life spans of all African trees. Some baobabs in Limpopo province are already over 3,000 years old. On average, baobab trees found in Vhembe are between 300 and 500 years old.

Venda pots

ON THE SIDE >> The Artists' Route
This self-drive or guided tour takes you to the studios and galleries of the Tsonga and Venda artists of the area. Vhembe is famed for its sculptors, potters, weavers and drum makers. You can meet the artists and see their work.

Section ❷
Wylie's Poort to Thohoyandou
Distance 101km
Driving Time 5hrs
Highlights Tshipise, rural villages, Nwanedi Nature Reserve

When the R523 reaches Wylie's Poort you will arrive at a T-junction. Turn left onto the N1 and head north in the direction of Musina. This road is the busy main route to Zimbabwe, so watch out for trucks and traffic. The views are gorgeous, with great sweeps over the mountains and a lovely winding road.

After 30km turn right on the R508 to **Tshipise**, which leads into a busy road that goes through a series of laid-back **rural villages**. Watch out for chickens and cows, children and pedestrians. The landscape here is a wonderful combination of mountains and bushveld, with enormous baobabs, umbrella-thorn trees and tracts of mopane trees.

After 34km you will reach Tshipise Forever Resort, set in pleasant gardens with hot springs, water features and pools. A distinctive koppie towers protectively over this long-established, family-friendly resort, which is a great spot to lunch or overnight in the guesthouses, self-catering rondavels or in the camp site that is set among baobabs, mopani, red bushwillow and jackalberry trees. The resort is a good stopover if you're heading into the Kruger National Park — the Pafuri Gate is 105km away.

From Tshipise, it's about 50km to Thohoyandou, and the rural scenery is pretty. After about 70km, you pass the **Nwanedi Nature Reserve**, which is good for a break and a wander. The reserve has two scenic dams and a lovely waterfall. You can go on game drives or take to the water on a kayak or in a canoe.

Continue along the R508 towards Thohoyandou, which lies northeast of Makhado and is a colourful urban centre for surrounding farms and villages.

TIP

The 9,300ha Nwanedi Nature Reserve is worth a stop for its fabulous mix of dams and waterfalls, baobabs and ancient Venda mythology. Check out the baobabs and the beautiful umbrella-thorn trees. Take a picnic down to one of the two dams — Nwanedi Dam or the smaller Lupepe Dam — and spend some time at the tumbling Tshihovhohovho Falls. Nwanedi offers game drives and kayak and canoe trips, which are great for boat-based birding and general chilling. There is overnight accommodation and camping.

LAND OF LEGEND
Circular route around Makhado via Elim and Thohoyandou

Section ❸
Thohoyandou to Makhado
Distance 103km
Driving Time 5hrs
Highlights Thathe Vondo forest and Lake Fundudzi, Wylie's Poort Pass and Hendrik Verwoerd Tunnels, Mashovhela Lodge, Shiluvari Lakeside Lodge and Albasini Dam, Zoutpansberg Skirmish Route

Head out of Thohoyandou on the R523. You'll feel your spirits lift as you drive through the colourful villages and markets, past rivers and dams and tea plantations. This is where you get to slow right down to Limpopo time. There'll be lots you want to photograph – just remember to pull over safely and put on your hazard lights.

After travelling along the R523 for about 30km, you will see the entrance (on your right) to the holy forest of **Thathe Vondo** and sacred **Lake Fundudzi**. This fascinating reserve is under threat as a result of deforestation and agriculture, but remains an important Venda cultural site, and it's worth staying for a picnic and a stroll. Pay your respects to the Venda people at the Phiphidi Waterfall where *zwidudwane* – waters sprites – are said to frolic.

ON THE SIDE >> Sacred spots
The holy forest of Thathe Vondo is the burial ground of ancient Venda royalty. The forest has beautiful giant hardwood and yellowwood trees, ferns, thick undergrowth, creepers and amazing bird life. You'll also find here the sacred Lake Fundudzi, place of birth and creation in Venda culture. One of the few true inland lake systems in South Africa, Fundudzi is formed by the waters of the Mutale River and has no obvious outlet. It is said to be guarded by a giant python, who is honoured annually with the ritual Domba dance.

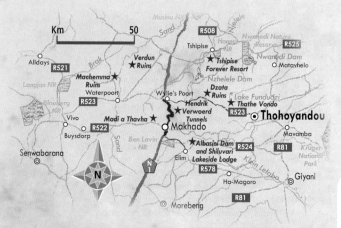

Further along the R523, you can also stop and see the Dzata Ruins, which are in need of some TLC. These ruins were once the capital of the Venda people, ruled by the great Thohoyandou, whose name means 'head of the elephant'.

Continue along the R523 through villages and mountains for about another 60km, until the road ends in a T-junction. Turn left onto the N1 to Makhado. You'll drive down the historic **Wylie's Poort Pass** and through the **Hendrik Verwoerd Tunnels**, a spectacular gateway that cuts through the mountain and has been used as a passage from the north since the Iron Age.

ON THE SIDE >> Did you know?
Wylie's Poort was named after Lieutenant C H Wylie, who surveyed it for a road in 1904. The pass has since been made largely redundant by two tunnels built in the 1960s. These are the Hendrik Verwoerd Tunnels that take you through the mountains.

A great stopover or refreshment spot is **Mashovhela Lodge**, which is about 16km before Makhado. You drive about 6km into the game reserve, where a lovely old stone-and-thatch lodge offers good food and cheer. The name *mashovhela* means 'the place where the drums are heard' in Venda, and the Mashovhela Pools here are considered sacred. You can take a hike through the reserve to see the pools, and enjoy a night under the stars on an astronomy safari. Mashovhela also arranges guided cultural tours in the area.

Mashovhela Pools

ON THE SIDE >> Mashovhela's magical drum
According to a Venda legend, King Thohoyandou, the man who forged the Venda nation, had a mystical drum, *ngoma lungundo*, which he played when his enemies approached, killing them off one by one with each drumbeat. Alas, the drum was stolen from the royal kraal and is said to be living as a spirit in and around the rock pools at Mashovhela, 'the place where the drums can be heard'.

Continue down the N1 to Makhado and don't forget to buy some fruit from the many roadside stalls along the way. The Vhembe district produces litchis, bananas, mangoes, nuts, tea and coffee. For a fabulous lunch before heading into town, take a left about 8km before you reach Makhado and drive up the mountainside to Mountain View Hotel. Their Explorers Restaurant has a deck with amazing views and they serve good South African fusion cuisine.

If you are looking for a good spot to relax out of town for a few days, head east to Elim and stay at **Shiluvari Lakeside Lodge,** an eco-friendly lodge with a generous porch and a comfortable lounge-bar-dining room area with gorgeous views onto the **Albasini Dam.** Their food is fabulous fusion and their décor reflects the artistic traditions and crafts of the local Tsonga and Venda people. They also have a fab spa.

Shiluvari will arrange guided tours in the area, including the Artists' Route and the **Zoutpansberg Skirmish Route** on which local historian and personality Charles Leach takes you on a fascinating adventure back to the South African War and the last bloody days that played out here in the Soutpansberg. Visit graves, battle sites, lookout points and historic buildings.

TIP

The place where the drums can be heard is also the place where the stars can be seen. Enjoy an astronomy safari with local astronomer Kos Coronaios. You head out at night into the bush, gather round a fire and take a tour of the stars through a giant telescope. Visit the Southern Cross, Africa's most famous astro icon, swirl around the Milky Way, stop off at Jupiter's moon and Saturn's rings, and drop in at Orion. You can stay over at Hammock Camp, an under-the-stars experience where you sleep in hammocks alongside a waterfall.

LAND OF LEGEND Contact details

Artists' Route
contact Madi a Thavha (see below)
Blouberg Nature Reserve
015 295 2829
Explorers Restaurant
015 517 7031
Forever Resorts Tshipise
015 539 0634, 015 539 0651 or 015 539 0658
www.forevertshipise.co.za
Leshiba Wilderness
011 483 1841
www.leshiba.co.za
Limpopo Birding Route
015 276 1131
www.limpopobirding.com
Madi a Thavha Mountain Lodge
015 516 0220 or 083 342 4162
www.madiathavha.com
Makhado (Louis Trichardt) Information Services
087 805 8633
www.louistrichardtinfo.co.za
Mashovhela
012 991 6930
www.mashovhela.com
Nwanedi Nature Reserve
015 290 7355, 015 290 7339 or 015 290 7336
www.wildliferesorts.org
Shiluvari Lakeside Lodge
015 556 3406
www.shiluvari.com
Zoutpansberg Skirmish Route
015 516 5455

Regional info
www.golimpopo.com
www.limpopohappenings.co.za
www.nightjartravel.com
www.safarinow.com
www.sa-venues.co.za
www.southafrica.net

Baobab trees line the route

PADKOS

My favourite padkos hamper is filled with many of the fruits for which the Vhembe area is famous — sweet naartjies, grapefruit, bananas and avo spread on a fresh roll with a squeeze of lemon. And biltong — wet and thinly sliced. And I always take a little gas burner so that we can make espresso.

THE DRY NORTH
Johannesburg to Cape Town

The Northern Cape has the distinction of being the province with the lowest population density in South Africa, and it achieves this from both ends of the spectrum – by being sparsely populated and by being insanely big. Thus, the best way to do this trip is to put a good few kilometres behind you on the first day, and the last, to ensure that you spend most of your time in the heart of the Northern Cape.

Granted, there is beauty to be found in the Free State before and the Western Cape after, but both of these warrant separate journeys. The true Northern Cape experience lies between Kuruman and Calvinia.

Within this range you will find vast, rolling desert sands where the Kalahari encroaches, Martian outcrops where the Orange River Valley shatters the earth, and infinite desolation in the flat fields of the Karoo. This fierce, weathered landscape houses by far the friendliest people in South Africa – a genuine triumph of human spirit.

Take a mountain bike, your hiking boots, a camera or even just a stack of good books and a cooler full of treats. It doesn't really matter how you choose to experience the Northern Cape, as long as you remember to take your sense of adventure, and your sense of wonder.

Total Distance 1,960km
Driving Time 28hrs

Section ❶
Johannesburg to Witsand Nature Reserve
Distance 730km
Driving Time 8hrs
Highlight:
A ranger-guided night walk in the Witsand
Nature Reserve
SEE PAGE 174

Section ❷
Witsand Nature Reserve to Riemvasmaak Hot
Springs via Keimoes
Distance 290km
Driving Time 5hrs
Highlight:
Daydreaming in the warm water while
gazing through the 'Africa'-shaped piece of
sky revealed by the rocky cliffs beyond the
hot springs
SEE PAGES 174–175

Section ❸
Riemvasmaak Hot Springs to Augrabies Falls
National Park via the 'new' bridge
Distance 40km
Driving Time 2hrs
Highlights:
The incredible Martian landscapes
approaching the Orange River
The highly photogenic contrast between
animals as tall as giraffes and the flat
landscape
SEE PAGES 175–176

Section ❹
Augrabies Falls National Park to
Loeriesfontein via Pofadder
Distance 440km
Driving Time 7hrs
Highlights:
The sense of smallness and solitude that the
vast open spaces along the road through
Pofadder and Kliprand will inspire in you
The possibility of seeing bat-eared foxes
SEE PAGE 176

Section ❺
Loeriesfontein to Cape Town via Calvinia
Distance 460km
Driving Time 6hrs
Highlight:
The incredible beauty of the N7 between
Clanwilliam and Piekenierskloof Pass
SEE PAGES 176–177

THE DRY NORTH
Johannesburg to Cape Town

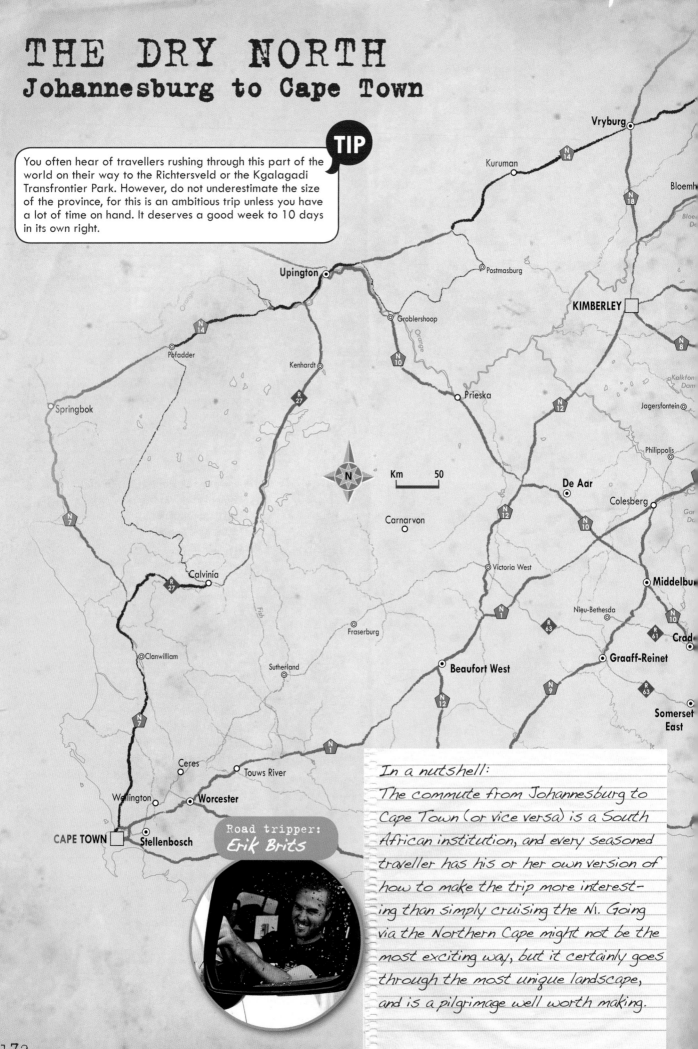

TIP

You often hear of travellers rushing through this part of the world on their way to the Richtersveld or the Kgalagadi Transfrontier Park. However, do not underestimate the size of the province, for this is an ambitious trip unless you have a lot of time on hand. It deserves a good week to 10 days in its own right.

Road tripper:
Erik Brits

In a nutshell:

The commute from Johannesburg to Cape Town (or vice versa) is a South African institution, and every seasoned traveller has his or her own version of how to make the trip more interesting than simply cruising the N1. Going via the Northern Cape might not be the most exciting way, but it certainly goes through the most unique landscape, and is a pilgrimage well worth making.

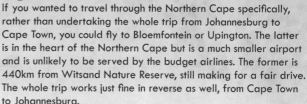

Logistics

If you wanted to travel through the Northern Cape specifically, rather than undertaking the whole trip from Johannesburg to Cape Town, you could fly to Bloemfontein or Upington. The latter is in the heart of the Northern Cape but is a much smaller airport and is unlikely to be served by the budget airlines. The former is 440km from Witsand Nature Reserve, still making for a fair drive. The whole trip works just fine in reverse as well, from Cape Town to Johannesburg.

Driving conditions

Most of the trip will be done on gravel roads that are in relatively good condition. Thus a family sedan will be able to complete the trip, but some detours will be required between Witsand Nature Reserve and Riemvasmaak to avoid the soft sandy roads where a vehicle with more clearance is essential, and a vehicle with 4x4 traction is preferable. The ideal vehicle for this trip, in order to be confident in exploring all areas, would be a vehicle with high clearance, rugged tyres and advanced traction control (such as 4x4 or electronic wizardry). Note that run-flat tyres and low-profile tyres tend to have a higher risk of damage by the rugged gravel used on the roads in the more mountainous regions, so it is advisable to drive cautiously off the tarmac to avoid slashing a tyre.

In the more remote parts of South Africa, the general rule of thumb is to avoid passing up the opportunity to fill your tank, as the fuel supply is not guaranteed, and the Northern Cape falls within this rule. However, this is a matter of 'rather safe than sorry', as the fuel situation is not dire by any stretch of the imagination.

More important, purely for trip enjoyment, is to avoid passing up the opportunity to fill the snack box! The vast distances with a complete lack of humanity can become frustrating if you become hungry or thirsty.

Pet-friendly rating ★ ☆ ☆ ☆ ☆

1 = least suited 5 = most suited
Pets are not allowed in national parks.

Child-friendly rating ★ ★ ★ ★ ☆

1 = least suited 5 = most suited

Low-slung vehicle-friendly rating ★ ★ ☆ ☆ ☆

1 = high clearance 5 = lowest slung

Don't miss

- Riemvasmaak
- Augrabies Falls National Park
- Witsand Nature Reserve.

Emergency service numbers

Emergency (from a landline) 10111
Emergency (from a cellphone) 112
AA roadside assistance 086 100 0234 or 083 843 22 (24 hours)

Best time

Being a province of extremes, the Northern Cape tends to be too hot in summer and too cold in winter, but just right in spring or autumn. In this part of the world, locals turn their air conditioners off when summer temperatures drop below 30°C, so we think in this case the summer warning is warranted. Winter days are mostly beautiful, warm and crisp, but winter nights can get bitterly cold.

SUMMER			AUTUMN			WINTER			SPRING		
D	J	F	M	A	M	J	J	A	S	O	N

Background reading

Karoo and other stories by Athol Fugard is a good way to obtain a bit of cultural insight.

TIP

The Orange River offers a range of rafting possibilities. Closer to the |Ai-|Ais/Richtersveld Transfrontier Park the river is very placid, so much so that the commercial trips here are done in Canadian canoes and not in the usual 'crocs'. Below the Augrabies Falls, the section at the Gorge near Verloorsdrif features wilder water and is rated up to grade 4 – perhaps only for the more experienced. For groups of mixed experience, the section in the Augrabies Falls National Park is a good compromise.

THE DRY NORTH
Johannesburg to Cape Town

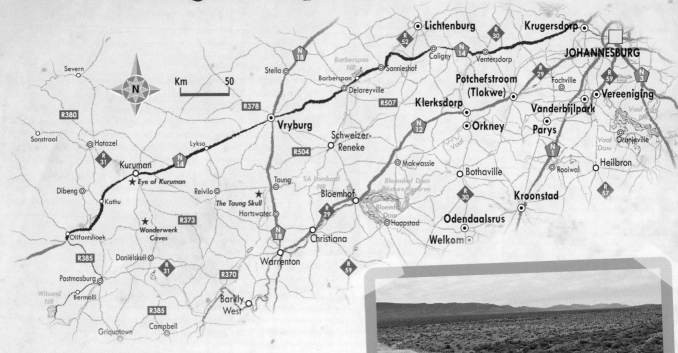

Section ❶
Johannesburg to Witsand Nature Reserve
Distance 730km
Driving Time 8hrs
Highlight A ranger-guided night walk in the
Witsand Nature Reserve

The road to Witsand Nature Reserve runs through
Ventersburg, Coligny, Sannieshof, Delareyville and Vryburg, before you get to Kuruman. Although there are
probably many nooks and crannies one could explore
along the way, Witsand is a long drive away, and it is
best to cover a fair distance on the first day. Getting
this behind you on day one means that the major part
of the trip is spent in the heart of the Northern Cape.

From Kuruman, the landscape starts changing to more
typical Kalahari scrubland, and once you turn off to
the **Witsand Nature Reserve** (just beyond Olifants-
hoek), the beauty of the area comes into its own.
There are more trees than you would expect and,
depending on the time of year, it could actually be
quite green. The transition from red Kalahari sands to
the whiter large-grained sand around Witsand is surprising, and that's not the only trick this sand has. If the
sand is dry enough, the large grains make a roaring
noise as they tumble down the dunes. Be sure to ask at
the main office about listening to the Brulsand.

Spend at least one evening watching the sun set from
the top of the dunes. From the parking lot at the end of
the road, it is a steep, but short climb to the top of the
dunes, and it is a breeze sliding back to the car after
dark. Also make sure you do the **guided night walk** – it
was free the last time we were there. You will certainly
be amazed – both by how much the guide knows about
things he can only hear in the dark, and by how much
life there is crawling around on the dunes.

Witsand Nature Reserve

Section ❷
Witsand Nature Reserve to Riemvasmaak Hot Springs via Keimoes
Distance 290km
Driving Time 5hrs
Highlight Daydreaming in the warm water while
gazing through the 'Africa'-shaped piece of sky
revealed by the rocky cliffs beyond the hot springs

The second leg of the road trip heads off to Riemvasmaak, and the scenic beauty of the trip lies right
at the beginning and right at the end, with a large
stretch of 'flatland' in the middle. So, don't rush off –
rather, enjoy the transition back to red Kalahari sand
again, keep an eye out for the larger birds, and
treat the road with respect so that you don't get
stuck in the sand.

When you leave Witsand, at the dirt road, instead of
turning back the way you came in, turn right and continue until you come to the first 'major' dirt road coming in from the right. This road runs around Witsand
and the first section is alive with interest, particularly
the gnarled acacias full of sociable weavers' nests.

After about an hour (if you are doing it at the right
speed) the landscape flattens out and it is time to
get a move on to Upington and then Riemvasmaak.

Ignore your GPS when it tells you to head north out of Upington, but rather follow the course of the Orange River through Keimoes if you are on the north bank, or via Kakamas if you are on the south bank — it doesn't really matter which route you choose.

Upington is the biggest town you will go through, and is a good place to restock. It is likely to have most convenience needs, whereas most of the smaller towns are very unlikely to have what you need, save for the bare essentials.

The road to **Riemvasmaak** starts off quite tame, and just when you start wondering what all the fuss is about, the landscape rises up dramatically (if you're curious, have a look at the topography on Google Maps). The area is a warren of mountains and canyons — hard to describe in words, but certainly one of the hidden jewels in the country. The scenery is similar to that of the renowned Richtersveld, but condensed into a much smaller space, making it ideal for those who don't want the commitment of a two-week drive into the wilderness.

TIP

The chalets at Riemvasmaak have been built as semi-detached 'twins'. In other words, there are two adjoining units per site. If you are in a smaller group, consider reserving both sides of the dual chalets nonetheless, as you have come to a very remote place and may not want to share your evening with strangers.

ON THE SIDE >> Sociable weavers
Although some birds build bigger nests, nothing matches sociable weavers for the size of their colonies. Some of these colonies house over 100 pairs. Pygmy falcons are the most common co-inhabitant, but a range of other birds, including finches, lovebirds, barbets and chats, also use these nests — and for good reason. During hot summer days, the outside chambers offer cool relief from the scorching sun, while at night the central chambers remain cosy and warm.

Section ❸
Riemvasmaak Hot Springs to Augrabies Falls National Park via the 'new' bridge
Distance 40km
Driving Time 2hrs
Highlights The incredible Martian landscapes approaching the Orange River; the highly photogenic contrast between animals as tall as giraffes and the flat landscape

When you head off to the Augrabies Falls National Park, your GPS will keep telling you to head back the way you came, but please don't. If you have stayed over at the hot springs, you would probably have explored much of this area already, but it is a spectacular **scenic drive** to get to the bridge over the Orange River. From here, you are soon back on tar and will be at the falls in a flash.

The Augrabies Falls National Park holds much more to discover than just the waterfall for which it is named. There is a big stretch of land below the falls that is open to vehicles and offers game drives through some beguiling country-side. In this arid landscape, game is not abundant, but this part of the trip is as much about the landscape as it is about the game. You can also explore this section on a bicycle or on foot, on either one-day or over-night trails.

This area is heaven for **photographers**, with endless skies, intense **contrasts**, and deeply saturated colours in the rocks, the sand and the sky. The best treat is finding **giraffes** standing like skyscrapers in the **flat open areas** near the falls.

Spend a day or two here, enjoying the **hot springs** and exploring the mountains and desert on foot, on your bike, or in a 4x4.

There are three 4x4 trails of varying difficulty in the area, but you don't have to be in a 4x4 to enjoy the main road through this beautiful landscape. There is a day-walk from the hot springs that allows you to immerse yourself in this amazing landscape, and then the roads here just beg to be explored on a mountain bike.

Giraffes at Augrabies Falls National Park

175

THE DRY NORTH
Johannesburg to Cape Town

The circular 5km Dassie Trail is one of the most rewarding hikes, and if you feel up to the challenge, the 40km Klipspringer Trail will leave you breathless.

The park also extends above the falls, but this section is less accessible. One way of doing it is by boat with Kalahari Outventures. They run a 9km stretch through this section of the park. In fact, the take-out point is just a few hundred metres above the falls, so don't miss it.

Section ❹
Augrabies Falls National Park to Loeriesfontein via Pofadder
Distance 440km
Driving Time 7hrs
Highlights The sense of smallness and solitude that the vast open spaces along the road through Pofadder and Kliprand will inspire in you; the possibility of seeing bat-eared foxes

The second last leg of this road trip takes you into another world altogether. Here you will be forgiven for thinking that the earth is indeed flat as you drive through mile upon mile of **emptiness...** but herein lies the appeal. The trick is to take it easy, drive slowly, and be on the lookout for little creatures like tortoises and **bat-eared foxes**. Get out of the car occasionally and enjoy the empty space. In an ever-fuller planet, it is becoming a scarce commodity. Oh, and of course, the first town you will be driving through is Pofadder ('puff adder'). It's not much of a town, but it's one of those iconic places you have to tick off your list, and the people are usually very friendly.

One of the highlights of this section is the Loeriesfontein Windmill Museum. The collection of 27 windmills on display in the small Hantam Karoo town of Loeriesfontein is one of a kind.

Section ❺
Loeriesfontein to Cape Town via Calvinia
Distance 460km
Driving Time 6hrs
Highlights The incredible beauty of the N7 between Clanwilliam and Piekenierskloof Pass

Hantam House in Calvinia is a lovingly restored historic building in Hope Street, across the road from the giant red postbox, another landmark in the town. The small museum has displays of a range of utensils and furnishings used in everyday life way back before cars and electricity, and the shop is a treasure-trove for those who like to unearth the unusual in out-of-the-way places and includes a good range of pottery and enamelware.

Augrabies Falls

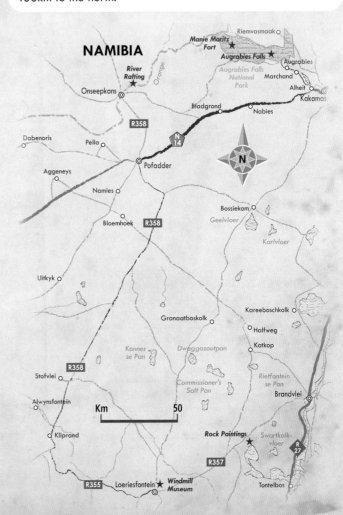

176

The home stretch runs through one of the most scenically diverse parts of the country, and there are a number of alternatives, from the coastal route to the road over the Cederberg. This is traditionally known as one of the most **beautiful parts of the country**, but after the trip you've just undertaken, you may well find yourself hankering for a bit more dust and a little less green.

Furthermore, these areas are easily accessible from Cape Town, even just for a weekend, and by the time you've arrived here you will have a fair number of kilometres under the belt, so it is no sin to hit the N7 on the last day and just drive on to Cape Town.

THE DRY NORTH Contact details

Augrabies Falls National Park
054 452 9200
www.sanparks.org
Hantam House
027 341 1606
www.calvinia.co.za
Kalahari Outventures
082 476 8213
www.kalahari-outventures.co.za
Loeriesfontein Tourism Information
027 662 1119
Loeriesfontein Windmill Museum
027 662 1023
www.loeriesfontein.co.za
Northern Cape Tourism
053 832 2657
http://experiencenortherncape.com
Riemvasmaak Hot Springs
054 337 2804
www.greenkalahari.co.za
Witsand Nature Reserve
053 313 1061
www.witsandkalahari.co.za

Regional info
www.namakwa-dm.gov.za/tourism/
www.nightjartravel.com/regions-towns/northern-cape
http://experiencenortherncape.com

Bat-eared foxes

SURFING ROAD TRIP
Cape Town (via Lambert's Bay) to Mdumbi

As a surfer who grew up in the frigid waters of Cape Town, it took two trips to Indonesia, an extended sojourn through Central America and many furtive missions abroad to realise that the ultimate surf trip to be had is right here in South Africa.

True, you can't fault the repetitive perfection of Indonesia or the intensity of Hawaii. But few destinations in the world offer you such a variety of quality surf that's so easily accessible as good old Mzansi. From dolphins and board shorts on the Wild Coast to the big-wave reefs and icy perfection of the West Coast, the diversity South Africa bundles into 2,500km of coastline is mind-boggling.

The N2 highway is the key to this surfing odyssey and connects the major surf regions in a convenient route running southwest to northeast. Jeffreys Bay (or J-Bay) remains the focal point on any surfer's map of South Africa and we flock there like homing pigeons. But in doing so you bypass a number of turn-offs and back roads that lead to many more amazing beaches and incredible waves that are best explored at a leisurely pace in your own vehicle.

Collectively these routes make South Africa the ultimate place to be a surfer. After seven years of editing the country's premier surfing magazine, *Zigzag*, I'm more convinced of this than ever.

Total Distance 1,535km
Driving Time 20hrs 25mins

....

Section ❶
Cape Town to Lambert's Bay
Distance 265km
Driving Time 3hrs 35mins
Highlights:
Elands Bay and Baboon Point
Secluded beaches along the R365
Muisbosskerm open-air restaurant
SEE PAGE 182

....

Section ❷
Cape Town to Gansbaai
Distance 180km
Driving Time 2hrs 25mins
Highlights:
Vintners Surf Classic Contest
Kogelberg Biosphere Reserve
Big waves and whale-watching in Hermanus
SEE PAGE 183

....

Section ❸
Stilbaai to Mossel Bay
Distance 130km
Driving Time 2hrs 10mins
Highlight:
Start of the Garden Route
SEE PAGE 184

....

Section ❹
Mossel Bay to Plettenberg Bay
Distance 138km
Driving Time 2hrs 25mins
Highlights:
Victoria Bay
Gericke's Point beach walks and snorkelling
Steam Whistle Stop Café
Robberg Peninsula and Nature Reserve
SEE PAGES 185–186

....

Section ❺
Plettenberg Bay to Jeffreys Bay
Distance 204km
Driving Time 2hrs 30mins
Highlights:
The world-famous waves of Supertubes
Jeffreys Bay Surf Museum
Cape St Francis Wild Side
SEE PAGES 187–188

....

Section ❻
Jeffreys Bay to Chintsa West
Distance 414km
Driving Time 4hrs 50mins
Highlights:
Nahoon Reef
Wild Coast Jikileza
SEE PAGE 189

....

Section ❼
East London to Mdumbi
Distance 204km
Driving Time 2hrs 30mins
Highlights:
Mdumbi Point and Backpackers
Lwandile hiking and surfing
SEE PAGES 190–191

SURFING ROAD TRIP
Cape Town (via Lambert's Bay) to Mdumbi

Road tripper:
Will Bendix

In a nutshell:
In search of the
perfect wave: from the
West Coast to the Wild
Coast, an epic journey
for surfers and beach
lovers alike.

Logistics
This trip can be done as a fish-hook, so you can fly into Cape Town, drive up the West Coast and then back down and up along the East Coast. Or you can easily do chunks of the trip by flying in to one of the regional airports. The international airport is in Cape Town, and there are local airports at George, Port Elizabeth and East London.

Driving conditions
The N2 is generally well tarred and in very good condition. A vehicle with normal clearance is fine for most routes, but low-slung cars will struggle along some of the West Coast and Wild Coast dirt roads. No matter what car you drive, it's best to take it slowly on these roads and carry an extra spare tyre if you've got the space. Some surf spots are remote and a couple of hours away from decent medical help, so make sure you have a well-stocked first-aid kit. Avoid driving at night along the Wild Coast.

Pet-friendly rating ★ ★ ☆ ☆ ☆
1 = least suited 5 = most suited

Child-friendly rating ★ ★ ★ ★ ☆
1 = least suited 5 = most suited

Low-slung vehicle-friendly rating ★ ★ ☆ ☆ ☆
1 = high clearance 5 = lowest slung

Don't miss
- Elands Bay and the R365 north
- A unique seafood feast at Muisbosskerm south of Lambert's Bay
- Camping on the edge of the sea at Victoria Bay
- The world-famous waves of Supertubes
- The Jeffreys Bay Surf Museum
- The Wild Coast and Mdumbi, home to one of the coolest backpackers in the world

Emergency service numbers
Emergency (from a landline) 10111
Emergency (from a cellphone) 112
AA roadside assistance 086 100 0234 or 083 843 22 (24 hours)

Best time
Autumn into early winter (April to June) offers the best combination of sublime days and good swell along both the east and west coasts. Mid- to late winter (June to August) offers exceptional waves, especially along the east coast, but it's going to be a trade-off with the weather. Expect low temperatures and an equal combination of sunshine and rain. Jeffreys Bay can get especially chilly after a cold front when the southwest wind chill causes temperatures to plummet dramatically.

SUMMER			AUTUMN			WINTER			SPRING		
D	J	F	M	A	M	J	J	A	S	O	N

Background reading
Zigzag magazine, www.zigzag.co.za

Don't forget
Your wetsuit. The water gets freezing up the West Coast but warms considerably along the East Coast. A 3/2mm suit is a good all-rounder for the latter but if you're going in the heart of winter, you'll want to pack a 4/3mm. Temperatures can warm up considerably along the East Coast in summer. All you'll need on those days is your board shorts or bikini.

ON THE SIDE >> In the water
Just as driving has the rules of the road, surfing has its own set of rules and sticking to them will make for a pleasant journey. Keep in mind that many of the surf spots mentioned here have locals who have spent their lives dedicated to these waves. Be respectful of this and you'll generally have no problems.

Sharks are a reality in South Africa and you need to be alert, but don't let this deter your enjoyment. They're really not very interested in us and when you add up the numbers, chances of an incident are still miniscule.

There are many more waves than the ones mentioned here. Go exploring and carve out your own route.

SURFING ROAD TRIP
Cape Town (via Lambert's Bay) to Mdumbi

Section ❶
Cape Town to Lambert's Bay
Distance 265km
Driving Time 3hrs 35mins
Highlights Elands Bay and Baboon Point, secluded beaches along the R365, Muisbosskerm open-air restaurant

Long before the iconic waves of Jeffreys Bay became world famous, a colder, kelpier pilgrimage began 800km away on the West Coast. **Elands Bay** was first surfed by pioneering Cape Town surfer John Whitmore and friends back in 1957 when wetsuits had yet to be invented and the dirt road from Piketberg would take five hours to traverse in a VW Kombi.

Despite the blazing sun and freezing water, the wave was too good to resist and quickly established itself in local surf lore. By the early 1960s there was a steady stream of cars bouncing, sliding and getting stuck along the farm roads leading to this new mecca.

Nowadays the road to Elands Bay is easily covered in a couple of hours from Cape Town via the tarred R27 or along the N7 to Piketberg then the R366 to the coast, but other than that, not much else has changed. Unlike many West Coast dorpies, development at Elands Bay has been slow and kept relatively in check. Aside from the annual Crayfish Festival at nearby Lambert's Bay, the biggest occasion in town is when a new swell rolls in from the Atlantic, closely followed by an influx of wave-hungry pilgrims.

If the waves aren't happening, you can scramble up the mountain at **Baboon Point**, a provincial heritage site and home to Elands Bay Cave, which hosts some excellent examples of San rock paintings. There are endless hours of beachcombing to be had on the southern side of the headland, but heading north is where the real adventure lies.

The **R365** between Elands Bay and Lambert's Bay is 44km of shuddering dirt road that cuts across farm land and rolling sand dunes. The briny smell of the ocean hangs thick in the air and the beaches are hard-packed with mussel shells. This is the real *Weskus* — rugged, raw and desolate — where you can find your own **secluded stretch of sand** and drop off the map. It's also home to a series of temperamental but occasionally excellent waves that can be world class on their day. Farmer Burgers is the best known of these beaches and is imaginatively named after the farmer — a Mr Burger — whose land it borders. Farmer Burgers breaks hard over a shallow reef and is worth having a look at when Elands Bay is dead flat. Even if the waves aren't great, the rocky little bay makes for an idyllic location to spend the afternoon.

Lambert's Bay is the end of the road and home to an average but consistent beach break called Yo-Yo's that breaks left and right and bounces you all the way to the shore. The dirt road north of Lambert's Bay may beckon the intrepid surf traveller, but we'd recommend a vehicle with high clearance and a lot of patience before going further.

ON THE SIDE >> Muisbosskerm
The ultimate post-surf chow down can be had along the R365, but you're going to have to plan in advance. **Muisbosskerm** is a one-of-a-kind seafood restaurant nestled on the beach 5km south of Lambert's Bay. Phone the big number on the signboard to book a place for lunch or dinner (the restaurant is only open if 15 people or more have booked). If you are travelling en masse and have a big enough group, they will open the restaurant and cook up a seafood storm just for you. It's an eat-all-you-can affair of crayfish, mussels, line fish and other saltwater delights plucked from the ocean and done with an assortment of legendary local recipes like waterblommetjies and hanepoot korrelkonfyt. Sink a cold beer under the thatch lapa as the sun drops over the Atlantic and you may never want to leave. Nor do you have to — Muisbosskerm also offers accommodation with good camping sites and a small cottage on the farm land bordering the open-air restaurant.

Fishing boats in Elands Bay

Section ❷
Cape Town to Gansbaai
Distance 180km
Driving Time 2hrs 25mins
Highlights Vintners Surf Classic Contest, Kogelberg Biosphere Reserve, big waves and whale-watching in Hermanus

Koeël Bay

The coastal area between the Boland and the Overberg lies just beyond Cape Town and is often overlooked as a destination for visiting surfers but is home to a variety of waves that lie tucked away between imposing mountains and rolling winelands. This makes it an ideal region to explore, with its scenic roads that hug the coastline. The local surfers even have an annual wine makers' surfing contest, the **Vintners Classic**, where scoring a good barrel is guaranteed one way or the other.

Exiting Cape Town past Somerset West, take the R44 through Gordon's Bay. The road then snakes along the coastal cliffs with spectacular views over False Bay that continue as you round the corner into Koeël Bay. This exquisite stretch of beach is framed by the Hottentots-Holland mountain range and **Kogelberg Biosphere Reserve**, with the best surf found on the western side of the beach beneath a series of caves. It's a steep hike down the path but well worth it for the quality waves that bounce off the cliff and wedge up into a tubing right-hander.

The Kogel Bay Resort is a well-run camp site directly off the road. It spills onto the beach, making this an attractive stopover even if you just want to get away for the weekend. The idyllic location does come with a couple of warning labels, however. The beach can have strong rip currents and was the site of a fatal shark attack on a bodyboarder in 2011. Shark spotters have since been deployed to the area but are not always on duty. If you're feeling especially brave, there's a powerful left point break that comes to life in huge swells on the opposite end of the bay and is appropriately named Paranoias. Approach with caution.

The R44 continues along the coast and takes you deeper into the Boland's waves. Pringle Bay has the occasional good peak in a southeasterly wind, and Betty's Bay can throw up some great beach breaks in a westerly. There are also decent waves at the Kleinmond River mouth when the swell is small. Continue along the R44, turn left on to the R43, and you will join up with the N2 again, making a neat loop. Alternatively, you can branch off onto the R43, which will take you to Hermanus with its fallback wave, Voëlklip. The R43 continues all the way through to Onrus and Gansbaai. There are some very good waves in the Gansbaai region, like Toilets, a crunchy left barrel, but you are going to have to put in your time to score these spots at their best.

ON THE SIDE >> Big waves at Hermanus
Hermanus is famous for the huge **whales** that pull up inside Walker Bay and bask mere metres from the rocks, but it also boasts another massive attraction that you won't find in any tourist brochures. The bay is home to a notorious **big-wave reef** that only kicks into gear on the largest winter swells, when waves topping twenty feet come steaming in from the Indian Ocean. Watching surfers tackle these giant peaks from the safety of the cliffs is like having a front row seat at the Colosseum and offers an equally spectacular alternative to breaching whales. If you're lucky you'll get to see both – the prime whale-watching season from June to November coincides with the best winter swells that roll through until late August. Only get amongst the action yourself if you're extremely competent and have a set of iron lungs for the inevitable wipeouts.

SURFING ROAD TRIP
Cape Town (via Lambert's Bay) to Mdumbi

Section ❸
Stilbaai to Mossel Bay
Distance 130km
Driving Time 2hrs 10mins
Highlight Start of the Garden Route

Just where exactly the **Garden Route** begins is still a hotly debated topic among locals, but everyone agrees that the coastline stretching from Stilbaai to Plettenberg Bay is some of the most beautiful in the world. And the good news for surfers is it comes laden with waves.

Heading east on the N2 past Heidelberg are a number of easy-to-reach holiday towns, the most famous of which is Stilbaai, home to a classic right-hand point break. It lies at the end of the R305 on the western side of the town. Turn right over the bridge and travel for 4km along Main Road. The point is located just inside the Skulpiesbaai Nature Reserve opposite the NSRI station and turns a solid southwest swell into thigh-aching long rides that end at the break wall.

TIP

> The rip current washing down the point can become horrendous — sometimes it's easier to just get out and walk back up the point rather than battle against the liquid treadmill.

If Stilbaai is small, turn right onto the Jongensfontein road and head west for 10km until you reach Groot-Jongensfontein where an exposed reef serves up rippable waves when the wind is light or from the northwest. It's conveniently close to the Jongensfontein Municipal Camp Site, which has excellent facilities to match the view, making it a great place to bunk down whether you're pitching a tent, parking your caravan or looking for a self-catering apartment.

The coastline heading east towards Mossel Bay is made up of rolling hills, farm land and nature reserves, with the best waves found sheltered inside large headlands. This is great for funnelling the dominant southwest winds into perfect offshore conditions, but makes it hard for the prevailing southwest swells to sneak in. Rare east or southeasterly swells produce excellent waves at Vleesbaai, which has been compared to Bruce's Beauties for sheer perfection and length of ride when it does work. You can reach Vleesbaai by heading approximately 5km out of Stilbaai on the R305 and then swinging right at the T-junction. From there it's a circuit board of unmarked dirt roads heading east until you reach the R325. Cross the Gourits River and follow the Vleesbaai signposts that will take you to the small coastal town. Be aware, however, that Vleesbaai is located on private land and access is restricted, but day visitors are generally allowed.

Searching for the right surf spot

TIP

> It's a fun drive along the back roads even if you get a bit lost — just ask for directions at one of the authentic farm stalls along the way and buy some delicious home-made goodies while you're at it. Alternatively you can rejoin the N2 from Stilbaai and simply turn right at the Vleesbaai turn-off.

Section ④
Mossel Bay to Plettenberg Bay
Distance 138km
Driving Time 2hrs 25mins
Highlights Victoria Bay, Gericke's Point beach walks and snorkelling, Steam Whistle Stop Café, Robberg Peninsula and Nature Reserve

Mossel Bay was the first place that Europeans, led by Bartolomeu Dias, landed on South African soil way back in 1488. It later became famous for its historic Milkwood 'postbox' where early explorers would leave messages for one another tied to the famous tree. The initial excursion ended abruptly for Dias though, when he was chased away in a hail of stones by unimpressed locals. The resident surfers today are generally a friendlier bunch and there's a strong local scene focused around the town's two main waves, Inner Pool and Outer Pool, which are easily located in front of the Point Caravan Park at the end of Point Road.

To get there, take the R102 turn-off from the N2 and head east along Louis Fourie Road until you reach the centre of town. Turn right into Marsh Street until it finally becomes Point Road. Inner Pool is where the 'lighties' learn to surf and the fun waves are a hotbed of talent on any given day. Outer Pool is a more demanding reef break with a notoriously shallow inside reef that can throw up wide barrels or smear you across the rocks.

There are a number of other surf spots in and around Mossel Bay, but the next real gem is **Victoria Bay**, 57km northeast along the N2. Vic Bay, as it's commonly known, is clearly signposted and easily reached from the N2 turn-off. The winding road drops deep into a valley and spits you out onto a small boulder-strewn beach flanked on either side by lush mountains. The bay is home to a consistent right point that is the cornerstone of surfing in the region and makes for a dramatic setting as waves smash up against the rocky cliffs then roll for hundreds of metres into the sheltered cove. Local surfers have been known to get a bit tetchy with visitors, but if you take it easy there shouldn't be any hassles.

This is definitely a place you want to spend a few days and there are numerous options to bunk down in. The best is Land's End on the tip of the point, where you can literally roll out of bed and into the line-up – it doesn't claim to be 'the closest accommodation to the sea in Africa' for nothing. Owner Rod Hossack is a wealth of local knowledge and can tell you what the surf will be doing better than any wave forecast simply by licking his index finger and sticking it in the air. Land's End has a variety of exceptional self-catering apartments, all with their own sun deck or verandah.

Wilderness Beach

Alternatively, the Victoria Bay Caravan Park boasts one of the most spectacular views along the Garden Route. There are a number of sites on the hill, overlooking the bay with Wilderness in the distance. Holidays can get chaotic, but being lulled to sleep by the roar of the ocean then watching the sun rise from your tent with dolphins slicing through the waves below makes for an unforgettable experience.

The road between Victoria Bay and Plettenberg Bay is pockmarked with waves, but they are relatively average or fickle. When the swell is small and easterly, **Gericke's Point** offers a nice alternative. It's a hollow left that breaks off the western side of a sandstone outcrop and favours the northeast wind, which ruins most other waves in the area. Those in the know also call Gericke's Point one of the Garden Route's best-kept secrets, thanks to its stunning **beach walks** past sandstone cliffs that are actually fossilised dunes. The point also makes a brilliant vantage point to spy passing whales, and there is excellent **snorkelling** and plenty of sea life around the rock shelf on low tide.

To get to Gericke's Point, take the Swartvlei turn-off from the N2 approximately 5km before Sedgefield. Park at Swartvlei beach and walk southwest towards the rocky outcrop – you can't miss it. Swartvlei is also gorgeous, and southern right whales are a common sight from July to August, but visitors are warned about leaving valuables unattended in the car.

TIP

There isn't much in terms of surf in nearby Sedgefield, but the **Steam Whistle Stop Café** serves one of the best breakfasts and coffees along the Garden Route and can be found on Owl Street just off the main road. It's located at the old train station that used to service the Outeniqua Choo-Tjoe. The pies are almost as legendary as the decommissioned locomotive.

SURFING ROAD TRIP
Cape Town (via Lambert's Bay) to Mdumbi

Buffelsbaai, 5km before Knysna, is home to a slow rolling point break and a great place to detour before heading on to Plettenberg Bay. Plett is far more famous – or infamous – for the annual Matric Rage than it is for waves, but there are some good breaks in the area. The Wreck lies nestled inside the Robberg Peninsula and occasionally serves up excellent beach break peaks. To get there, turn right into Piesang Valley Road off the N2, approximately 500m before the main traffic circle leading into Plett, and follow the road until Robberg Road, where you turn right again. Follow Robberg Road all the way to the **Robberg Nature Reserve** and then turn left to access the beach. You'll find it at the bottom of a long flight of wooden steps.

The **Robberg Peninsula** sticks into the sea like a barnacle-encrusted finger and provides an epic setting to spend the day. If you're surfed out, take a scenic hike around the nature reserve trail. It takes you along the tip of the peninsula and offers amazing views that explain why early Portuguese explorers named Plett 'Bahia Formosa', or Beautiful Bay.

TIP The Surf Café is a little gem located in Piesang Valley that serves amazing food and is the social hub of the local surf scene. They host regular bands and Open Mic nights, and it's the perfect place to hit if you're feeling hungry or in search of a good time – or both.

Moving east into the thick of the action, the Wedge is a popular spot for bodyboarders – it's just in front of the landmark Beacon Island Hotel. Swells refract off a clump of rocks here and bounce up unexpectedly over a shallow sandbank. It's a tricky wave that offers plenty of entertainment even from the beach as unsuccessful riders get launched into the air by the hectic backwash.

Heading northeast past the Wedge is Lookout, an average spot that stretches into Keurbooms Beach, which can produce excellent waves but is known to be sharky.

ON THE SIDE >> The power of nature

Lookout Beach has experienced both sides of fame and fortune at the hands of nature. After the dramatic floods in 2007, dubbed 'the 20-year storm', the Keurbooms River mouth was diverted towards the rocks along Lookout Point. This ruined the beach for holiday-makers but created a dream wave for surfers, as sediment flowing out the estuary built up along the rocks and sculpted a world-class wave. Imagine living next door to a go-cart track all your life then waking up one morning to see it has transformed to Le Mans. It wasn't long before the 'Plett Superbank' was giving J-Bay a run for its money.

Torrential rains in October 2012, however, reversed the process. Intense flooding forced another river mouth to open up further north along the beach, quickly shifting the flow of sediment away from the rocks. The mouth has since closed up, the wave disappeared and the beach re-appeared. Nobody knows if the Superbank will ever come back, but locals can often be found at the top of Lookout Point, staring wistfully out to sea and wondering when the next 20-year storm is coming.

Robberg Peninsula

Section ⑤
Plettenberg Bay to Jeffreys Bay
Distance 204km
Driving Time 2hrs 30mins
Highlights The world-famous waves of Supertubes, Jeffreys Bay Surf Museum, Cape St Francis Wild Side

Driving east from Plettenberg Bay along the N2, the Outeniqua mountain range creeps closer to the coast and you find yourself wedged between mountain and sea. You know you're approaching Jeffreys Bay when you start to see the iconic red aloes that frame the road and the dense smell of fynbos fills the air.

J-Bay used to be nothing more than a small Afrikaans fishing dorpie, a lonely outpost licked by the salty sea breeze and frigid southwest winds that howl off the mountains in winter. Then in the 1960s John Whitmore discovered the endless waves that roll down the point, and the floodgates opened.

Local and foreign surfers flocked to this new Holy Grail as the conservative fishing village unwittingly became a hotbed of 70s counterculture. Surfers camped in the towering sand dunes for months on end, while farmers locked up their daughters and grabbed their shotguns. Tensions quickly rose between the new immigrants and the local community. The town was reportedly even under surveillance by the CIA thanks to the influx of narcotics and some of surfing's most eccentric characters — like multi-millionaire Bunker Spreckles, who was heir to a sugar baron fortune, Clarke Gable's stepson and an ardent disciple of LSD.

By the early 1980s tensions had reached breaking point. Ironically it was J-Bay's first major surfing contest, the 1984 Country Feeling Classic, that bridged the divide. As the sport entered a new era of professionalism, local residents came round to the fact that this surfing thing was actually good for business, and the town has never looked back since.

All of J-Bay's best waves are easily located off Da Gama Road, which runs parallel to the ocean. If you are approaching from the western side of town, take the R676 turn-off from the N2 and follow the road until it becomes St Francis Street. As you near the ocean, turn left into De Reyger Street, and then left again into Da Gama Road. Follow Da Gama Road for approximately 1.5km and then turn right into Pepper Street. The short cul-de-sac ends at the iconic board-walk overlooking J-Bay's finest wave, Supertubes.

Even if you're not a surfer, watching **Supertubes** in full cry from the boardwalk is a beautiful sight to behold. Long bands of swell that have travelled all the way from Antarctica finally make landfall at the top of the point, also known as Boneyards. The wave then screeches down the rocks at breakneck speed, gaining momentum as all the energy gets squeezed into the bay, where the wave tubes relentlessly towards Impossibles, the end section of the wave.

Riding the waves

Supertubes was actually deemed 'impossible' to ride by the early pioneers who opted to surf the Point instead — a far more mellow version of perfection that lies tucked further down inside the bay. You can either walk there from Supertubes or continue along Da Gama Road and then turn right into Tacoma Road. Park in the parking lot and the wave is directly in front of you. On really big days you may be lucky enough to get a ride all the way from Boneyards to the Point, a distance of over 1km, but you'd better make sure your legs are up to the task.

> **TIP**
> Supertubes is often affected by the northwesterly 'Devil Wind' on winter mornings. The wind blows up the wave face and creates a fierce cross-chop that makes it difficult to ride. Rather head east around the corner to Magna Tubes or Kitchen Windows, which operate nicely in these conditions.

There's no lack of accommodation or places to eat in J-Bay and the town is awash with surf shops. A great budget option is Cristal Cove, conveniently located within two minutes' walk from Supertubes. They offer everything from dorm beds to self-catering units. It's a friendly, well-run place and comes highly recommended. If you want to live it up with a plush sea view, there are a number of excellent options right on the beach overlooking Supertubes. African Perfection has B&B suites and rooms, while Beach Music offers singles, doubles and the penthouse at affordable rates.

For the best fish and chips in town, hit the legendary Trawlers Take Away along Da Gama Road. Then there's InFood, a deli and restaurant with an amazing menu — plenty of healthy alternatives and organic options. The coffee alone is worth the visit. If you're looking for a big night out, the Mexican is the place to be and gets really raucous during the holiday season. Line your stomach with some of their tasty Tex-Mex grub while you're about it.

SURFING ROAD TRIP
Cape Town (via Lambert's Bay) to Mdumbi

If the intensity of J-Bay gets too much, it's time to visit Cape St Francis. Head back out of town towards the N2 and turn left onto the R102 that takes you to Humansdorp. Turn right onto the R330 and follow the road for 25km until you reach Cape St Francis, with its iconic lighthouse on the tip of Seal Point. Seal Point has nowhere near the world-class status of Supertubes, but it's a long, fun wave that has the advantage of getting swell when J-Bay is flat. The beach break at the bottom of the point can serve up grinding tubes when the sandbanks are aligned. Cape St Francis has managed to retain the feel of a small village and is a far more laid-back experience than Jeffreys Bay, making it a great place to spend a holiday.

ON THE SIDE >> The Wild Side
The **Wild Side** is an exquisite stretch of coast, flanked by private nature reserves, that starts on the eastern side of **Cape St Francis**. There are several hiking trails all the way to Oyster Bay, approximately 20km away. Along the way you will pass historical Strandloper middens and fish traps near Thysbaai. You may also see some secret waves that break hard over an assortment of reefs in the area, but bring your A-game: these waves are for advanced surfers only. If you prefer your scenery with less exertion, the rocks at the start of the Wild Side are a spectacular place to have a sundowner.

TIP

Visit the **Jeffreys Bay Surf Museum** for a fascinating overview on how the town has evolved over the decades. The museum houses a number of vintage surfboards and historical photos documenting the beachfront from when it was just rolling sand dunes and donkey cart tracks to the

Cape St Francis Lighthouse

PADKOS

Some home-made pizza from the night before is hard to beat. We've got a pretty good recipe down too — caramelised onion, aubergines or butternut, olives and feta all taste even better the next day. Make an extra one for the road, along with a flask of coffee, and you're set. My favourite stop on my surfing route is Nanaga on the N2. I'm not much of a meat eater, but they do the best ever *roosterbrood* with fillet that alone is almost worth the drive from Cape Town or Durban. The coffee is also pretty damn good.

Section ❻
Jeffreys Bay to Chintsa West
Distance 414km
Driving Time 4hrs 50mins
Highlights Nahoon Reef, Wild Coast Jikileza

The N2 from Jeffreys Bay takes you through Port Elizabeth, and then inland past Grahamstown, before dropping back down to the coast through King William's Town and on to East London.

Nahoon Reef is the epicentre of surfing in East London and is located at the end of the Nahoon River. It's a consistent, powerful wave around which many East London surfers have developed their style. There's also a good inside break called Nahoon Corner that prefers a high tide and more east in the swell. The area is home to a number of other good waves but if you're looking for a real slice of Eastern Cape paradise, head for the **Wild Coast Jikileza**.

Located off the N2, the Jikileza route comprises a number of idyllic bays, beaches and points that are connected by a maze of roads. You can easily visit the area from East London, but the best thing to do is base yourself at one of the little villages like Chintsa West, home to the legendary Buccaneers Backpackers. Getting there is a bit tricky, and they strongly advise not following the 'shortest route' on your GPS. Rather take the East Coast Resorts Road (R102) off the N2, which will take you past the Crossways Spar and Retail Park and on to the T1. As you dip up and down the verdant hills, you'll catch glimpses of the ocean beckoning in the distance. Continue along the road until you see the Chintsa West turn-off, then turn right and follow the road for approximately 1km before turning left into the Buccaneers dirt road.

Buccaneers sits above the Chintsa estuary and offers a variety of accommodation with spectacular views. A favourite is the tented camp. It has tents with single or double beds built onto a deck among the milkwood trees overlooking the estuary and beach. It can get rowdy during varsity holidays and long weekends, but most other times it's blissfully mellow. The beach out front has some average waves, but if you head towards the rocks on the south side, there is a high-quality reef break that works in big swells. It's a shallow, demanding spot that you should only surf on a high tide. There are a myriad other quality waves in the area but all require a drive.

Yellow Sands is at the mouth of the Kwelera River and offers a fickle but good right point break on the outside and a speedy beach break in front of the river mouth. To get there from Chintsa, get back onto the T1 and head southwest, following the Kwelera River signs. Yellow Sands is a great place to set up camp for the day and has braai spots overlooking the surf. If you want to stay a little longer, there is an excellent camp site on the opposite side of the river, with the beach literally on your doorstep.

Between Yellow Sands and Chintsa is Queensberry Bay, a classy right reef that can offer exceptional waves when there's a good swell running and the wind is from the northwest. Glen Eden is a fairly good beach break around the corner from Queensberry – just walk west around the point. Both spots are reached by the T6 via the T1.

Surf culture

SURFING ROAD TRIP
Cape Town (via Lambert's Bay) to Mdumbi

Section 7
East London to Mdumbi
Distance 204km
Driving Time 2hrs 30mins
Highlights Mdumbi Point and Backpackers, Lwandile hiking and surfing

As you snake over the twisting Kei River Pass, you are entering South Africa's last untouched surfing frontier. The Wild Coast is riddled with high-quality waves that were first explored by intrepid surfers as far back as the 1970s. They would navigate the non-existent roads in their VW Kombis and Beetles, somehow making it to the coast, and come back with tales of perfect virgin waves ridden only by dolphins. Although the roads have improved in relative terms, the region remains largely untouched by surfers thanks to its isolation and the perceived threat of sharks. There is reason to be cautious – Port St Johns in the north has had several fatal attacks in the past five years – but other spots have been surfed for decades without incident.

You could spend years exploring the Kei's surf potential along its washboard dirt roads, but we'd recommend cutting straight to the chase and heading for Mdumbi. Getting there is relatively straightforward. Take the turn-off for Coffee Bay 5km before Mthatha on the N2. Drive towards the coast, following the Coffee Bay signs all the way. The road is mostly tarred but watch out for wheel-eating potholes and the obligatory cows. As you dip down towards the sea, the parched landscape becomes flecked with subtropical bush. After 70km there's a signposted turn-off for Mdumbi, and from here it's another 25km along a dirt road that gets rough in places but generally isn't a problem if you take it slowly. The road eventually deposits you at the **Mdumbi Backpackers**, perched on a hill overlooking a majestic river and beach.

It's an exceptional place to stay for a number of reasons: from the traditional Xhosa huts kitted out in rustic comfort to the fact that 30% of the business is owned by local employees, with 10% of all profits going back to the local community. Best of all, one of South Africa's finest waves is just a short amble down the hill.

Mdumbi Backpackers

TIP

You're a long way away from any convenience stores, so bring supplies. Mdumbi Backpackers make delicious meals but do not run a shop and encourage you rather to support the local community. Beers and basics can be purchased from the nearby spaza. Don't miss out on the eat-all-you-can fish braai once a week.

Mdumbi Point comes alive during deep winter swells in similar conditions to J-Bay, except here you'll be surfing only with a handful of mates and the resident dolphins. The surf can get phenomenal depending on the sandbanks that build up against the rocky point. At its best you're looking at a ride of 500m and more that takes you deep into the bay. The beach break also has fun peaks in summer, and if you're up for a mission, **Lwandile** is another top-quality point break a one-hour hike northwards along the coast. You'll know you're there when you reach the next major headland running into a bay with a long beach.

Former pro surfer Justin Saunders and his wife Lee-Anne also run the highly recommended Swell Tours from their lodge in Mdumbi. They offer everything from accommodation to exploratory trips of the surrounding coast, and you're guaranteed to get the best waves with Justin leading the way. Coffee Bay is a 45min drive west and is a far more raucous affair, with a few average waves set against spectacular scenery. If you're looking for a party, it's the place to go, but Mdumbi makes an excellent base from which to explore the rest of the Transkei and meet like-minded travellers. There's still an untapped wealth of waves out there waiting for the adventurous.

ON THE SIDE >> Wild water
The edge of the continental shelf lies closer to the Wild Coast than anywhere else in South Africa. This makes it notorious for shipwrecks and freak waves that smash up against the cliffs and have been known to claim the lives of unsuspecting fishermen. If the sea is wild, rather admire from a distance.

End of a long surfing day

SURFING ROAD TRIP Contact details

African Perfection
042 293 1401
www.africanperfection.co.za
Beach Music
042 293 2291
www.beachmusic.co.za
Buccaneers Backpackers
043 734 3012
www.cintsa.com
Cristal Cove
042 293 2101
www.cristalcove.co.za
Elands Bay Hotel
022 972 1640
www.elandsbayhotel.co.za
InFood
042 293 1880
www.infood.co.za
Jongensfontein Municipal Camp Site
028 755 8015
www.campsa.co.za
Kogel Bay Resort
021 850 4172
Land's End Guesthouse
044 889 0123
www.vicbay.com
Mdumbi Backpackers
083 461 1834
www.mdumbi.co.za
Muisbosskerm
027 432 1017
www.muisbosskerm.co.za
Point Caravan Park, Mossel Bay
044 690 3501
www.visitmosselbay.co.za
Steam Whistle Stop Café
044 343 1052
www.visitsedgefield.com
Swell Tours
082 893 7717
www.swelltours.com
The Mexican Grill and Restaurant
072 447 7148
The Surf Café
044 533 6801
www.surfcafeplett.com
Trawlers Take Aways
042 293 1353
Victoria Bay Caravan Park
044 889 0081
www.victoriabaycaravanpark.co.za
Yellow Sands Caravan Park
043 734 3043
www.yellows.co.za

Regional info
www.capewestcoast.org
www.cintsa.com
www.elandsbay.co.za
www.gardenroute.co.za
www.gardenrouteadventureguide.com
www.hermanus.co.za
www.hessequa.net
www.jeffreysbaytourism.org
www.kogelbergbiospherereserve.co.za
www.lambertsbay.co.za
www.plettenbergbay.co.za
www.stilbaaitourism.co.za
www.wildcoast.co.za

GOLF ROAD TRIP
Ballito to KwaZulu-Natal/Wild Coast border

I spent my youngest years in Durban. Some of my earliest memories are of knocking plastic golf balls around our yard with a set of 'knock-down' irons.

Pitching those plastic balls up and down the lawn; chipping around sandy flowerbeds; hitting knock-down wedges out from under thickets of coastal bush; and taking in full lungs of sultry sea air that drifted in from the Indian Ocean — this was when the very tangible, visceral, sensual (it always seems to engage *all* of your senses) nature of KwaZulu-Natal golf was impressed upon me.

The great travellers have always told us that the most enriching travel experiences are often a result of not just notching up the clichéd 'sights and sounds' of the journey but also getting to grips with the more subtle smell and feel and taste of the things we experience along the way.

I've been lucky to have played some of the best (and the worst/un-engaging) golf courses around South Africa. For me, golf in KwaZulu-Natal, especially golf along the coastline, seems to be like one of these enriching travel experiences. You can see it, hear it, smell it, feel it, and even taste the salty Indian Ocean air and sweet hints of sugar cane wafting around an elevated tee, or curry at the 19th hole.

Of course, what makes it all so damn fantastic is that there is a bunch of great quality golf courses (some of them superb) dotted along the KwaZulu-Natal coastline. And a road trip here could very well be South Africa's ultimate golf experience.

Total Distance 225km
Driving Time (excluding golf and stopovers) 3hrs 30mins

....

Section ❶
Ballito to Durban
Distance 45km
Driving Time 1hr
Courses to be played Simbithi, Zimbali, Beachwood
Highlights:
The Litchi Orchard
Cocktails at the Lighthouse Bar
Views of ocean and lagoons driving south along the M4
Sunrise cycle/run/walk along Durban beachfront promenade
uShaka Marine World
Other courses en route (Prince's Grant, Umhlali, Mount Edgecombe, Royal Durban, Durban Country Club)
SEE PAGES 196–197

....

Section ❷
Durban to Pennington
Distance 75km
Driving Time 1hr
Courses to be played Selborne, Umdoni Park
Highlights:
Sunrise swim in the Indian Ocean at Scottburgh
Other courses en route (uMkomaas, Scottburgh)
SEE PAGES 197–198

....

Section ❸
Pennington to KwaZulu-Natal/Wild Coast border
Distance 105km
Driving Time 1hr 30mins
Courses to be played Southbroom, Wild Coast Sun
Highlights:
Horse ride/beach walk along the Trafalgar Marine Reserve shoreline
Oribi Gorge Nature Reserve (zipline at Oribi Gorge)
Other courses en route (San Lameer, Port Shepstone, Margate, Port Edward).
SEE PAGE 198

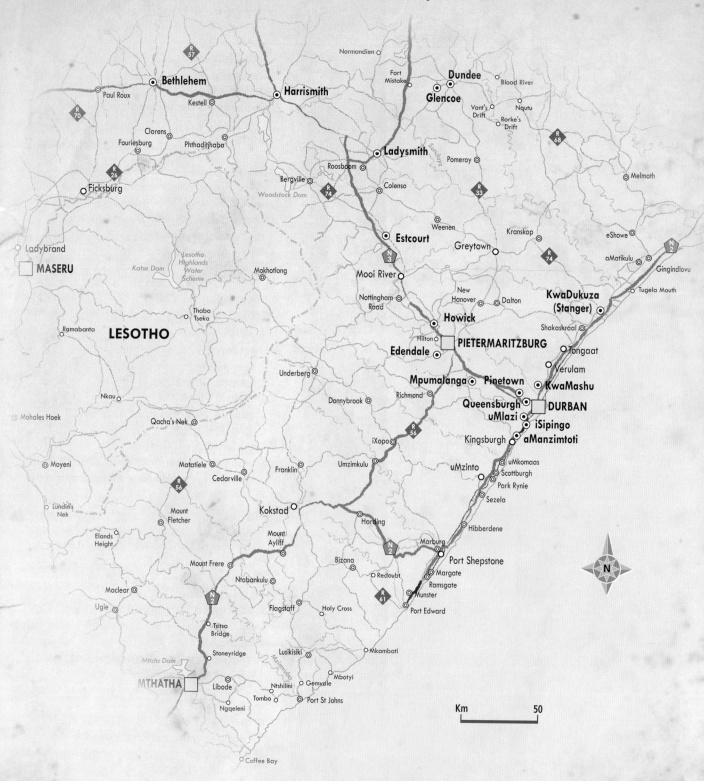

ON THE SIDE >> Right place, right time
In the 2012–13 season, the South African Sunshine Tour hosted a remarkable six tournaments co-sanctioned with the European Tour (one of the two biggest tours in the world). That is more than any other country at the moment, and it shows the confidence the professional golf world community has for South Africa's golf courses and golf culture.

PADKOS

If travelling along the KwaZulu-Natal coastline, you'd do well to make some of these quirky, tasty treats part of your trip:

Sugar cane: Small bundles of sugar cane can be bought from informal vendors along the North Coast roads, often next to the sugar cane plantations. It's messy eating – but an iconic KwaZulu-Natal snack.

Bunny chow: A Durban 'bunny' is a half-loaf of bread hollowed out and filled with mutton, lamb, chicken or bean curry, and a side portion of grated carrot, chilli and onion salad. Again, it's messy eating, but an essential Durban experience. Ask a local where to buy the best.

Samoosas: Half a dozen of these savoury pastry snacks (lamb, chicken, potato or sweetcorn filling) go splendidly well with a road trip. The best are the home-made variety bought from local markets or home-industry style eateries. Delicious with a saucy chilli dip or mango chutney.

Fish and chips: Fish and chips have always represented a certain anti-opulence in food. In much of Africa, the best food experiences are often found at informal, hole-in-the-wall eateries. And the same rings true for fish and chips along the KZN coastline. Often, the most delicious parcels – wrapped in newspaper or in polystyrene boxes – are found at small takeaways or at corner cafés in quaint seaside suburbs.

Road tripper:
Paul Winter

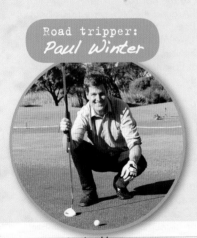

In a nutshell:
Playing golf and travelling along the KwaZulu-Natal South and North Coast is arguably South Africa's ultimate golf road trip.

Logistics
This road trip is designed to be done as a linear trip from north to south along the KwaZulu-Natal coastline. Ideally, you'll fly into Durban (King Shaka International airport), pick up a rental car at the airport, and then head north towards the start at Simbithi Country Club or Ballito (same area). From here, you'll play Simbithi on the first full day, followed by a different course every day (or every second day or so) as you head south – Zimbali, Beachwood, Selborne, Umdoni Park, Southbroom, and the Wild Coast Sun. The selection of courses listed here reflects the diversity of golf available to travellers. However, there are a number of other courses in the area that are spectacular and well worth playing if you have time.

Driving conditions
You'll need a car with lots of space for golf bags and kit. The roads and towns get frantically crowded over the festive season (December/January). You'll always be a few minutes away from shops/restaurants/accommodation along this route.

Pet-friendly rating ★ ★ ☆ ☆ ☆
1 = least suited 5 = most suited
Best leave the pooch at home.

Child-friendly rating ★ ★ ★ ☆ ☆
1 = least suited 5 = most suited
Potentially excellent (★ ★ ★ ★ ★) if there's someone to hang out with the kids while you're playing golf.

Low-slung vehicle-friendly rating ★ ★ ★ ★ ★
1 = high clearance 5 = lowest slung

Don't miss
- Cocktails or cold beers at the Lighthouse Bar, uMhlanga (beautiful view of the Indian Ocean)
- At least a few dips in the Indian Ocean – there are lifeguards on duty at most of the popular beaches
- The Oribi Gorge Nature Reserve
- Cycle/run/walk along the Durban promenade

Emergency service numbers
Emergency (from a landline) 10111
Emergency (from a cellphone) 112
AA roadside assistance 086 100 0234 or 083 843 22 (24 hours)

Best time
The best time to play is late summer, autumn, and even winter, when there is less rain, less wind and milder temperatures.

SUMMER			AUTUMN			WINTER			SPRING		
D	J	F	M	A	M	J	J	A	S	O	N

Background reading
Most courses in KwaZulu-Natal are well represented online, with up-to-date green fees, news of weekly club competitions and more. *Golf Digest* magazine publishes an informative and well-researched South African Top 100 courses guide (www.golfdigest.co.za) every year. More information is available on the website of the KwaZulu-Natal Tourism Board (www.zulu.org.za).

Don't forget
Remember to book and confirm all tee-off times. As per good golfing etiquette, give yourself plenty of time to be ready for your start time, and respect the club's dress code.

GOLF ROAD TRIP
Ballito to KwaZulu-Natal/Wild Coast border

Section ❶
Ballito to Durban
Distance 45km
Driving Time 1hr
Courses to be played Simbithi, Zimbali, Beachwood
Highlights The Litchi Orchard, Cocktails at the Lighthouse Bar, views of ocean and lagoons driving south along the M4, sunrise cycle/run/walk along Durban beachfront promenade, uShaka Marine World, other courses en route (Prince's Grant, Umhlali, Mount Edgecombe, Royal Durban, Durban Country Club)

Okay, so let's assume we've just arrived in Ballito, the small town on the North Coast of KwaZulu-Natal. A few hours ago, our flight touched down at King Shaka International. We picked up our rental car and drove the few minutes north along the N2 to end up here. For a golfing road trip like this, we chose a large sedan with lots of room for three or four adults — plus golf bags and luggage.

Tonight, we've chosen to stay at the four-star Forest Lodge, a three-bedroom luxury home on the Simbithi Eco Estate itself, right next to the golf course.

We haven't any plans for this afternoon, so we head for a late lunch at the **Litchi Orchard**, which is a popular, farm-style eatery and market that uses lots of locally grown produce in their dishes. (They also sell boxes of litchis in season, picked from their orchard of about 300 litchi trees.) We aren't travelling with the kids this time, but they would have loved the resident gang of mongooses.

In the afternoon, the Indian Ocean looks spectacular. We shoot down to the Salt Rock beach and tidal pool for a swim. While we're contemplating how life could not be better, a pod of dolphins appears just beyond the surf line. We claim this as the official send-off for the journey.

The next day, we get down to business at **Simbithi**. Due to its very short length (under 4,500m) and number of par-3s (13 in total), Simbithi has the qualities of an extremely high-quality mashie course — but with the design (by Peter Matkovich), prestige, aesthetics and technical challenge of a championship 18-hole course. Simbithi is an excellent 'warm-up' for a golf trip. Of course, your short game needs to be in great shape, especially for holes like the par-3 17th. It's named *isiqhingana*, which is Zulu for 'the tiniest island'. Unless your pitching is spot on from the tee here, your ball will end up in the water!

After playing Simbithi, we phone and confirm our tee-times for tomorrow's round at Zimbali. On advice from a local, we eat at the nearby Crayfish Inn, which does great seafood. Around the table, we talk about the five fantastic courses in the area that we don't have time to play — Umhlali, Prince's Grant, Mount Edgecombe, Royal Durban, and Durban Country Club. That night, we stay at Fairmont Zimbali Lodge on the Zimbali Coastal Estate.

The next day at **Zimbali** (which was recently ranked 25th on the *Golf Digest* magazine's acclaimed Top 100 Golf Courses in South Africa list), we feel the effect of playing golf at sea level. We all normally play at higher altitudes, so we're used to our drives and tee shots flying further in the thinner air. Zimbali is a delight to play and the views out over the Indian Ocean are spectacular. There seems to be something in the air at Zimbali that proclaims, '*this* is the KwaZulu-Natal golf experience'. Carts are compulsory here, but we'd walk this course dozens of times if we could.

Simbithi

Lighthouse Bar

Section ❷
Durban to Pennington
Distance 75km
Driving Time 1hr
Courses to be played Selborne, Umdoni Park
Highlight Sunrise swim in the Indian Ocean at Scottburgh, other courses en route (uMkomaas, Scottburgh)

After Zimbali, in the afternoon, we continue the road trip south to the coastal town of uMhlanga. Instead of the quicker route via the N2 highway, we opt for the slower, more **scenic M4 coastal route**. The contrast of the bright green of the coastal bush with intermittent views of the blue Indian Ocean is unforgettable.

In uMhlanga, we're booked into the Oyster Box Hotel. We check in, and meet up for cocktails at the hotel's **Lighthouse Bar**, where we have a panoramic view of the beach, the ocean, and the lighthouse just out front. After that, we eat at the vibey Gringos Mexican Canteen, near the hotel. The next morning, in order to make our tee-off time at Beachwood, we have to leave early. It's not easy missing out on a French toast breakfast at the uMhlanga Surf Lifesaving Club, which is highly recommended by locals.

It's only a few minutes (under 10km) from uMhlanga to **Beachwood**. Driving along the M4, you have to take the Virginia Airport (Exit 5) off-ramp and backtrack slightly to get here. If there was a course in KwaZulu-Natal that could be called a links-style layout, then it's Beachwood. An interesting aspect of the course is that it lies at the southern end of Virginia Airport, so it's interesting to watch the light aircraft taking off directly overhead. Beachwood's signature hole is the par-4 6th – a very demanding 410m dogleg left, which is set high in the dunes. Coastal bush, a stream and a water hazard all have to be negotiated en route to the green.

We've just had three fantastic rounds of golf in three days, and this afternoon we begin Section 2 of our road trip. As we negotiate our way through Durban and head south, we make one last stop at a hole-in-the-wall type of take-away joint, and purchase four traditional bunny chows for the road. The 'bunny' is a kind of fast-food curry served in a hollowed-out half-loaf of bread and held in high esteem by Durbanites.

For the sake of the road trip, just after aManzimtoti we get onto the slightly quieter R102 and track the coastline down past uMkomaas, Green Point, and then into **Scottburgh**, where we'll be spending the night at Eden River Lodge.

After three days of golf in a row, we schedule the following day as a 'rest' day – which is to be spent milling around Scottburgh's beachfront and soaking up the spirit of the South Coast.

Two factors conspire to make **mornings a good time to swim** along this coastline. First, the sun rises out of the sea (eastern horizon), so you'll often be swimming with a gorgeous sunrise in front of you. Second, the sea's surface would probably have been combed smooth by the prevailing land breezes that blow gently through the night and into the morning.

We again spend the night at Eden River Lodge. Then, the next day, we drive the 20 or so minutes south along the R102 to play **Selborne**. The golf here is excellent. But what makes the experience even more engaging is that a round can be shared with bushbuck, grey duiker and rare blue duiker, as well as other wildlife like monkeys and mongooses, and apparently there are over 160 species of birds. Selborne demands a high degree of course management, and there are a number of par-4s that require weighing up the odds of going for the green with one long risky tee shot, or playing it safe and taking a guaranteed two to get there.

ON THE SIDE >> Extras
- A **walk, run or cycle along the Durban beachfront promenade** – Bike and Saddle do guided cycle tours along the Durban beachfront
- **uShaka Marine World**
- Big Rush swing at Moses Mabhida Stadium
- Rickshaw ride

Teeing off

After another night at Eden River Lodge, the next morning is spent playing **Umdoni Park**. All of the dozens of reviews that have been written about Umdoni Park mention something along the lines of the course being an 'undiscovered gem of the South Coast', or 'one of South Africa's most underrated'. And this is all true. It is a fantastic, feel-good (quite short) and fun 18 holes. The front nine holes run along the coastline, with the back nine stretching inland through Umdoni's indigenous forest vegetation.

Umdoni Park means we've come to the end of Section 2 of our road trip — from Durban to Pennington. We haul ourselves back into the car, and cruise off into Section 3 — driving slightly inland for a few kilometres along the R102, and then linking back to the coastline, joining the R620 and easing into Shelly Beach.

ON THE SIDE >> uMkomaas

One of the special courses along the South Coast is uMkomaas. It's a quaint, quiet, good-quality 18-hole layout much adored by its members. What makes uMkomaas rather remarkable is that this is where the well-known PGA golf professional, Tim Clark, grew up and learned to play. Clark is one of South Africa's greatest golfers. He has won several events on the Major tours around the world, and achieved international acclaim when he won the 2010 Players Championship, which is considered the golfing world's 'Fifth Major'.

Section ❸
Pennington to KwaZulu-Natal/Wild Coast border
Distance 105km
Driving Time 1hr 30mins
Courses to be played Southbroom, Wild Coast Sun
Highlights Horse ride/beach walk along the Trafalgar Marine Reserve shoreline, Oribi Gorge Nature Reserve (zipline at Oribi Gorge), other courses en route (San Lameer, Port Shepstone, Margate, Port Edward).

Shelly Beach is a little town that turns out to be a hub of activity along this coastline. Here, on the first night of Section 3 of our trip, we check into Izotsha Creek, just inland of Shelly Beach.

The next day we tee off at **Southbroom**, host to the South African Women's Open in 2013. Unfortunately, rain affected much of the event, but a strong international field of players from over 20 countries and featuring multiple tournament winners on the Ladies European Tour still showed up. There are a handful of remarkable holes at Southbroom, but the signature 112m par-3 4th hole is an absolute beauty. The hole overlooks the ocean, and when you're standing on the tee box, you can hear the waves crashing against the rocks just below. There are bunkers all around the green, and the wind plays a huge part in deciding which club you'll be using on the day.

After the golf, we drive south for a few minutes to **Trafalgar beach** and **Marine Reserve** (which is just next to the Mpenji Nature Reserve). You really seem to be able to connect with the sea and the earth here. Apparently, **horse riding** on the beach can be arranged through Selsdon Park Estate (Marina Beach). That night, we stay at the Coral Tree Colony, a modern colonial-style guesthouse that actually overlooks Southbroom's 12th green.

We've played six courses now, and can't wait for the Wild Coast Sun Country Club, which lies in wait for us tomorrow. It's technically not in the KwaZulu-Natal province, but just over the Umtamvuna River, which forms the border between KwaZulu-Natal and the Eastern Cape. Many would agree that by playing the **Wild Coast Sun** at the end of our trip, we've saved the best for last. The course is set out over terrain that includes everything a golfer could want — hills, ravines, rivers, dams, lakes and waterfalls — and the views from most of the holes are something truly special. Although quite short in length, it is one of South Africa's most testing layouts, especially when the wind picks up. The signature 168m par-3 13th is played across a waterfall gorge to a green that is partly hidden by rocks and patches of coastal bush.

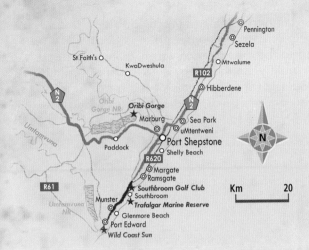

ON THE SIDE >> A bad day

In 2001, after a terrible day at the Wild Coast Sun's Nashua Masters, which saw him miss the cut, professional Hennie Otto decided his clubs weren't worth keeping. He promptly left the course, pulled over at the Umtamvuna Bridge, snapped every club in his bag, stuffed them in his tour bag, and threw everything into the river!

ON THE SIDE >> Ziplining

If you have the time, a visit to the nearby **Oribi Gorge** is well recommended. Wild 5, an adventure company based here, offers a Wild Slide (**zipline**), which spans across the bottom of the gorge 165m below.

ON THE SIDE >> Midlands golf

If the abundance of golf on offer along the KwaZulu-Natal coastline hasn't been enough for you, the KwaZulu-Natal Midlands region, which is about an hour's drive inland from Durban, has plenty to offer:
Gowrie Farm (www.gowriefarm.com)
Victoria Country Club (www.victoria.co.za)
Bosch Hoek Golf Club (www.boschhoek.co.za)
Mooi River Country Club (www.mooirivercountryclub.co.za)
Howick Country Club (033 330 3422)
Sakabula Country Estate (www.sakabula.co.za)

Beachwood (Durban Country Club)
031 313 1777
www.dcclub.co.za
Big Rush
031 312 9435
www.bigrush.co.za
Bike and Saddle
031 813 5633
www.bikeandsaddle.com
Eden River Lodge
082 892 5986
www.facebook.com/EdenRiverLodge
Gringos Mexican Canteen
031 811 4258
www.facebook.com/GringosMexicanCanteen
Izotsha Creek
082 447 5147
www.izotshacreek.co.za
Oyster Box Hotel
031 514 5000
www.oysterboxhotel.com
Selborne Golf Estate
039 688 1896
www.selbornegolf.co.za
Selsdon Park Estate/Marina Beach (horse riding)
083 301 2941
www.marinabeach.co.za
Simbithi Golf Estate
032 946 8360/1
www.simbithi.co.za
Southbroom Golf Club
039 316 6051
www.southbroomgolfclub.co.za
The Coral Tree
039 316 6676
www.thecoraltree.com
The Litchi Orchard
032 525 5118
www.litchiorchard.co.za
Umdoni Park
039 975 1615
www.umdonipark.com
uShaka Marine World
031 328 8000
www.ushakamarineworld.co.za
Wild 5
039 687 0253
www.oribigorge.co.za
Wild Coast Sun
039 305 9111
www.suninternational.com
Zimbali Golf Estate
032 538 1041
www.zimbali.co.za

Regional info
www.zulu.org.za

Wild Coast Sun Country Club

IN DEEP WATER
Cape Town to Maputaland

I learned to dive in Cape Town, and had logged almost a hundred dives before my first trip to Aliwal Shoal. I rolled off the boat into pea-green, ice-cold water and wondered what the fuss was about. That was until, at about 8m, I hit the thermocline and emerged into warm, gin-clear water and saw the whole reef laid out before me with myriad colourful fish flitting past my mask. Seriously, we had 30m plus visibility — mind-blowing stuff for a Cape Town girl. I strongly recommend learning to dive in cold, relatively surgy conditions, and then treating yourself to the sheer joy of warm, calm water and great visibility. So that's how I have structured this route. Some of the highlights of this road trip are great diving, sea birds, whales, penguins, turtles and laid-back locations.

Total Distance 1,810km
Driving Time 22hrs

Section ❶
Cape Town to Gansbaai
Distance 170km
Driving Time 2hrs
Highlight:
Penguins
Two Oceans Aquarium
Shark cage-diving
Whales
SEE PAGE 204

Section ❷
Knysna to Port Edward
Distance 1,020km
Driving Time 12hrs
Highlight:
Sardine run
Dolphin- and whale-watching
SEE PAGE 205

Section ❸
Port Edward to Maputaland
Distance 620km
Driving Time 8hrs
Highlights:
Sardine run
Protea Banks
Raggies and tiger sharks
Aliwal Shoal
Coral reefs
Humpback whales
Turtle breeding
SEE PAGES 206–207

IN DEEP WATER
Cape Town to Maputaland

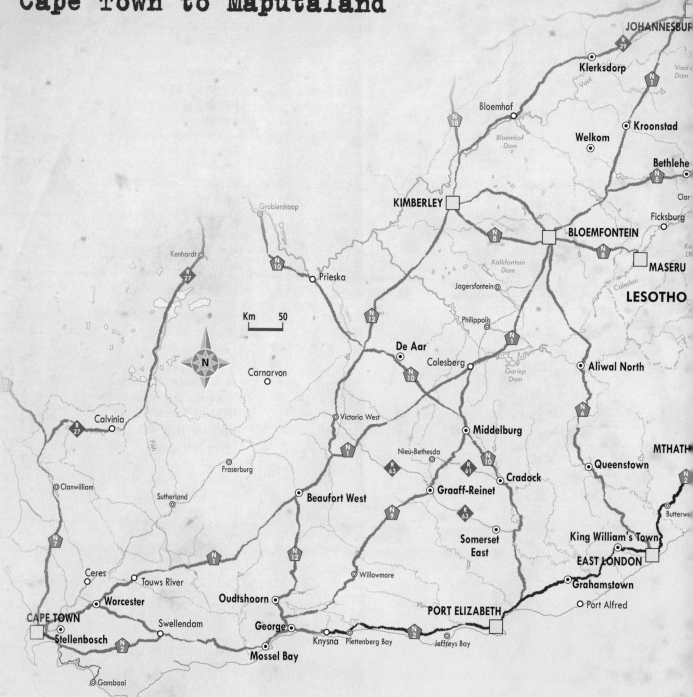

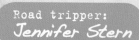

Road tripper:
Jennifer Stern

In a nutshell:
An odyssey through the
marine biomes of South
Africa, from the chilly kelp
forests of the Cape to the
balmy subtropical coral
reefs of Maputaland.

Logistics

You can drive the whole route, but there are long stretches that, while scenic and interesting, do not offer great diving. So, if you are serious about the diving and only the diving, do Section 1 and either drive to George or head back to Cape Town and fly to George. Then drive to Port Elizabeth and either continue up the coast or fly to Durban and head down the coast for the sardine run and the South Coast, and then up the coast to Maputaland.

Driving conditions

The route pretty much follows the N2. From Cape Town to East London the roads vary from twisty-turny scenic drives to superhighways, but they are all tarred and all in pretty decent condition. Once past East London, depending on the route you take, the condition of the roads can vary from atrocious to fantastic. The Kei Cuttings, which descend steeply down to the Kei River and up the other side, used to be a nightmare, but the road works are finished and the road is now great. But roads along the Wild Coast are generally a tad challenging (see pages 90–97). The road from the KwaZulu-Natal South Coast to Durban and beyond is fine and only starts becoming a bit challenging as you enter Maputaland.

After the Tsitsikamma toll road between Plett and PE you're free from toll roads until you cross the Umtamvuna River into KwaZulu-Natal. The coastal R61 is a toll road between Ramsgate and Port Shepstone. It's clear till past Durban and then, heading up the N2 towards Maputaland, you will go through three toll gates.

Pet-friendly rating ★ ☆ ☆ ☆ ☆

1 = least suited 5 = most suited
Best leave the pooch at home.

Child-friendly rating ★ ☆ ☆ ☆ ☆

1 = least suited 5 = most suited

Low-slung vehicle-friendly rating ★ ★ ★ ☆ ☆

1 = high clearance 5 = lowest slung

Don't miss

- Kelp diving
- Two Oceans Aquarium
- Shark cage-diving
- Protea Banks
- Sardine run
- Aliwal Shoal
- Turtle beaches

Emergency service numbers

DAN SA Emergency 080 002 0111 (from within SA only) or 082 810 6010
DAN SA non-emergency enquiries 086 024 2242 or 011 266 4900, www.dansa.org
Cape Town NSRI Emergency 021 449 3500
Hermanus NSRI Emergency 082 990 5967
Mossel Bay NSRI Emergency 044 604 6271
Port Elizabeth NSRI Emergency 041 507 1911
East London NSRI Emergency 043 700 2100
Durban NSRI Emergency 031 361 8567
Richards Bay NSRI Emergency 035 753 1991, 035 905 3401 or 035 905 3444
General Emergency (from a landline) 10111
General Emergency (from a cellphone) 112
AA roadside assistance 086 100 0234 or 083 843 22 (24 hours)

Best time

Any time is a trade-off but I think winter gives you the most pluses and the fewest minuses. The diving in False Bay is great, the white sharks are at Dyer Island, the raggies at Aliwal and the diving and weather in Maputaland are both great. The sardine run is in winter, and the coast from Cape Town to Plett is *vrot* with southern right whales. However, in summer you get the breeding raggies at Sodwana, humpback whales off Maputaland, great diving on Cape Town's west coast, and generally warmer weather.

SUMMER			AUTUMN			WINTER			SPRING		
D	J	F	M	A	M	J	J	A	S	O	N

Background reading

Dive Atlas to South Africa and Mozambique, Fiona McIntosh, MapStudio
www.nightjartravel.com/scuba-diving

IN DEEP WATER
Cape Town to Maputaland

TIP

Do **not** be tempted to join in the locally popular activity of perlemoen poaching while in this area.

Section ❶
Cape Town to Gansbaai
Distance 170km
Driving Time 2hrs
Highlights Penguins, Two Oceans Aquarium, shark cage-diving, whales

Except for very deep dives, diving in Cape Town means coming to terms with kelp, but getting tangled up in kelp is about as likely as getting tangled up in trees in a forest – not impossible, but not a major threat. So just ditch that one imaginary demon. Kelp forests are beautiful, with fabulous, extremely colourful invertebrate life. The water is chilly so make sure you have a decent wet suit or a dry suit. In summer, you will probably dive the western seaboard, and in winter, probably False Bay. My favourite sites are Coral Gardens or Geldkis in the west and Partridge Point or Castle Rocks in False Bay. If the weather is really bad, dive in the kelp tank at the **Two Oceans Aquarium** – it's close to the real thing, but you can wave at the tourists.

Two Oceans Aquarium

From the N2 heading east, take the R44 towards Strand and continue around the eastern edge of False Bay – the views are awesome. Percy's Hole and Kruis are best in summer after a good southeaster, but the entry is a bit tricky, so they're not good spots to dive without a local. There is a great little **penguin** beach at Stony Point just after Betty's Bay if you didn't check out these cute little guys at Boulders while you were in Cape Town. After going through Kleinmond, turn right onto the R43 and pass Bot River Lagoon on your right. Check out the Overberg road trip (see pages 62–69) for more information on this area.

Continue through Gansbaai and, after 2km, turn right into Kleinbaai, where the small harbour is just littered with **shark cage-diving** boats. Shark cage-'diving' is not a diving activity at all, but you do get to stick your head underwater and see one of the world's greatest predators, so don't turn your nose up at it just because you don't need to be a certified diver to partake. If you're here in winter, you are unlikely to miss the **whales**.

From Kleinbaai, join up with the Overberg route (see pages 62–69), go back to Cape Town and fly to George, or head back to Stanford, and then take the R328 to the N2. Stop at the Ou Meul Bakery in Riviersonderend for great pies and excellent coffee and then continue to Knysna (see Garden Route road trip, pages 70–81).

ON THE SIDE >> Kelp and the two oceans

Many people claim that the Indian and Atlantic oceans meet at Cape Point but the official meeting place is Cape Agulhas – the most southerly point of Africa about 60km east of Gansbaai as the gull flies. And, while the Cape Town tourism marketers may whinge, the kelp tells the true story. Kelp is abundant on the West Coast, from Swakopmund, around Cape Point to Agulhas. East of Agulhas there is no kelp, so the ocean really does change character at this wild and stormy spot. It's a drive of about 90km from Gansbaai, and a great photo op. Stand there looking directly out towards Antarctica, say goodbye to the Atlantic on your right and say hello to the Indian Ocean on your left. From here on east and north, the average sea temperature increases gradually.

Penguins

Section ❷
Knysna to Port Edward
Distance 1,020km
Driving Time 12hrs
Highlights Sardine run, dolphin- and whale-watching

Whale-watching

Dive the *Paquita* at Knysna Heads, but only on slack tide, preferably high. There's not much left of the wreck, but there's lots of pretty marine life. No kelp, though. If the conditions are good, there are a few great dive sites in the ocean outside the Heads, but there is currently no dive operator in Knysna. (This may change, so check with the tourism bureau.) You can also snorkel inside the lagoon and, if you spend enough time flolloping around the shallow reefs and the pilings of the various jetties, you may see an endangered Knysna sea horse. They're very chilled little guys so, if you see one, look but don't touch.

TIP

Do a boat-based **dolphin- or whale-watching** trip from Knysna or Plett, and check the Garden Route road trip (see pages 70–81) for loads of other activities. If you decide to drive between Sections 2 and 3, check out the Frontier Country (see pages 82–89) and Wild Coast (see pages 90–97) road trips.

From Knysna to Plett is a pleasant drive through some pretty forest and past lots of great little farm stalls. Plett has one or two nice shore dives and a host of great boat dives. It's a kelpless environment, with colourful invertebrates, but the fish are almost all red or silver as they are further west. There are some great dives off Port Elizabeth and the water is definitely a bit warmer, but it takes a real expert to spot the subtle differences in the floral and faunal assemblages compared with further west. What is a nice comparison, though, is the difference between diving inside Algoa Bay and diving the 'Wild Side' to the west of Cape Recife. ProDive has operations in both Plett and PE, and Ocean Divers operates from PE.

From Port Elizabeth, the coast curves and starts heading north-south instead of east-west. From here it's worth flying to Durban, renting a car and driving south. But if you want to drive up, read the warnings about this route in the Wild Coast road trip (see pages 90–97).

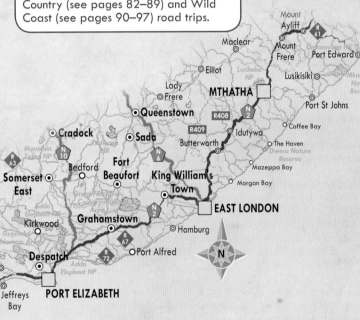

Km 50

The east coast of South Africa is warmer than the west coast because of the southward-flowing Mozambique Current, but in winter the current sometimes moves further out to sea, allowing the cold water flowing up from Antarctica and the west coast to move further inshore. And with the cold water come millions of sardines, followed by millions of bigger fish, gannets, gulls, seals, sharks, dolphins and even Bryde's whales. It's a movable feast of note and the biggest migration on earth in terms of biomass. And diving the **sardine run** is the holy grail of sub-aqua action. So plan to be somewhere along the Wild Coast or the South Coast towards the end of June or the beginning of July and check out what the local marketing gurus call 'the greatest shoal on earth'. It's a bit hit and miss as the dive operators have tried tying the sardines to a pre-arranged schedule but they are surprisingly immune to

threats of no-show penalties. The best places for basing yourself for a sardine run excursion are Port St Johns and Mbotyi on the Wild Coast, and Port Edward on the South Coast.

IN DEEP WATER
Cape Town to Maputaland

Section ❸
Port Edward to Maputaland
Distance 620km
Driving Time 8hrs
Highlights Sardine run, Protea Banks, raggies and tiger sharks, Aliwal Shoal, coral reefs, humpback whales, turtle breeding

Some years the **sardine run** is better off the South Coast and some years it's better off the Wild Coast. Blue Wilderness and African Watersports offer full-service sardine run charters as well as other diving for the rest of the year.

From Port Edward, take the R61 north. After 35km take exit 39 to Shelly Beach. This is the launch spot for Protea Banks. **Protea Banks** is not for sissies — it's deep (top of the reef at about 36m), it's far out to sea (about 7.5km offshore) and, the best part, it's the favourite hangout of hammerheads, Zambezis (bull sharks), **raggies**, **tiger sharks** and a host more big toothy fish.

Head back to the R61 and travel north for about 70km to Park Rynie, which is the launch site for Landers Reef. Or carry on for a further 12km and turn off to uMkomaas for the launch for **Aliwal Shoal**.

These dive sites look, at first glance, like real coral reefs as they are filled with all the gorgeous colourful reef fish (like Nemo and his mates). But they are not coral reefs. They are rocky reefs with coral growing on them — an important distinction. Aliwal is not as deep as Protea, nor quite as far out to sea, but it's also a good shark-diving spot. Tiger sharks are around most of the year, although they are more dependable in summer, and in winter many parts of the reef are transformed into a veritable singles bar for raggedtooth sharks who hook up for a while before the females head north to gestate, and the males head south to ... I dunno? Talk about rugby? Fin wrestle?

Durban is another 40km or so north. The diving in Durban Bay is okay but not as good as it is further south or further north. However, you can have a fun dive in the uShaka aquarium and even take the kids snorkelling in an open tank with sharks (gulp) just the other side of a glass barrier. From Durban, I would just head straight up to Sodwana Bay, with one stop. If you are either particularly fond (or particularly scared) of sharks, stop in at the Sharks Board at uMhlanga, about 20km north of Durban. It's an illuminating and instructive experience and should make you realise that sharks have far more to fear from humans than humans do from sharks.

Sodwana waters

The **coral reefs** at Sodwana Bay are among the most southerly in the world — courtesy of the Mozambique Current that keeps the water above the required 20°C. It's great diving, but it can get rather crowded on high days and holidays, as there are a number of dive camps, dive lodges, dive schools and dive charter operators at Sodwana. Reefteach has a great little self-catering spot and offers the usual dive charters with a bit of flair. It's about 360km from Durban, all on a good tarred road (but with lots of speed bumps).

There is a shorter, more scenic dirt road from the N2, so if you want to take that, ask about it when you book your stay.

For peaceful, quiet and uncrowded diving, you need to travel further up the coast to either Rocktail Beach Lodge or Thonga Beach Lodge. Each lodge has only one boat with restricted launch times, and they take great pains to avoid each other, so it is an exclusive dive experience – and both lodges offer a high level of service (I got pretty spoiled here with someone carrying my gear, washing my gear and feeding me yummy food between dives). So they are a bit pricey, but there are inexpensive camp sites nearby and you can dive with either of the lodges if the boat is not full with their guests.

In summer you can hear **humpback whales** singing and, at night, you can walk along the beach to watch **turtles** laying their eggs or hatching and waddling back to sea. Whale sharks are not guaranteed to make an appearance, but they swim through pretty regularly. The beautiful Kosi Bay is just a bit further north, with great snorkelling in the lagoon mouth (but watch the tides).

Diving with sharks, Protea Banks

IN DEEP WATER Contact details

African Dive Adventures
082 456 7885
www.afridive.com
African Watersports
039 973 2505
www.africanwatersports.co.za
Aliwal Dive Centre
039 973 2233
www.aliwalshoal.co.za
Blue Flash, Cape Town
073 167 6677
www.blueflash.co.za
Blue Wilderness Diving
039 973 2348
www.bluewilderness.co.za
Bubble Blowers
083 306 2550
www.scubaafrica.co.za
Dive Action
021 511 0800
www.diveaction.co.za
Marine Dynamics
079 930 9694
www.sharkwatchsa.com
Mbotyi River Lodge
082 674 1064 or 039 253 7200
www.mbotyi.co.za
Ocean Divers International
041 581 5121
www.odipe.co.za
Pisces Divers
021 786 3799
www.piscesdivers.co.za
Pro Dive
041 581 1144
www.prodive.co.za
Reefteach
035 571 0231 or 082 339 6920
www.reefteach.co.za
Rocktail Beach Camp
011 807 1800
www.wilderness-safaris.com
Seal Expeditions
082 253 5678
www.sardinerun.com or
www.facebook.com/sealexpeditions
Sharks Board
031 566 0400
www.shark.co.za
Thonga Beach Lodge
035 474 1473
www.thongabeachlodge.co.za
Two Oceans Aquarium
021 418 3823
www.aquarium.co.za

Regional info
www.gansbaaiinfo.com
www.gardenroute.co.za
www.tourismcapetown.co.za
www.visiteasterncape.co.za
www.zulu.org.za

First edition published in 2014 by MapStudio™ South Africa

ISBN (Print) 978-1-77026-518-9
ISBN (ePub) 978-1-77026-519-6
ISBN (ePdf) 978-1-77026-520-2

Managing Director Drew Sherwood
Publisher John Loubser
Project Manager Genené Hart
Commissioning Editor Elaine Fick
Editor Thea Grobbelaar
Designer Nicole Bannister
Cartographer Genené Hart
Proofreader Joy Clack
Reproduction Hirt & Carter, Cape Town
Marketing marketing@mapstudio.co.za
Feedback research@mapstudio.co.za
Photo credits © 2014 All images by Shaen Adey except the following:
Nicole Bannister, 185; Big Game Parks, 147a, 149b; Mike Boehme, 190; George Brits, 170, 172, 174, 175, 176, 177; Richard Chipps, 165; Cleopatra Mountain Farmhouse, 128a; Dyer Island Cruises, 62, 205a; Ezemvelo KZN Wildlife, 145; Carrie Hampton, 144b, 147b, 148, 149a, 151; Bridget Hilton-Barber, 164, 166, 167, 168, 169; Matthew Holt, 106, 111, 112, 114, 116, 118, 122, 134, 137a, 138; Kate Mason, 195; Fiona McIntosh, 35, 100, 200; Sue McWilliam, 143, 156; Hector Pringle, 162; Mandy Ramsden, 109, 117, 130, 132, 136, 137b, 139; Red Carnation Hotels, 197; Chris Sharpe, 10, 17b, 45, 65, 72, 84, 92, 202; Simbithi, 196; Jennifer Stern, 68a; Sun International, 192, 199; Alan van Gysen, 183, 184, 187, 191; www.sxc.hu, 198.

Printed and bound by Paarl Media, South Africa
ePdf and ePub available from www.mapstudio.co.za/eBooks.php and major online retailers

MapStudio™
Unit 3, Block B, M5 Park, Eastman Road, Maitland, 7405
PO Box 193, Maitland, 7404
Tel: 0860 10 50 50
www.mapstudio.co.za

Maps © 2014 MapStudio™
© MapStudio™ 2014